OUT OF ARCHITECTURE

Out of Architecture is both a call to reassess the architecture profession and its education, and a toolkit for graduates and working architects to untangle their skills, passions, and value from traditional architectural practice and consider alternate pathways.

Written by design professionals and expert career consultants, this book is informed by numerous client accounts as well as the authors' own stories and routes out of architecture. The initial chapters follow the narrative of a typical architecture training in the US, highlighting the many highs and lows, skills honed, and ultimately the huge disconnect that can occur between architectural education and practice. Subsequent chapters explore a disillusionment with the profession, unhealthy work cultures, mentorship, working with lead architects, toxic perfectionism, and the notion of a "calling." Authors then present the hopeful accounts of many architects who escaped a profession known for its grueling working conditions to find fulfilling, well-paying, creative jobs that better utilize the skills of architecture than the architectural profession itself. Written in a unique combination of storytelling and analysis, this patchwork of client and author stories makes for an immersive, provocative, and enjoyable read.

A wide range of architecture students, graduates, educators, and professionals will recognize themselves within the pages of this book and find prompts to reassess their working practices, teaching styles, and the profession itself. It will be of particular value to those students skeptical of joining the architecture workforce, as well as those further along and considering a career change.

Erin Pellegrino and **Jake Rudin** co-founded Out of Architecture in 2018. Out of Architecture is a career consulting firm helping architects and designers find challenging and creatively fulfilling roles beyond the bounds of traditional architectural practice.

T0383387

"*Out of Architecture* does not simply problematize architecture as a profession that devours its young through overwork and underpay because of their passion for design. Drawing on their experiences as students, working designers, and career consultants, the authors give practical advice, moral support, and proven alternatives to conventional practice. They show how to rebalance life and work by reimagining and repurposing design values and skills already learned. Amidst the Great Resignation and stirrings of collective action among architectural workers, *Out of Architecture* could not be more timely or necessary."

– Mary N. Woods, Professor Emerita, History of
Architecture, Cornell University

"Yes, the authors of this book are career consultants; yes, they have MBAs; yes, this book is an extension of their consulting practice. But do not be deceived. The practicality of their advice is more than matched by the humanity they bring to their narrative and the love they show for architectural sensibilities. Any architectural graduate who is honored to be part of a club – yes, an aesthetic bootcamp, but one that nevertheless yields the best of friends and the most amazing insights – but is dismayed by the tasks they will or do perform in the profession, has to read this book."

– Peggy Deamer, Professor Emerita,
Architecture, Yale University

"As a creator who has shifted my practice and career profoundly over the last few years, I found *Out of Architecture* to be a critical book for any concerned professional in the world of architecture. As our world is changing, disciplines are evolving, and architecture as a practice needs to adapt. This is a precious book for anyone looking to understand the motivations behind the changing tide of the profession."

– Dror Benshetrit, Founder of Supernature Labs

OUT OF ARCHITECTURE

THE VALUE OF ARCHITECTS BEYOND TRADITIONAL PRACTICE

Jake Rudin *and* Erin Pellegrino

Routledge
Taylor & Francis Group

LONDON AND NEW YORK

Cover design by Noura Alhariri and Out of Architecture

First published 2023
by Routledge
4 Park Square, Milton Park, Abingdon, Oxon OX14 4RN

and by Routledge
605 Third Avenue, New York, NY 10158

Routledge is an imprint of the Taylor & Francis Group, an informa business

British Library Cataloguing-in-Publication Data
A catalogue record for this book is available from the British Library

Library of Congress Cataloging-in-Publication Data
A catalog record has been requested for this book

ISBN: 978-1-032-29296-0 (hbk)
ISBN: 978-1-032-29294-6 (pbk)
ISBN: 978-1-003-30092-2 (ebk)

DOI: 10.4324/9781003300922

Typeset in Garamond
by Deanta Global Publishing Services, Chennai, India

Out of Architecture did not start as a business; it began well before that as a group of individuals seeking to make change and find their way through their early years in a love affair with architecture. Of that original group, none has been more impactful in the creation of this book than Rachel Bacus.

Rachel's journey from school into the working world through firms of many scales and sizes was one of the key resources as we developed the idea for Out of Architecture. As an architectural designer, Rachel worked on projects from embassies to airports and all stages of the architectural process. During her time at university, core to her thesis, she held a strong fascination for all things sensory – studying the ways in which the built environment can create unique phenomenological experiences. After six years of working in traditional firms, she realized her passion for sensory design on a new adventure out of architecture and established Bacus Vineyards.

Throughout the years, Rachel has been a constant supporter, collaborator, friend, and spouse. She has lent her stories to a number of sections in the following pages and this book would not have been possible without her.

Thank you, Rachel.

CONTENTS

ABOUT THE AUTHORS

Erin Pellegrino and Jake Rudin co-founded Out of Architecture in 2018. Out of Architecture is a career consulting firm helping architects and designers find challenging and creatively fulfilling roles beyond the bounds of traditional architectural practice.

ERIN PELLEGRINO

In addition to her work as co-founder of Out of Architecture, Erin Pellegrino is the founder and principal of Matter, a design/build studio that explores design problems through graphic design, furniture, and small-scale architectural work. Matter has completed award-winning projects in architecture, product and brand design, and has been recognized globally.

She holds a Bachelor of Architecture from Cornell University, a Master of Architecture II from the Harvard Graduate School of Design, and an MBA from the Quantic School of Business and Technology.

Erin has been recognized with an Autodesk BuildSpace Fellowship, First Prize in the 2021 Rethinking the Future Design Awards, an AIA New England Design Honor Award, a Core77 Design Award in Built Environment, two Architizer A+ Awards, a Paul M. Heffernan International Fellowship, and a nomination for the EU Mies Van der Rohe Award. Her work on Alpine Shelter Skuta was featured on the cover of Phaidon Press's publication *Environmental Living*. Early in her career, she trained in the offices of Tod Williams Billie Tsien Architects and Studio Gang.

Erin is also a Visiting Lecturer at Cornell University and leads design/build studio and fabrication courses at New Jersey Institute of Technology. In 2018, NCARB named Erin their inaugural Scholar of Professional Practice, recognizing her commitment to incorporating issues of ethics and equity into architectural training. Cornell then recruited her to redesign and teach the department's Professional Practice course, where she merges the course's traditional curriculum with a consideration of issues like fair pay, self-efficacy, and gender and racial disparities in the profession.

JAKE RUDIN

Beyond his role as co-founder of Out of Architecture, Jake Rudin is a member of the Innovation and Advanced Creation teams at Adidas where he leads digital technologies, pattern engineering, and computational design. He holds a Bachelor of Architecture from Cornell University, a Master in Design Studies (with a concentration in Technology) from Harvard University's Graduate School of Design, and an MBA from the Quantic School of Business and Technology.

Jake has created a number of award-winning projects throughout his design career, including footwear designs that were featured in Fast Company, built projects that received Architizer A+ Awards, photography named Wanderlust Travel Photo of the Year and Nikon's Best of College Photography, and a Historic Preservation Award for his work restoring a Richard Meier-designed home. Prior to pivoting out of the architectural field, Jake worked around the world for firms including Massimiliano Fuksas Architects, ZGF, and the Shenzhen Institute of Building Research.

Additionally, Jake has extensive professorial experience, teaching and coaching in architecture and design fields at universities including Harvard, Cornell, Northeastern, and Portland State University. He is currently actively involved in the startup community mentoring and advising early stage startups across EdTech, InsurTech, AECTech, and others.

ACKNOWLEDGEMENTS

This book, and by extension our work with Out of Architecture, would not be possible without the immense support of the people who taught, mentored, guided, and pushed us to where we are today. You have made us better designers, professionals, and people, through your guidance, rigor, and teachings. Thank you to Ben Nicholson, Taylor Lowe, Mark Cruvellier, Andrea Simitch, Mary Woods, Alessio Rosati, Davide Marchetti, Mark Morris, Hanif Kara, Vince Mulcahy, Medina Lasansky, Aleksander Mergold, Brian Beeners, Beth Kunz, Panagiotis Michalatos, and Allen Sayegh.

Having the idea to write a book is easy, but actually turning it into one is a humbling and difficult process. This experience has been both a challenging and rewarding one. Thanks to Amanda for her incredible ability to bring clarity to our thoughts. We especially want to thank Erin's aunt, Linda Morrison, for her insightful edits, unwavering support, and enthusiasm during this process, as well as during our days as fledgling designers. Thanks to Noura Alhariri for helping to keep the business of Out of Architecture turning while our attentions were otherwise occupied by this project. Another wholehearted thank you to Charlie Firestone for keeping the tools whirring at Matter during our many strategy sessions and editing passes.

We would also like to thank our families, who have provided invaluable insights and patiently sat through countless retellings of these stories. Jake would like to say thank you to Rachel, Mom, Dad, and Daisy. Erin would like to say thank you to Aunt Barbara, Uncle Michael, Aunt Angel, and Uncle Gary.

We must also acknowledge the willingness of our clients, friends, students, and colleagues who have confided in us their struggles and allowed us to share versions of their stories in this book. Your trust in us is humbling and your stories continually inspire us.

Finally, there is no person who would have wanted to see this through to fruition more than Erin's mom, Lynda Pellegrino. Unfortunately, Lynda passed away while we were writing this book. Thank you for your unwavering belief that we could do anything. I love and miss you, Mom.

CLIENT ENDORSEMENTS

"What I find important is that they talk about a wide variety of professions that a person with an architectural education can turn towards. It is amazing to find oneself surrounded by people from different countries and in a different moment of their professional life and feel connected to them by an architectural background and similar struggles in the job market. The advice that Erin gave about women not applying for jobs when they don't fulfill 90–100% of the requirements was super insightful to me!"

– Elzbieta P., Gdańsk, Poland

"Jake and Erin were crucial in helping me navigate the daunting world of environment and concept design. As an architect-turned-artist, I had struggled to find sustainable work that I could excel at. Jake and Erin presented me with many tangible forms of support, including consultation, connections and help with salary negotiation. They helped me find personal confidence by showing me paths and options that were previously clandestine. I have found it very difficult to move from one industry to another, but these two helped me find great work at a competitive rate."

– Ben L., Portland, OR, USA

"Working with Out of Architecture was fantastic. They helped me understand the value that I brought to my previous employers. I am still working within standard design practice, but my position has improved drastically. I could not have gotten there without their help."

– K.N., New York, NY, USA

"Out of Architecture offers a unique perspective for my transition from conventional architecture to tech and more VR-focused design. Leaving the familiar field of architecture can be a daunting undertaking, yet Out of Architecture gave me the support and camaraderie as well as actionable steps to make it happen. They helped me in understanding my own skill set and how to communicate it effectively in a non-architectural context."

– V.N., Toronto, Canada

"I truly wish I had known about OOA 4 years ago when I pivoted from Architecture to Tech. I felt so alone in that journey but meeting Jake and Erin showed me that there is a community of former architects willing to help and guide others who may want to leave the field. Jake and Erin served as the much-needed cheerleaders and advisors at the tail end of a long search.

I think the most important thing I learned from working with Jake and Erin was to not be shy about my value and what I bring to the table. I'd lost touch with not only my self-worth but also with my own values. I have just started this new job and I had forgotten that work could feel this good. Work is fun again! I am happier, better paid, surrounded by supportive, smart, and motivated people! I'm thrilled I found OOA. Erin and Jake are delightful people to work with and I love how they are creating positive change. If you are miserable in architecture – you can do other things. If you are miserable in your current role – you can change that. And Jake and Erin can help!"

– Helen L., San Francisco, CA, USA

"I decided not to look for a job, instead I will work on my own! I am already working on 4 projects!!!! I have you and Jake to thank for giving me the strength to believe in myself. I haven't gotten far yet but at least I have started the climb. Like you taught me – I have value, and that when looking for a job, I am not looking for charity. Even though I am young and have much, MUCH to learn I still have a lot that I am bringing to the table."

– Tere M., Guatemala

"I'm able to do more compelling and impactful work while being better compensated, so it's a good combination. It's shocking how a museum exhibit designer can make so much more than a licensed architect constructing utility plants for a big tech company. I hope to stay at this position for a long time and develop my skills using form making and digital media to tell stories and bring emotion to users. These skills should put me in a good position if I am looking for work in a wider range of design roles in the future."

– B.F., Portland, OR, USA

"I found what I wanted to do in the process of searching for a new position, rather than knowing what I want to do going into the search. At the beginning of this process, I had a very limited idea of what I really wanted or what is out there. After continuously reframing and refining my narratives, resume, and portfolio to the different set of roles, and engaging with the recruiters and managers at different companies I was able to define what I really value and make an informed decision on my career. For the first time in my life, I can say I am genuinely excited about my next job!"

– J.S., New York, NY, USA

"Erin and Jake's multi-faceted consulting talents have given me just the career kickstart I needed! They are thoroughly organized and remain consistent with their words, actions and values. They are a fountain of career knowledge, not just in the realm of architecture, but also with the courses of design, technology and construction related fields. They are capable of breaking down the deafening weight of finding 'the perfect job' into modest achievable steps. Thank you, Erin and Jake!"

– Sarah E., Florida, USA

"Jake and Erin's experience in the professional design realm offered clear and insightful direction during a process that can be filled with ambiguity, and doubt. The decision to make a career-change comes with a host of emotions. The thought of blazing your own trail, cross-pollinating your own unique skill-sets, and turning a new page in your life can be invigorating. But then you look at that blank page and different thoughts begin to propagate. 'where do I start?' 'How do I build a new professional network?' 'Am I turning my back on my investment in my education and experience?' In my own case, Out of Architecture helped shine a light on the value of my education and experience, while still offering healthy direction on the gaps that I would need to fill in my career journey. Landing that new gig is still up to you, but it sure does help to have these two in your corner."

– Jody B., Portland, OR, USA

Client Endorsements

"Though I didn't end up getting out of architecture, I really enjoyed this process. It was a pleasure getting to know the two of you, learning about your experiences both in and outside of the industry, and receiving a crash course on the many fields and roles that are related to the discipline."

– C.H., Boston, MA, USA

"I knew pretty early on that architecture wasn't for me. I could tell how much my peers enjoyed what they were doing – how committed they were to their craft. I never made such a connection during my time at school or in the workplace, and this didn't sit well with me.

I knew I was meant to be spending my time doing something that I strongly cared about, something I could make a meaningful impact on. From the beginning of the job hunt to the final negotiations, Out of Architecture had my best interests in mind and helped me navigate this transition with confidence. One thing I knew for sure was that I loved being creative and my design education would help me adapt to other artistic fields. The question was, how would I make that transition happen? Speaking with Out of Architecture helped shape my perspective. We started by unpacking the steps needed to make new connections, lock in meetings, and scope out opportunities to network with the people that could help me get to that next step. Each conversation became a stepping-stone that aligned me with yet another contact and gave me added motivation to push my creative boundaries."

– Yenny H., Boston, MA, USA

"I was changing careers from landscape designer to the software and tech industry. Out of Architecture guided me through each step of the whole interview process. They helped me reorganize my interview strategies so that I had a chance to fully express my potential and capabilities in this position during the on-site interview. I highly recommend Out of Architecture if you want to switch careers to other fields from the AEC industry. Switching careers is not easy, but I am sure Out of Architecture's knowledge will inspire and guide you to success."

– Y. L., Portland, OR, USA

"Before talking to Out of Architecture, I felt as though my architecture role wasn't allowing me to push boundaries and explore modern methods of design. After our conversations, I realized that many of the skills I consider secondary, are actually those that give me an edge outside the industry. This was just the push I needed to change industries for my perfect role, and they helped every step of the way."

– T.R., Sydney, Australia

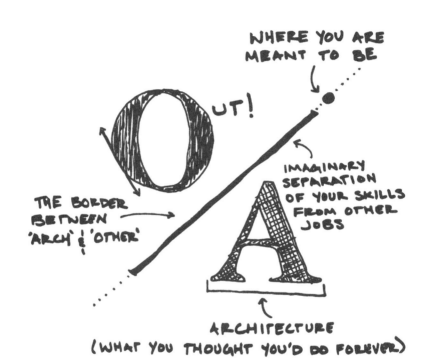

WHERE YOU ARE
MEANT TO BE

OUT!

THE BORDER
BETWEEN
'ARCH' & 'OTHER'

IMAGINARY
SEPARATION
OF YOUR SKILLS
FROM OTHER
JOBS

ARCHITECTURE
(WHAT YOU THOUGHT YOU'D DO FOREVER)

INTRODUCTION
OUT OF ARCHITECTURE

Nothing compares to those first few months of architecture school. You find yourself fully immersed in this strange, mysterious, beautiful world of possibilities you've never imagined. While the world around you remains the same, you begin to see it completely differently. It is the same world that has always been here, yet it is filled with possibilities you never *could* have imagined, if not for the new ways of seeing the world – the new perspectives that transform ordinary things into feats of design ingenuity. The everyday world suddenly becomes a space of magic. As every architect knows, however, it's not easy. The long work hours, the mounting pressure to perform, and the stress of pushing yourself beyond any semblance of your previous limitations – mental, physical, and emotional. These all take a heavy toll. And yet, you're willing to sacrifice – to scrape and claw your way through – because, at that moment, you love architecture more than you've ever loved anything else.

So, what drives these architects – the same designers who once overflowed with passion and awe – to Google "I don't want to be an architect anymore?" To search for "giving up architecture," "leaving architecture," or even "is the architecture profession dying?" We suspect most architects won't be surprised

DOI: 10.4324/9781003300922-1

to learn that these search strings are so common that they autocomplete in a Google query related to the profession of architecture.

This juxtaposition of love and despair is more than an interesting paradox. It *is* the profession.

From our vantage – as career consultants who help creatively driven architects and designers find roles that challenge and fulfill them beyond traditional practice – this type of toxic love affair with the architecture profession is alarmingly common. Client after client comes to us harboring both a deep passion for the art of architecture *and* a secret desire to leave the profession for good. For many architects, a sense of deteriorating mental, physical, and financial health leaves them no choice. For others, their core values – things like an intense focus on aesthetics, elegant practicality, and community improvement, all of which should be perfectly aligned with the field – feel out of place in the day-to-day grind of professional architecture. What very few students understand until they enter the profession is that 90 percent of the business of architecture is comprised of things other than art. And that is exactly what we discovered when we left the sanctity of architecture school to pursue traditional careers.

At first, we rolled with the punches.

Then, we rebelled.

We wanted to challenge the idea of a "typical" architecture career – one that so often leaves people feeling trapped and unhappy. We knew that the things we loved about architecture could all be separated from the profession, carried over into other fields and projects and careers. And we saw that the types of discussions in so many architecture offices had little to do with the passion we felt for the art form and more to do with the constant, crushing weight of being overworked and undervalued. As trained architects – people who understand how to operate within strict parameters, how to generate innovative and unexpected solutions, and how to channel apparently impossible challenges into beautiful, practical results – we quickly realized that our design training could be useful beyond professional architecture. We realized that a career is really just another design problem.

The title of this book, *Out of Architecture*, has dual meanings. First, we aim to support those who are feeling unfulfilled by their careers in the field. Those of us with formal training in architecture often find ourselves disenchanted with the profession but anxious about the prospect of leaving the field. Therefore, this book – and our work in general – uses a common design language to provide curated resources, success stories, and moral support to demonstrate the feasibility of a career "out of architecture." Second, as trained architects smitten with the process of design, we strive to highlight the value of an architectural education – the versatility of the skills that come "out of architecture." This book follows our successful company of the same name to unite these two missions. In the following pages, we demonstrate how the unique ways of thinking that come "out of architecture" can help architects to realize their true career potential, particularly when that means positioning themselves in careers beyond the scope of traditional architectural practice.

#

Out of Architecture is a collection of stories united by our contention that the disconnect – the tragic love affair so many experience in the rift between the art and the profession of architecture – is a product of particular practices that move from an educational setting into the workplace. In this book, we argue that the traditional studio approach to architecture education often leaves students with a skewed and underdeveloped sense of their own value as workers. Specifically, one's movement through school is often experienced as a kind of love affair with design, making the shift into the practice of professional architecture jarring, and even traumatic. However, despite the value architectural training can bring to a number of non-architecture career paths – ranging from tech development to fashion design to corporate consulting – many architects understand their deep dissatisfaction as unavoidable. They feel trapped between a rock and a hard place, unable to reconcile expectation with reality, and are uncertain about whether, when, and how to leave the profession.

Out of Architecture traces the reasons for this problem, connecting them to antiquated models like the history of "the gentlemen's profession" and the concept of architecture as a "calling." While these problems are deeply embedded in the traditional understanding of architecture – and can thus seem inescapable from within the profession – they simultaneously illuminate some of the unique skills and the remarkable resilience that architects bring to their work. It is crucial that architects and architectural training programs begin to recognize the transferability of the skills associated with architecture, including not only design skills but also things like project and team management, effective communication, and the ability to solve complex problems. Through the experiences of our clients, we demonstrate that embracing these components of architecture can allow trained architects to enjoy a range of career opportunities that better align with each individual's unique values.

#

This idea of value is central to *Out of Architecture* and our company in general. A deceptively small word, value has a range of definitions that often come into competition with one another when we begin to truly explore the possibilities for our careers. *Out of Architecture* approaches value from two primary directions. The first approach – and the one that often elbows its way into the center of career conversations – is the value that workers offer to employers. For trained architects, this value is vast and variable but simultaneously under-appreciated and unimpressive. General design skills, for example, offer an obvious example of the value of architectural training for a plethora of professions. The transferability of the architect's way of thinking is less often recognized but no less valuable. Design requires us to trust our intuition and our training. It asks us to immerse ourselves in problems so that we can solve them comprehensively, using all of our faculties. If a particular direction isn't working, we explore the other options, because if the project's not right, you feel it in your bones. This visceral design sensibility reaches far beyond the cognitive processing of "good" and "bad," "beautiful" or "ugly." Yet, architects and architecture students often miss the value of that kind of intuition. Most architects are proactive, creative, innovative, skilled problem solvers. We are characterized by a nimbleness that allows us to investigate a problem, choose the right tools – or easily learn new ones, if necessary – and apply independence, confidence, and ingenuity to find a solution. We are well-equipped to work in teams to synthesize complex information into clear and engaging output, whether that manifests as a building, a brand, a shoe, or an understanding of how a company is managed.

In other words, architects not only bring the tools of architecture to any job, we also bring complex, creative problem-solving skills that are invaluable to any employer in the contemporary marketplace. And, by the way, employers focused on current market trends know this to be true: as Julee Everett wrote for *Product Coalition*, "There's a shift underway in large organizations, one that puts design much closer to the center of the enterprise. But the shift isn't about aesthetics. It's about applying the principles of design to the way people work."[1] Architects

Introduction

and architecture students are perfectly positioned to offer this valuable asset to a broad spectrum of companies, and those industries are hungry for it.

The second approach to value requires more self-reflection. By virtue of our training, architects across the board bring similar kinds of skills and approaches to our projects. The ways we each value our time and energy, on the other hand, are necessarily unique. This is not about training, and it has nothing to do with the marketplace. It is a question of nurturing the self. Architecture students are often expected to move through school and into the profession without truly considering our own priorities. This can lead to a misalignment between the vision we hold for our lives and a career that demands constant sacrifice. There is no faster or more direct route to resentment, despair, and burnout.

We believe it is unreasonable and unnecessary to ask workers to put their values aside. By reflecting on what it is we each value most – and then letting those values take center stage in our career choices – we can each bring our careers into harmony with the lives we imagined for ourselves before we were told that traditional architecture practice was our only option. For those who have already spent years paying their dues at a traditional firm, the idea of a radical career change may seem unrealistic. But we know it is possible because we have seen it over and over again. Throughout this book, we will describe people whose circumstances led them to value everything from a flexible schedule to a humanitarian cause to a more generous paycheck. These are real – though anonymized and often composited – clients who reflected on what was important to them and took action to prioritize their values. And they did it by recognizing the value their training in architecture could bring to companies beyond the boundaries of the traditional profession.

#

We see this understanding of value as intuitive – something we are taught to ignore by our peers, some professors, and the professional architecture marketplace. As individuals who are naturally drawn to financial discussions, we began to notice the disconnect between the value we knew we could bring to the marketplace and the things that were important to us. We wanted financial stability. We wanted to feel as though our work was valued in our workplaces. We wanted healthy settings for collaboration and freedom to create and innovate within the parameters of particular projects. And so, we became the first clients of a new business we now call Out of Architecture.

We are architects who ran the gauntlet of late-night studios, professional degrees, post-professional education, licensure, exams, paid and unpaid internships, and firms, large and small – we understand what it means to merge purpose with profession. The things we loved about the study of architecture didn't always translate to the architecture workplace. And although we each hold MBAs, we quickly learned that you don't need an advanced business degree to see that the business of architecture is severely lacking. What we found was that everything we learned – and loved – could be carried with us to careers in all kinds of amazing industries.

Once we got out, we started to teach others how to see themselves beyond the bounds of a single industry. When you work with incredible candidates, they achieve incredible results. Our previous clients have taken their expertise into industries that include tech, fashion, startups, sportswear, industrial design, finance, and game design. This is the experience we bring to this book, and we place it in conversation with an analysis of the successes and failures of contemporary architectural education. Since we continue to teach at the college level, we have a bird's eye view of the perspective of new designers entering the profession within the past decade and those approaching graduation now, and we supplement that perspective with years of experience offering professional career coaching outside the field.

While we discuss our experience throughout the book, one particular point bears mention in this opening chapter. A few years ago, while Erin was teaching a course at Cornell, a number of high-profile cases emerged involving sexual harassment and abuse in architecture.[2] Suddenly the whisper network that had existed for decades came to the fore, and the profession had to face the fact that many talented male architects were known for more than just their work – they were also well-known for their mistreatment of the women they employed. In a meeting to explore the implications of this #MeToo moment, Erin raised the point that the Professional Practice course did not include a unit – or even much explicit discussion – on the ethics of the field. The conversation that ensued was part of the reason Erin was asked to take over the course. Erin was younger than many of the faculty who had taught the course in the past, and the administration saw this as a benefit – after all, the field was reckoning with a series of revelations about the abuses of older white men. It spoke to the disconnect between the expectations of a rising generation of young architects and a tradition of prioritizing the visions of the old guard in power at the expense of the health and safety of younger designers. What better way to address this issue than to promote an up-and-coming, young designer committed to changing the field and architectural education for the better? So, Erin took over the Professional Practice course, a role that allowed her not only to support the young professionals in training at Cornell but also to experience from a faculty position many of the struggles that young designers face in the transition from student to professional.

Jake, too, continues to teach while building a career outside of architecture as a member of the Adidas Advanced Creation Technologies team – fabricating, designing, digitizing, model-making, and exploring all aspects of footwear. This position has given him an inside track to understanding the ways companies beyond the scope of traditional architecture firms operate in terms of recruitment, hiring, and employee expectations. And Rachel, the additional contributor to this book, has spent years working in traditional architecture firms, building a deep understanding of the function – and dysfunction – common in more traditional roles. She recently made the leap out of architecture to start her own vineyard, putting her love of design and curated experiences at the forefront of this endeavor.

Together, we have collected a range of experiences and stories that illustrate the value of architecture as well as the field-embedded challenges of traditional practice. As architects, we were frustrated with the business aspect of our field. We decided to build new careers focused on helping people identify what they value about architecture and their lives.

#

This book is composed of the stories from these disparate experiences. Many of them are mined from our own encounters as architecture students, architects in the field, and designers working in fields outside of architecture. Others are borrowed from the experiences of our clients, included with permission and anonymized or compiled into client composites that illuminate, in human terms, the damaging trends of the mainstream architectural profession. *Out of Architecture* weaves together these narratives to offer a concrete perspective, not only on the value and fulfillment architects can find in non-architectural fields but also on the reasons that so many find the profession unfulfilling, disheartening, and even traumatic.

We approach this task from a perspective that is, perhaps, unexpected within traditional architecture publications. That is, we approached the writing of this book as a journalist might, focusing on the experiences that make architecture a unique educational and professional endeavor rather than on the images and figures often packed between the covers of traditional architecture books. We are all highly invested in beautiful design. But this book is not about that. This book is about the scars that linger on many who practice architecture. And it is about addressing these scars with concrete, actionable approaches to healing.

#

We have always been clear that *Out of Architecture* needed to be a solution-focused book. Although we believe that many of the horror stories we have encountered deserve the attention of the field, this book balances those problems with an analysis of their root causes and individual-level solutions. Of course, no book can offer a one-size-fits-all proposal for the myriad career issues experienced by architects and architecture students – we know because this is exactly the work we do in our company, and our years of operation have made it abundantly clear that each individual person is unique in their values, goals, skills, and struggles. And yet, we have observed clear patterns of experiences that demand to be shared, that offer potential ways of reconceptualizing approaches to the practice of architecture and architecture training.

In order to fully contextualize the ambivalence about architecture that many of our clients experience, we begin this book by tracing the progression of a typical architecture student from a deep, passionate love of the architectural art form through to the unsettling emotional experience of beginning a career in the profession. This section, Part One: The Disconnect, is offered as a narrative collage, illustrating both general circumstances and particular examples from our own and our clients' experiences. Through these narratives, we demonstrate that, while every architecture student's experiences are unique, there are common threads among them that highlight the skills, abilities, and personality traits common to architecture students and graduates – and that there are common problems encountered by architects in a range of job settings.

Next, we move to Part Two: Why Is It Like This? Part Two is comprised of a series of five chapters, each of which explores one major causal factor in the feelings of ambivalence common to new architects. We focus first on the often-unintended negative consequences of the family model of both studio education and many design firms, then move on to a discussion of the harmful assumptions at play behind the idea of "the gentlemen's profession." In these chapters, we argue that these traditional approaches to architecture carry increasingly negative implications for architects, particularly for those entering the profession today. We then discuss issues of the self and community in architecture, first highlighting the paradox of the insecure overachiever – the architecture student who is infinitely valuable to a creative economy but who fails to see their own worth – and second discussing the challenges of forming healthy teams within the architecture workplace. We conclude Part Two by challenging architects, students, and educators to leave behind the concept of "the calling" that often pits passion against fair pay.

Finally, in Part Three: Your Career Is a Design Problem, we offer a series of case studies. Each case study represents a composite client, meaning that these chapters are not based on real individuals but instead draw from the types of personalities, values, goals, and challenges that we have seen as trends in our clients over the years. These chapters represent both a variety of client types, ranging from "the techie" to "the fashionistx," and a variety of career levels. Through these case studies, we demonstrate the various approaches we take with our clients, in hopes of demonstrating some of the potential ways of reframing and reimagining what a career out of architecture might look like. We then conclude the book by offering some overarching takeaways while calling on the field of architecture and architectural education to broaden its approaches to career placement, recognizing the changing nature of the field of architecture as well as the trend in other industries toward a focus on design.

Out of Architecture will illuminate some possibilities for architecture's future – not by revolutionizing the field but by empowering those who love it to take its best principles elsewhere. As architects who love this art form, we are deeply invested in the power of design. We know architects love their craft – we talk with them about it every day. We hope these lessons provide a new perspective on architecture – a perspective that centers value and that considers not only the value architects provide to others but the value that architecture should provide to its own practitioners.

NOTES

1   Julee Everett, "Use These 3 Techniques to Grow Your Product Mindset," *Product Coalition*, September 2020. Retrieved from https://productcoalition.com/3-steps-to-grow-our-product-mindset -10cf90e18125.
2   Robin Pogrebin, "5 Women Accuse the Architect Richard Meier of Sexual Harassment," *The New York Times*, March 13, 2018. Retrieved from www.nytimes.com/2018/03/13/arts/design/richard-meier -sexual-harassment-allegations.html.

THE DISCONNECT

PART ONE
THE DISCONNECT

Over the past decade, a staggering number of online articles have detailed the problem of burnout in the architecture profession. So common is this state of total fatigue – physical, mental, creative, and emotional – that news of early-career architects leaving the profession hardly registers as news.

So how do we reconcile the inability of the architecture profession to sustain its practitioners with the intense passion that characterizes architecture students early in their studies? What transforms a group of people once so deeply in love with their craft into a virtual horde of design zombies?

In Part One: The Disconnect, we trace the trajectory of architecture students from love to disillusionment. Bringing together stories from our own experiences and those of our clients, we detail the stages of a typical architecture student – from love to stress to confusion to disillusionment. And they are as common as the burnout they so often cause.

DOI: 10.4324/9781003300922-2

CHAPTER 1
LOVE AT FIRST SIGHT

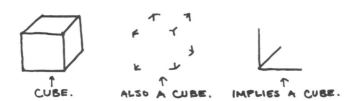

CUBE.   ALSO A CUBE.   IMPLIES A CUBE.

Anne Smith died a few days before Christmas in 2004. New Jersey winters are never particularly hospitable, and the day after she died, a nasty storm rolled in. It froze the ground and left a blanket of snow in its wake. Holding a graveside service was out of the question. After a series of phone calls between the funeral director and Anne's family, they settled on the only alternative that seemed feasible. It wasn't ideal, but they were out of options.

One gray, frosty Thursday afternoon, they layered coats and scarves with their funeral clothes and trekked up the snow-packed hill that led to East Brunswick's Frost Woods Memorial Park Mausoleum.

The funeral director ushered in Anne's family and friends out of the cold wind. And while the untreated concrete building did provide some shelter from the biting chill of the December air, it was not a space that anyone would describe as warm. The temperature was as cold as the space's atmosphere. It was, after all, a brutalist building on a hill. In the snow. Full of dead people.

"A building for dead people," Anne's 12-year-old granddaughter thought aloud, her voice a blend of horror and curiosity. Directed toward the building's blood-red carpet, her voice was barely a whisper. By the time it bounced around the walls of the space, it was somehow loud enough to be heard across the room.

"Shh," her father said sternly, wrapping a gloved hand around the child's shoulder. "Be quiet." *Be quiet, quiet, quiet*, his voice echoed. Her father withdrew his hand and shoved it back into his coat pocket. Even with his gloves on, his

DOI: 10.4324/9781003300922-3

hands were too cold, the child thought. She sympathized. It was freezing, and her own small mittens were doing little to protect from the frost.

Around them, other whispers reverberated.

"It's so cold," someone said.

"She always hated the cold," a voice replied. "She would hate this."

No, she wouldn't, the 12-year-old thought – because she's dead. This time she kept the sentiment to herself. There were no secrets in this space. Whispers were somehow transformed by these stone walls. Softly spoken ideas became unbearably loud in this place that was somehow both full of people and horribly empty.

The unbearable resonance became even more apparent as the service progressed.

Grandma had loved to sing. She had loved music in general. To honor her, the family arranged to have a choir participate in the service. This would have been a lovely touch for the outdoor service they had originally envisioned. Instead, hymns that might have brought a sense of comfort and familiarity to those attending the service banged around the chilly interior. They struck the dull gray walls, bounced to the glass ends of the building, and circled back against every frigid, hard surface before assaulting the ears of those who had come to pay their last respects. It was terrifying and horrible.

Grandma would have hated it.

There, in the freezing stone space, shivering against the temperature and the choral cacophony, the 12-year-old finally understood what death was. It felt icy and still and somehow lonely, even with all the people.

She had wanted one last moment with her grandmother, and she had understood that this would happen at the funeral. But now it seemed no trace of her grandmother remained. Her most powerful memory of her grandma was her perfume – "the most important part of any ensemble," Grandma used to say. But this level of cold deadens one's acute sense of smell. The 12-year-old breathed in as deeply as she could, but no trace of her grandmother remained in the air – even that had been stolen by this crucifix-shaped building full of death.

Anne Smith had been a seamstress, a dressmaker, and the first designer in the family. She had studied fashion design at Parsons in New York City in the 1940s, and she was the first person who taught Erin to make. She was someone who crafted things. In her hands, an idea became a muslin pattern, which then took on the tactile silkiness of satin or the soft stiffness of wool suiting. To that fabric, she applied a series of highly technical processes that are invisible to most people, processes designed to give the appearance of ease, so that years of training disappear into the effortlessness of a beautiful garment. Her work represented the intersection of style and utility – a thing that people live their lives in.

It's popular now to call people like her – like us – "makers," but she probably wouldn't have used that term to describe herself. She made beautiful goods that enhanced people's lives. If you've ever put on a suit that's been perfectly tailored to your frame, or a dress that was made especially for your body, you know that the change is more than clothing. It changes your outlook. It makes you feel different, better. It opens up possibilities of who you could be and what you could do.

Architecture does that too.

Erin didn't know that yet. But she had felt the power of architecture on that late December afternoon as she sat, fearing she might freeze. The voices of the singers echoed violently around her, and even though she didn't have the language to explain it,

she felt in her bones that buildings are more than just places.

It would be years before she would learn the term "phenomenology." She hadn't dreamt of exploring "the architecture of the invisible" or of thinking about the ways our bodies intertwine with space. But she knew then that space has a profound effect on our relationships, our experiences, and our stories.

#

Most architects can relate to this feeling of being plunged, headfirst, into a love affair with the craft. Jake's headfirst feeling emerged when his budding love of design reared its head through the form and craft of woodworking. Dan Rudin studied jazz guitar in college. He supported himself by building guitars and selling them and passed that fascination with woodworking – with shaping a piece of wood, gorgeous in its own right, into an incredible, useful thing – to his son, Jake.

There was always music playing at the Rudin house. It was part of the space as much as it was part of the family that shared that space. In that context, he marveled over the way things physically come together to form new, more complex objects. He surrounded himself with form and beauty – from guitars to books to plants – curves and lines and shapes that dictate our relationship to a place.

Rummaging through the garage one afternoon, gathering scraps of wood and spare fasteners to tinker with, the toe of Jake's sneaker brushed a chunk of wood, dull from its years propped up in its corner.

"Hey, Dad?" he called out, as he grabbed a shop towel and wiped at the thick layer of dust. He coughed into the cloud but kept at the task.

Dan emerged from the warm glow of the kitchen and leaned against the doorframe. "What's up?" he asked, then paused, stepping into the room. "What do you have there?"

"I was going to ask you. What is this?" He looked back to the spot where the wood had been sitting and noticed several more. "What are all of these?"

His dad chuckled. "Well, as you can see, they aren't guitars. But they were supposed to be at some point."

It was as though lightning had struck Jake where he stood. He knew that his father had built guitars, but he had no idea that the supplies had been sitting here the whole time. The project would blend his love of music with his passion for building and his need to surround himself with beautiful things. "Can I build one?" he asked. "Will you show me how?"

Applying to architecture school requires a portfolio, and that process is daunting. There was no better way for Jake to demonstrate his passion for making beautiful, practical things than building a guitar. It would prove to be an exercise that solidified an investment he had already felt for some time. Once that guitar was ready for inclusion in a portfolio, it had transformed from a dingy brown piece of wood to a rich, warm, polished mahogany. And Jake's love for building had transformed into the love affair that would lead him to architecture school.

We bet you remember when you first learned about this field called "architecture," when you learned that it was something you could do – that an "architect" was someone you could be. That architecture school was a place you could study at.

Maybe you saw a romantic comedy with some dashing leading man, adorned with a yellow hard hat, leaning confidently over a set of blueprints. Now, you'd watch that scene with a little pang of annoyance, mentally highlighting everything Hollywood gets wrong about our craft.

Maybe you experienced a building that spoke to your soul, a grand cathedral, or a provincial cottage, or a high-rise, studded with steel and glass. You noticed that most people moved past, not even stopping to look. But you wanted to experience that structure. You wondered what the texture of the concrete felt like, or you had to step back to take in the massive scale. You wanted to know how this structure had been imagined, designed, and constructed. Maybe you happened to find someone who could tell you about the architect behind it.

Or, perhaps, a high school counselor suggested the career path to you, noting your interest in both art and physical sciences. The counselor probably didn't know much more than you did about what architecture might entail. They had probably seen that romantic comedy, too. But they pointed you in the direction of a few programs, and you set out to explore what this career option could look like.

Then, like us, you discovered architecture school, and nothing was ever the same.

#

"Build a cube," the professor had told us, and we wondered whether it was a trap. We suspect you have had this experience, too. You walk into the studio one day, early in your architectural training, to find piles of paper, chipboard, and basswood: "the cube project," it's commonly called.

You'd expected architecture school to involve a lot of time spent talking about buildings. But you were quickly disabused of that idea. In fact, "building" was now known as "the b-word." That didn't stop you from trying your hardest to impress.

Hunched over your collection of rudimentary supplies, you set out to build a perfect cube. Every angle should be perfectly square. Every side should be smooth and clean. This was easier said than done, given the materials available. But you persisted. Everyone measured it out. You put your edges together. You took care to be tidy with the adhesive. You tried not to be too obvious as you glanced around the room, sizing up your cohort, praying you measured up. Maybe you were even feeling good about your cube.

Then the professor came through. He had wiry gray hair, a little longer than you might have expected. In addition to the glasses on his face, he had an apparently identical pair on his head that he seemed to have forgotten about. His face barely moved as he peered through the small, circular, wire rims. He was an art professor, straight from Central Casting.

This was the first review. You'd spent a day working on the project, and you'd gotten a taste of that now-familiar sense of constantly looming deadlines.

Even at that early stage, there was never enough time. You could never quite achieve the perfection you imagined. You were nervous but excited for that first bit of feedback. The professor walked around the room, looking at everyone's cubes.

The girl with the pixie cut had beveled her edges, and you wondered why you didn't think to do that. Her cube was perfect. Every measurement was exact; every angle was precise. You were impressed – maybe a little envious, if you were totally honest with yourself.

The professor seemed underwhelmed. You thought you heard him say, "This is cute," before he moved on to the next student. "*What am I missing?*" you wondered. Her cube looked perfect. If he wasn't impressed with her work, how would yours hold up? Your palms began to sweat.

The professor continued his rounds. He was generally stoic, but he did provide some feedback here and there.

"Look at this glue joint here," he said to the hipster in the skinny jeans. "You're sitting this piece on top of here, so technically that's an eighth of an inch more than a cube."

At this bit of feedback, the hipster kid looked utterly defeated. You couldn't blame him. You would have been too. Glancing down at your project, you hoped you hadn't made the same mistake.

There was more of the same as the professor moved around the room. He didn't seem impressed by anyone, which at least leveled the playing field in a way. You heard him give unenthusiastic feedback to a third student, a fourth, a fifth.

Then, he reached the woman with the blue hoodie and the blonde ponytail. In a month or two, she wouldn't be dressed in such a bold color, but you hadn't yet learned that bright clothing stole attention from your project during review.

Your heart skipped a beat. Her cube wasn't really a cube; it was just three sides.

"This isn't a cube," the professor said.

"Well, it is, though," she replied. The silence stretched longer than it should have, and you sensed that he was intentionally drawing the review out. Discomfort hung in the air, and he seemed to like it that way. But the girl in the blue hoodie was not shaken.

He returned the not-cube to the table and asked, "Why?"

You suspected that she was right – the not-cube was actually a different form of cube – but you had no idea how to explain it. She tried to answer, but struggled to find the words. She said something about the general shape, about how the sides were square, and the joints in the basic arrangement of –

"Because it *implies* a cube," the professor interrupted, and you felt your mind expand in that moment. "You have enough in these three sides and three angles to demonstrate that there is a corner out here in space that is speaking to these other corners."

It was as though the room's discomfort was suddenly replaced with electricity. Other students' eyes widened. You saw a few slanted grins. Someone mumbled, "holy shit."

Of course, that was not the end of the cube project. Soon, you built a second round of cubes. Everybody was still aiming for perfection, but now you were all working with an entirely new concept of what a perfect cube might be. The studio felt different. What had been an exercise in following the rules was now a test of reimagining them. It had been made abundantly clear that the person who broke the rules most cleverly would be heartily rewarded with the praise we all so desperately sought.

During the next round, someone made only edges. Or maybe someone built half of the cube – a diorama. Someone else made half of the cube in black and the other half in white.

As the third round became the fourth round, then the fifth round, you kept pushing yourself. You kept pushing each other. And, sure, you were tired, but you were also alive with creative energy.

In the sixth round, the boy in the plaid shirt didn't build a cube at all. He drew his cube in perspective, and when the professor came around, the boy announced, "that's a cube." Then you noticed how much better your classmates had gotten at defending their experiments. You noticed how much they were learning. And you noticed it in yourself, too.

Maybe you were having trouble sleeping by that point. Somehow a series of cubes had blown your mind open, and all you could think about was whether a closed cube was solid or hollow: Schrödinger's cube.

The teaching assistant showed you all how to draw a cube, and you found yourself back where you started. You were full of assumptions about how to draw a cube, about what a "perfect" cube might look like on paper. Suddenly, you realized that the idea of drawing a cube raised more questions than it answered.

You drew a section cut the way you thought it should look. Then you looked at it again. *Is that the cutline? Do I just draw lines?* You glanced at the guy next to you, and he had filled his cube. *Did that mean it's solid?* You experiment with degrees of solidity, with what it might mean for the cube to be empty or translucent. You were eating it up, and it was the best thing you had ever eaten. Someone asked a question about the thickness of the cube's walls, which led to a discussion of the properties of the material, and you thought you'd loved architecture before. You had no idea. Now you were fully, thoroughly, hypnotically, irreparably in love.

And that was how you fell in love with architecture. Not casually. Not a little at a time. Head. Over. Heels.

#

It's not that you fall in love with architecture despite its difficulty. The challenge of it is part of that initial affair.

This is why so many architects remember their first all-nighter so vividly. It's a rite of passage, flavored with an odd cocktail of passion, weariness, frustration, and camaraderie. Or, at least, we hope your first all-nighter brought with it the kind of communal bonding that ours did. The instability of having your world rocked by a cube isn't something you want to experience in isolation.

Cornell's architecture department has a summer program for high school students called, simply, "Introduction to Architecture." Jake attended this program between his junior and senior year of high school. Programs like this have a final project that could more accurately be called a series of final projects. The varied array of tasks students were asked to complete was absurd, particularly given the perfectionism that most architects are driven by. Beautiful hand-drawn elevations and models were abandoned in the studio every evening, and students were ushered to dinner and the dorms.

The night before the final review, around 10:00 pm, Jake peeked into the hallway. No one was there. The stairwell was clear, too, and he made his way out of the dorm, being careful not to set off the door prop alarm, across the quad, and over the bridge to the studio entrance. Unlocked. He pulled the door open and heard a gasp from inside. With hair piled on her head in a messy bun, a girl sat hunched over an intricately detailed model.

"Oh my God, you scared me!" she said, moving her hand to her chest.

"I'm sorry," Jake said apologetically. "I just needed to – "

"Oh, I totally get it," she said and gave a dramatic sweeping gesture toward her half-finished structure. For a moment, Jake felt a little pang of jealousy. Her model was already incredible.

He grabbed a chair near the girl and took out the lead holder, a new tool that felt impossibly professional, and the drawing he'd been forced to put away a few hours earlier. He glanced over, and the girl had already fallen back into her work.

For the next few hours, they sat like that, mostly silent, with a focused intensity on the projects at hand. Occasionally, one of them would yawn or ask for the other's opinion. There were breaks to grab a snack from the vending machine down the hall, and as the night progressed and the loopy fatigue set in, there were occasional fits of laughter.

But mostly there was a sense of solidarity that Jake wasn't sure he'd felt before. It was the relief of feeling that someone else was on your team, that you were working toward the same goal with the same sense of passion and dedication, even though neither of you had experienced that level of determination before. It was destabilizing. So, it was comforting to know that someone else felt it too.

The way they talked about their projects, when they took a moment to look up from their work, was reassuring as well. They'd gotten critiques from the professors and teaching assistants – these often felt harsh, although they later realized that they barely knew what a harsh critique could be – and now they found themselves offering each other suggestions in a way that felt refreshingly supportive. They were working independently, but they were a team. There had been a sense of competition throughout the program, probably a natural outgrowth of programs like that. But this wasn't competitive. It was inspiring in a way that is particular to healthy, creative communities.

That energy powered them through the night.

Sometime around three or four in the morning – they'd lost track – the girl, whose name Jake now knew was Yenny, gave a grunt of frustration.

Jake looked up to see her, elbows on the table, one hand supporting her forehead and the other holding the thinnest piece of metal.

"I can't get this to stay," she said.

"What are you trying to do?" he asked and made his way around the table to where her model had transformed from the half-finished project he'd seen earlier in the evening to a remarkably detailed work of art.

She held the metal up, bridging the tiny door with the series of perfect stairs. "It's a handrail," she said. "I think it will help show the scale."

Honestly, it seemed impossible, but Jake could see what she meant. It was the tiniest detail, and maybe other students would have given up, but she had her heart set on affixing this minute piece of metal, a fraction of a millimeter thick, to her model. The problem, Jake saw as Yenny held the piece to her model, was that her hands were shaking.

"Let me try it," he offered, and she handed him the handrail. It was immediately clear that his hands were no more stable than hers had been. Exhaustion will wreak havoc on a person's fine motor skills.

In the end, they had to work together. She applied a new dab of glue to each end of the rail, and, together, they held the tiny piece of metal in place until the adhesive set.

Until the bond had formed.

#

That bond was about more than glue and a model. That friendship – and, more broadly,

the sense of being part of a creative community and a fraternity of architects – carried us through school. It made us push harder than we ever had before. It fueled a sense of dedication to our collective craft. It made us stubborn in the best possible way.

Of course, we had professors who encouraged this. We bet you did too. Those mentors taught us to never accept the idea of "impossible," to reject those who say it can't be done, who say, "It's too expensive," or "No one does it that way anymore."

Driven by the passion you've discovered for the art and the dedication you feel to this little community – the love you feel for them – you know you won't take "no" for an answer. You can't take "no" for an answer.

There is a tradition in the Cornell University College of Architecture, Art, and Planning, where we all completed our bachelor's degrees, called "Dragon Day." The tradition began in 1901, which makes it the longest standing college tradition in the United States. First-year students get an entire week off from classes the week before spring break. That time is dedicated to creating a massive dragon structure. Apparently, the dragon originally carried some loose symbolic connection to St. Patrick's driving the snakes out of Ireland. Students later would vaguely recall conversations connecting the tradition to anti-war protests.

Whatever its origin story, the important part of the ritual was the creation of a huge dragon that could be paraded around campus. The more advanced architecture students from the program dressed in garish costumes and chanted at the top of their lungs as the dragon passed by. Alumni sometimes visited and joined in the festivities. Professors silently judged the results. The dragons were meticulously documented and inevitably compared to one another. Perhaps no one literally shouted "Gooble, gobble, one of us!" but the sense of being initiated into an exclusive fraternity hung in the air nonetheless.

And at the end of the parade, tradition demanded that the dragon must burn.

Burning the dragon symbolized something truly profound about our journey into this art form. In the most tangible way possible, it demonstrated the confidence that because we had built this huge dragon once, we could always build it again. Our community of architecture students shared such a strong, intimate bond that we wouldn't flinch at the idea of building this towering, challenging, beautiful structure and then tossing it into a fire.

Then, in 2009, New York's state fire codes were updated. University administrators felt queasy about the idea of burning the dragon. That year, students burned the dragon's "nest," which was a clever workaround. They weren't planning to burn the *dragon*, they had assured administrators, and that was technically true. But that workaround left a legacy of resistance for the next year's "Dragon Day" participants. We were among those students, serving in the roles of co-president and construction manager.

From the outset, the university provost and fire marshal vetoed the burning of the dragon. They encouraged us to try an alternative. "Why not just spray some paint onto the creature?" they suggested. "Or maybe you could cover it. With a big cloth or something."

We did everything we could to keep from rolling our eyes. We saw this project as the first time we got to be our own clients. We weren't building this for our professors or the guest critics. We were building this for ourselves. For our cohort. For the advanced students and the alumni who had come before us. We would use Dragon Day to mark our entry into the fraternity of architects just as students had been doing for over a century.

So we were not thrilled about the idea of adding university administrators to our client list, particularly given what we saw as a list of banal concerns about a traditional bonfire. After a frustrating number of brainstorming sessions and what felt like even more meetings with the provost, we finally found a way to appease them. We would make the structure out of metal. It wouldn't burn, we assured them.

We spent countless hours working with our cohort to build a 53-foot-long dragon, its body covered with glistening scales. Alone, that aspect of the project had carried with it a host of problems. How could we create this steel structure in a way that would allow us to maneuver it? Where should we position the dragon carriers, to ensure we could keep the enormous beast off the ground? Would we have time to create and affix hundreds of individual scales to the structure?

And, always, droning in the back of our brains was the emotional baggage that balances the love of architecture in those early days of school: that incessant, nagging hunger for validation. Within the first few weeks of our program, our sense of taste had been dramatically destabilized. Often, we didn't know which way was up and which way was down, let alone which projects looked good and which were abysmally disappointing. It sometimes seemed as though the only people who knew were the professors, and as this sensation grew, we found ourselves trusting our own judgment less and less. The passion we brought to our art form only fueled this need for acceptance, which was magnified tenfold by the alumni investment in Dragon Day. This wasn't just for us. This was for everyone who came before.

This project, more than anything else we had ever worked on, was about upholding a promise to our community.

Of course, we were also energized by the build itself, the vision of what a huge dragon could be, and the highs and lows of the design process. We knew that this project would be good for us in the long run, as we battled through the administrative, political, bureaucratic, technical, mundane, and creative sides of design and project management.

By the time we burned the dragon — because much to the administration's chagrin, we had always planned to burn the dragon — our training in architecture was more than just love. We had concrete, material things we could point to that demonstrated our passion. We had new language to articulate our reasons for loving architecture. We had new ways to dream, more sophisticated tools to build the spaces we imagined.

As we struggled through these lessons, we never lost that feeling of passion. We still haven't. We felt ourselves transitioning into a new world where architecture was more than a dream. It was an identity.

Our younger selves may not have fully understood what our early experiences with architecture meant as we hovered in the icy chill of the mausoleum or manipulated the warm mahogany of that first guitar. But the things we would learn in architecture school – even from the very first days – forever colored our view of those experiences. These lessons, skills, and perspectives would irreversibly shape our perception of the past, our relationship with the present, and the way we would approach our careers in the future.

CHAPTER 2
AN EDUCATION

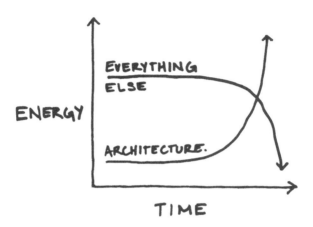

There was never any question of our passion for architecture – not that passion was enough. It wasn't even close. Passion might have kept you going through the fatigue, the frustration, and the gradual decline in your physical and psychological health. But if you wanted to keep your head above water, you knew you had to learn to swim.

This was never clearer than the day you held that first architecture design studio brief in your hands.

"Nihil," was printed at the top in bold, black letters. It meant "nothing" in Latin, you learned from the parenthetical below, its font much finer and yet somehow more unsettling. Your heart skipped a beat, flooded simultaneously with fear and excitement.

You scanned the description as the professor gave some vague instruction. Soon, even that level of clarification would feel like a luxury, but you were still new to architecture school. They were easing you in.

The brief continued by explaining that architecture is about "conceptual lenses," whatever that might mean, and "vast fields of information that make up

DOI: 10.4324/9781003300922-4

the world around us." It seemed a little dramatic, honestly, but your interest was piqued. There was something existential written there about earth, air, and water.

You were supposed to be "unfailing to unsee."

You rolled the phrase around in your head, wondering what it might mean, furrowing your brow. Unfailing to unsee. Okay, you think, just keep reading. Maybe the next part will be clearer.

Then came the actual instructions. You were to use five sheets of paper, the precise dimensions and weight specified in the assignment. You could do whatever you wanted with the paper, apparently, which gave you plenty of possibilities – listed were folding, cutting, drawing, and scoring. But you had to use exactly that amount of paper. To further complicate the assignment, you were not allowed to use any kind of adhesive or fastener.

What is happening? The assignment was disconcerting. But, you admitted to yourself, it was also kind of cool.

In the end, you were asked to create "a three-dimensional construct of nihil – nothing – at full scale."

What is the scale of nothing?

The past few weeks had brought about many mind-blowing experiences, and it had been somehow simultaneously mentally exhausting and viscerally energizing.

You had all been thrown into the proverbial deep end, and it was up to you whether or not to come up for air.

#

While you were sinking or swimming – no one could be sure which you were doing at this point – your class schedule threw you a lifeline. You strode, confident and relieved, into "Freehand Drawing." Amid the uncertainty of not-cubes and paper folded into nothing, you felt certain you could cling to your drawing skills.

Drawing made up a good portion of your portfolio when you applied to architecture school. You didn't want to brag, but when you were introducing yourself to another student earlier that day, you'd mentioned your love of drawing.

"I mean, I know I have a lot to learn here," you had said, "but I'm not worried about drawing."

You wanted to tell her that you had been the best at your high school. You'd even won an award during senior year. You didn't mention that part. You knew everyone would see soon enough how much you excelled in this particular area of architecture.

As soon as you had all gotten settled into seats in the lecture hall, your professor sent you all back out. You were to take your drawing sketchbook outside and bring back a sketch of something you observed on campus. Piece of cake, you thought. You had done this before, many times.

Perhaps you couldn't be faulted for not yet seeing the pattern of the entire early portion of architecture school. The point was to rattle you to your very core. If you had fully understood, you would not have gone into the situation with so much pride – with so much trust.

The warm air hit your face as you and your classmates streamed through the door and onto the walkway on the west side of campus. Summer was reluctant to give way to fall, but there was a hint of orange in the trees and that palpable sense of possibility that comes with every new school year.

Everyone split up and wished each other luck, and you spent some time wandering around campus with intention, searching for the perfect subject. There was an undeniable magical quality to drawing outside, in public. It conjured images of the great Renaissance artists, gazing out at pastoral settings, hovering a thumb in front of their face for scale. Finally, you plopped down – did Renaissance artists plop? – on the sidewalk in front of an ornate wrought-iron lamppost.

The fixture began to take shape on the page as you ran your pencil back and forth, sketching and shading the lines that made it elaborate without being too fussy. Very architectural, you thought.

You didn't have as much time as you would have liked, but you were pleased with your work. Back in the lecture hall, you proudly pinned up your drawing. It was really pretty.

"This drawing of the lamppost," the professor said when she reached your drawing. "It's darling. Very nostalgic."

You beamed with pride.

"We don't draw like this here."

You felt the blood rush up to your cheeks as your stomach flipped, then dropped. Casual humiliation – there was no other way to describe it.

"You will all unlearn this kind of drawing."

Back to the drawing board, so to speak. Except you weren't going back. You were going forward. You were "unlearning" how to draw – whatever that meant.

#

We piled back into studio, taking our places at the desks that were beginning to feel increasingly like our second homes. The teaching assistants distributed blank newsprint and asked you to retrieve your lead holders. Lead holders, you had learned last week, were holders for graphite with varying degrees of hardness and softness. We were instructed to sharpen them – something that took skill given their delicacy. And then, they taught us to draw.

"Draw a straight line," the lead TA said.

An end, a middle, and another end.

Trained architects know in our bones – the product of hours and hours of practice – the ends are extremely critical to the particular character of architectural drawings. There is a pointed emphasis on the ends.

But, of course, we didn't know that yet. We hadn't learned the precision that structures every aspect of this art form. So we drew our lines. We tried to draw them as straightly as possible, or we covered our imperfections by tracing back and forth over the line. Our past lives had taught us that a sketchy quality could cover a multitude of sins.

We were quickly dissuaded from employing that strategy.

In architectural drawing, every form on the page is marked by a balance of precision and humanity. There is a human hand behind the drawing, but that human hand is exact. It is perfect.

The only way to build that perfection is by drawing countless lines.

We filled pages of newsprint and our early sketchbooks with line after line, trying and failing, receiving correction with an increasing degree of grace and gratefulness. Sometimes a professor or teaching assistant physically placed their hand over ours. "Do you see what it should feel like?" they asked as they drew through our hands. This act of intense intimacy became quotidian in the daily repetition of drawing lines. This was the process, we understood, of learning how to do this thing we loved.

A line is a balance not only of geometry – a straight segment anchored by two points – but also of weight. The standard, yellow Dixon Ticonderoga #2 pencil is exactly in the middle of the spectrum, the lead graded HB denoting a "hard black" quality to the graphite. A thin, delicate line like that of a brilliantly sharpened 4H lead carries a lightness and slenderness reminiscent of something that can only barely be seen with the naked eye. Heft, largess, and prominence were readily conveyed by the softer, darker leads higher in the 4B, 6B, or 8B range. Of course, the pressure of the hand and consistency of speed can produce myriad effects for those advanced enough to control them.

Soon, the lines began to intersect. The corners began to cross. Then, they began to bend and curve.

"Fill the page with circles," the professor said. "Each circle should overlap the next by five millimeters. No more, no less." The focus that filled the room took on a material quality. A unique sound of silence layered with the textural scratching of pencils on paper. Occasionally, it seemed unbearably loud. Then came the sound of another human breathing over your shoulder or the burst of a correction spoken across the room.

Invariably, the silence would be broken by the sound of an alarm: "Radar," it's called on iPhones. A series of four sets of four electronic beeps, the first set loud, then quieter and quieter. Like an echo, but divorced from any space that might reasonably produce reverberations like those.

Beep-be-be-be-beep-be-be-be-beep.

"That's time."

We would look down at our finished work. At first, we were frustrated and disappointed. We hadn't finished the task, or our millimeters suddenly looked closer to centimeters. The whole thing looked like shit, and we knew it. It was miles away from living up to the standards of the program, let alone the standards we had for our own work.

Then round after round of practice transformed our abilities. One day we looked down and, if we squinted, we could see that we were getting somewhere.

Of course, there was rarely much time for gazing at your work with pride. Time was always a luxury.

"Now fill a new page. Circles again. But this time, draw with both hands at the same time."

No sooner did we master one task than we were pushed into the next. Each one seemed impossible until we did it. Each was punctuated with the beep-be-be-be-beep of the iPhone.

"Now fill the page with lines two inches long with half-inch gaps between the lines."

"Now write your name exactly four inches wide without measuring or lifting your hand."

Beep-be-be-be-beep-be-be-be-beep.

"Now write your name as a mirror image with both hands at the same time."

Beep-be-be-be-beep-be-be-be-beep.

Eventually, we moved on from those basics to parti diagrams and floor plans, to manipulating line weight and representing what can't be seen. Not that you're taught to do these things, per se. Not immediately anyway. You're just expected to figure it out.

A building flashed up on the projector. "You have three minutes to capture what's on the screen in your sketchbook."

Beep-be-be-be-beep-be-be-be-beep. Another one.

Then the second round. "Thirty seconds."

Then the third. "Ten seconds."

"Replicate this drawing in five seconds."

Beep-be-be-be-beep-be-be-be-beep.

We set out to unlearn drawing. That happened very quickly. The difficult part was the re-learning, realizing that our technical skills didn't match our vision, that time constraints were constant and looming, symbolized a little too perfectly by the Pavlovian response we developed to that iPhone alarm.

We learned, too, that our skills were not the responsibility of our professor, our teaching assistants, or our cohort. That you learned from doing and there was always more you could do. That the only way to get to where we wanted to go was to become our own worst critic and to let that inner voice push us beyond the limits we thought we had. That inner voice, and the outer voices of our fellow students, pushed us to be so much better. To learn the most valuable skills of our education.

#

It was a chilly afternoon in November, and architecture students buzzed around the building excitedly like bees around a hive. One student had taken a keen interest in the precise moment where concrete gave way to the brick of an exterior wall. A second was squinting up at the roofline while wandering around the corner of the building. He seemed to be looking for the best angle for a picture, Jake thought. He also thought the guy should watch where he was going if he didn't want to face plant.

Jake was observing his classmate from a ground position, where he was on hands and knees, sifting through the dust at the base of the structure. By this point, it was becoming clear that the professor's instructions to "document the site" meant more than simply taking photos that could be later found with a quick Google search. A particular piece of rock had caught Jake's eye. The way the bits of debris signaled the intersection of spirit and structure seemed apt for the space. He hoped it was a potential way to reimagine this very well-known building and add something new to the conversation. That was the real pressure with these site visits: to find something unique to contribute.

That morning at 7:30 am, the students had boarded a university bus and traveled 90 minutes to Rochester. In the late 1950s, the congregation of the First Unitarian Church had conducted a search for an architect. They began with Frank Lloyd Wright, elderly by then and apparently disinterested in the project, before sifting through several of the biggest names in architecture at the time. They landed on Louis Kahn, citing the congruence of his outlook with their denomination's theology. The building was designed and constructed over the next few years, not without controversy. It seemed even the most artistically conceived design sometimes displeased the client, and eventually, Kahn had to make concessions to appease the congregation. The process clearly worked, as the building was later recognized as a key work of twentieth-century religious architecture. It is frequently used as a case study for early architecture students.

Of course, the students knew very little of this at the time. They were often kept in the dark on matters of the architectural canon. At least these buildings weren't taught by name, and the observations of critics and theorists were never explicitly discussed until long after the site visit, if at all. Sometimes a professor would flash a diagram up on the screen and ask the students to draw it. Then, months or years down the line, Jake would recognize the particular shapes in a site visit to Buffalo, Manhattan, or the outskirts of Tompkins County.

It was a strange sensation, Jake thought, to have the core ideas of your academic field withheld. It was not something that seemed like particularly intuitive pedagogy, and he doubted that students in other fields were asked to grapple with their studies in this way. The idea was that students learned best through exploration, so they would be taken to site visits and asked to document what they observed. How many hundreds of pictures would those students take, collectively, at each location they visited throughout the program? How many textures would students try to transpose into words, only to realize that every linguistic description came up a bit short of the tactile sensation of being there? How many on-site ideas would later escape them when they tried to develop original materials for review?

This was the power of architecture, the realization that all the drawings and photographs in the world could never match the experience of a place.

All of it was beautiful. However, the point of the site visits was not to gain more of an appreciation for the art form they were all passionate about. That passion was a baseline assumption. The purpose was to develop skills of evaluation and to learn criticism – not in the "two thumbs down" sense but in the way that thorough analysis is crucial for effective problem solving. They were building the grammar of architecture through trial and error, asked to observe how experiments in stone and steel, glass and light, were made into social spaces. They were learning how to describe the details that ordinary people never even noticed.

"Panera this afternoon?" Erin asked, once they were settled into their bus seats and Ithaca-bound.

"You got it."

At Panera, you could buy one cup of coffee for a buck fifty and refill it as many times as you wanted. It felt like an illicit college secret, although it wasn't a secret at all. Panera had free Wi-Fi, and as long as you bought something when you first arrived, they usually didn't mind if you stayed a few hours. The restaurant was usually flooded with students from architecture and elsewhere on campus.

Jake and Erin had learned this intimately as they spent hours watching YouTube tutorials for 3D modeling software propped up by the hospitality of the casual dining chain. It had all begun one day in studio when Jake looked over to see another student with something similar to a not-cube idea – an approach that seemed illegal, but that was exactly the kind of rule-breaking that won you the praise of the faculty. The student was modeling their nihil in a program called Rhino, a 3D computer-aided design software.

"Woah," Jake said, barely masking his jealousy. "We can do that?"

"They never said we couldn't print onto one of the sheets of paper, right?"

It was right, and it was brilliant. That afternoon, Jake and Erin set up their laptops at Panera for the first time, determined to enter this brave new world of design technology.

Jake had always had a knack for tech, and while it wasn't Erin's favorite aspect of architecture, she picked up on the new software without much trouble. This was good, because aside from a rogue teaching assistant or two, they would never get direct instruction on the software programs they needed to use. This was part of the genius of the studio system. It was sometimes frustrating, but the professors let you figure things out on your own so you wouldn't be limited by the way they had taught you. You were left to sink or swim, so when you swam, you felt like Michael Phelps.

Unfortunately, this model for learning design technology resulted in a marked discrepancy between the "techies" and those who never quite got the hang of the software. The fortunate few had already experimented with some of these applications – some had entered the program with a working knowledge of the Adobe suite, or at least some sense of how to manipulate an image in Photoshop. Others found themselves completely lost and frustrated, with the understanding that this might not be "on the test" in architecture school but that some ability to use design and collaboration software would likely be an expectation in the workforce. A third group didn't think that far ahead and found ways to pick up just enough to get by.

#

Learning to put things on paper – by hand or computer – wasn't usually the final goal, so it usually wasn't taught in isolation, even from the beginning. What you created on paper had to be translated into three-dimensional, material objects.

The charge to design a full-scale nihil, for example, wasn't simply a problem of design, at least not as you had understood design before the "darling lamppost" incident. As you had understood it before, you drew 50 precisely overlapping circles, wrote dozens of pages of notes about the character of a tiny alcove you found hidden away in a church, or modeled a sheet of paper in 3D design software.

Now you realized that you needed some materials if you were going to create a nihil, a void – a space. The assignment called for 24-pound white paper, exactly 216 millimeters by 279 millimeters. Even an instruction so precise raised a host of challenges. What exactly is this paper? Where could you buy it? If you had to use five sheets, should you buy six? Seven? Ten? And how much did each of these sheets cost?

Of course, the punchline, if you could call it that, was that 216 millimeters by 279 millimeters is equal to 8.5 inches by 11 inches, and 24-pound bond is a fairly standard type of printer paper. Very shortly, assignments would demand much more in terms of logistical coordination.

The next project required larger sheets of paper, which had to be transported, somehow, from the art supply store to your dorm. You found yourself schlepping these sheets of paper up a hill, sandwiched between two boards but still terrified one might rip or fold. Perhaps you spent your last 20 dollars on those pieces of paper, and your near-empty bank account threatened to derail your project unless you could successfully transfer those sheets of paper from store to dorm to studio, pristine and intact, without even a trace of a curl on the corners.

And that's only the first step. Within a year or two, you were building a model of an urban complex, and at that point, it wasn't just paper you needed. Now it was necessary to coordinate the collection of a variety of materials: wood, plexiglass, acrylic, foam, fasteners, adhesive, and paint. You had to produce all of the design drawings and the files for fabrication.

Then, you had to book a time slot with the digital fabrication lab to mill out your site model. This meant accurately estimating the amount of time you would need and getting your file ready in time for your appointment.

It meant double checking that your adhesive was compatible with the other materials you planned to use. You had learned from your own previous mistakes that the right glue was not only a matter of safety, it was also a matter of time. There was no Beep-be-be-be-beep to tell you the time was up – although you still heard it in your mind – but you were intimately aware of every impending deadline, and you needed to make sure you bought an adhesive that would have time to dry before review.

While you were finishing your model, you also had to juggle your drawings. You had to schedule time in the plotting room. If you were short on money – as most students were – you needed to figure out the most efficient way to lay out your drawings. The plotting service charged by the linear foot, so if you could fit multiple drawings onto one sheet and have them cut out, you might be able to upgrade your lunch from generic to name-brand macaroni and cheese.

By this point, you were becoming competent at transporting huge pieces of paper without wrinkling or tearing them. That turned out to be a very useful skill, now that you had to move your drawings down to the review space and pin them up. You needed the ladder for that. You needed pins. You needed to make sure you could access the space and coordinate with other students, since that made it much easier to get bigger drawings up on the board. You needed to get out a pedestal for your model, and the model needed to be moved to the pedestal while maintaining its integrity – hopefully you used the correct glue. And once those basic tasks were done, there was always more to do.

Review was coming.

#

You learned very quickly about review.

The studio method is designed as a series of case studies that position your professor as your client. Clients don't give you designs. They give you criteria. And then it's up to you to convince them that your design suits their needs. You are responsible for post-rationalizing every design choice, developing the strongest argument, the best way to draw the red thread from problem to solution. It's tough. Incredibly intimidating. But an important lesson in how to work with clients in the real world.

The ultimate exercise in this kind of stakeholder management was review.

After the mad dash to pin your drawings and position your models and adjust the lighting and figure out your presentation, you were usually a sticky, sweaty mess. Hopefully you were finished in time to shower and change. If not, you would guzzle as much coffee as you could and sit there, feeling physically and psychologically uncomfortable, for the duration of the review session.

You and your classmates took your seats behind the Professor and Pals – whichever faculty, teaching assistants, or guest critics happened to be on slate for the day – and tried to keep yourself upright in your chair until it was your turn. The struggle to stay awake was no indication of your sense of camaraderie or interest. It was simply the effect of very little sleep and the fatigue of the emotional build-up.

And then, it was your turn.

You gave your seven-minute presentation to the panel of critics who were often both terrifying and fascinating in what they said and how they dressed. Regardless, you soldiered on, using every persuasive tactic you could muster and praying their blank faces weren't an indication of their level of interest.

"Everyone else so far has had a section model through the site," one of them said. "Do you have that?"

Maybe you produced that piece, or maybe you argued to the proverbial death that it wasn't part of the conceptual needs of the design presentation.

Then came their comments.

"I mean, this is just…"

A giant, terrifying pause.

"This is endlessly intriguing. There's something about this thing and its relationship to the human. I mean, just look, the model tells you something about the experience of moving through the space. But the drawings tell a completely different story about the quality of light and dark in the interior. Imagine what it would feel like to circumambulate the site at dusk."

Oh, thank God.

A flood of relief washed over your body. They didn't hate it.

Get it together. Don't be too obvious.

You were elated, of course, but part of the exercise was to stay calm, cool, and collected. You did your best to hide how much your emotions had hinged on those first words.

"And not only did you have time to build this intricate creation, but you produced a series of finely detailed sections."

"Fascinating. I see hints of blah blah blah," and you honestly couldn't even hear them by that point because a symphony of pure elation had exploded behind your eardrums. The review gods had smiled on you that day. You enjoyed that moment of praise – you needed it desperately – but you were always a tiny bit aware that this positive review was also a product of the colors you used, the outfit you were wearing, the smell, the ambient temperature, the side of the bed the critics had gotten up on that morning, and so on.

You had done great work, but you always did great work. And that only made it starkly clear that the review could never be about the projects themselves. This gave you the sense of being entirely out of control. This project's fate, a thing that made up your entire identity at that moment – that you had poured every drop of energy and love and money and time into – rested tenuously on something that felt as uncertain as the wind.

#

Architecture school is very good at making makers. We were molded into designers and thinkers who could synthesize a variety of skills and emerge with something elegant, in every sense of the term. Not only drawing and evaluating and building and critiquing and accepting critique and managing projects and presenting ideas, but all of those skills together in perfect balance.

Sometimes moving between the various demands of creating and managing and communicating and critiquing felt a little like whiplash. But what it produced in us was an intense connection with the design process. It nurtured an instinct for meta-thinking

– in our case, designing about design – which required us to synthesize the things we learned in technical classes with the ideas we learned in theory courses and the images and stories we studied in history lectures. We were saturated with information, and we learned to hierarchically arrange those concepts because it was the only way to cope with being pulled from one obsession to the next.

Architecture school not only taught us that; it made it second nature. The synthesis of what felt like a million ideas became a background to how we operated without the need for direction. We became self-starters by training and by instinct. Critical thinking became our only way of thinking. Of course, it often kept us from sleeping or woke us up in the middle of the night because our brains never really shut off. In school, that meant we stopped sleeping. We stopped eating well. We forgot that we had actual relationships with other humans – we were so completely consumed by the process of design.

And we loved it.

That state of suffering for our passion was the beauty and the bane of our training. And while we can and should celebrate the way of thinking that is unique to those trained in architecture, it is impossible to overlook the fact that our way of seeing the world was not the only notion we carried with us when we left school.

CHAPTER 3
THE DISCONNECT

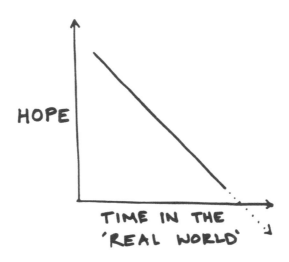

HOPE

TIME IN THE
'REAL WORLD'

Sheila Kingsbury's thick gray hair was gathered loosely behind her, but the wilder strands refused to be tamed. One escaped tendril drooped across her forehead, and Sheila tucked it back into her messy braid. A thick strand had also fallen behind her left ear, and the generally unwieldy mass of waves blurred the light behind her, giving a soft halo effect.

Immediately upon entering the space, Erin and Jake were overwhelmed by a fog of patchouli and the delicate clatter of the bracelet collection that adorned Sheila's wrist. With her voice soft and calm, she welcomed them to her home. They were swiftly escorted into an orange dining room, its walls peppered with tribal masks and an impressively scaled macramé wall hanging.

Erin's laptop felt somewhat anachronistic in the space, but she opened it and logged in as Jake arranged their sketches on the small table.

Their professor had noted Sheila's eccentricities, which were charmingly at home in upstate New York, when he prepped them to meet their client for the

DOI: 10.4324/9781003300922-5

first time. The commission, which wasn't technically as much a commission as a job handed to them by a mentor, involved designing a teahouse on Sheila's property. A year earlier, a tornado had torn across her five-acre property, flattening both her former tea house and a grove of beautiful old cherry trees. Sheila was having those trees milled so they could remain on the property in the form of the new tea house, but she needed someone to design the project. Jake and Erin were elated to have been chosen by their mentor, a close friend of Sheila's, and they had spent hours brainstorming, sketching, and eventually designing a rough concept model in 3D.

Now they sat at the table, cluttered with books and knick-knacks, as the two of them competently and enthusiastically explained their design concept to the client – their first client. They had finally made it.

Sheila seemed pleased enough as they presented their plans. They had taken care to match the brief, infusing the structure with the sense of organic spirituality they felt the client wanted and needed. The presentation was peppered with persuasive elements connecting the design to the history of the place and the traditions of tea ceremonies that would carry the spirit of the old building into the new structure. "A wooden structure in tribute to both the history of your land and the ceremony surrounding tea itself," they had concluded.

They waited eagerly for their client's response.

There was a pregnant pause, which Sheila broke by coughing lightly into a wadded up tissue she retrieved from her pocket. As she replaced the tissue, she smiled warmly at them. "Did you bring the construction drawings?" she asked.

It was a casual question, but carried a profound weight.

Jake swallowed hard. Erin just blinked. They had expected the kinds of feedback they got from their professors: some commentary on the strength of the conceptual design or, at least, approval to move forward with the project. Sheila seemed totally disinterested in that conversation. Or maybe she didn't realize they were expecting it in the first place.

Either way, her reaction caught them totally off guard. Jake stammered something about still being a work in progress. They wanted to make sure they were on the same page conceptually, Erin added, and they were planning to come back with the plans later. They felt shaky and confused, but mercifully Sheila didn't seem to notice. She offered them a cup of tea, appropriate, she sighed, for the creators of this new tea house, soon to be filled with community and love. They graciously declined, and she hugged each of them as they left.

The Disconnect

As they made their way to the door, their minds swirled with a sense of disembodied confusion. Their first years of architecture school had been eye-opening to say the least. They had learned not to mention buildings, "the b-word." There was a wry humor in the use of this euphemism, so counterintuitive for an architecture program that to use the term was to mark yourself an insider. Newbies and normies talked about buildings, they were taught. Architects talked about space and form.

And now, here they were, being asked to actually execute their ideas. The job was to construct an actual, well, b-word. Sheila wanted plans. She wanted to know, in detail, how this structure was going to be built.

On campus the next day, they debriefed with their mentor, recounting the awkward turn that the presentation had taken. They needed fully thought through construction drawings, they explained. They needed help figuring out how to answer Sheila's very practical questions.

Their mentor smiled a half-smile of something like commiseration. "You need to go talk to a structural engineer," he said, once he had shared the few, somewhat vague, suggestions he had. "You'll need someone to talk with you about this framing idea. Whether it will hold up over time. And I'm not sure about making the place two stories. Maybe it could work." He shuffled the sketches in his hands and squinted at them. "Yeah, you need to find a structural guy."

But at Erin and Jake's suggestion of a structural professor in the department, their mentor chuckled. "No, no," he responded jovially. "He'll just laugh at you."

Again, the students found themselves totally caught off guard. Why would he laugh? They had felt so confident about this project as they prepared to present the concept to Sheila, and now they were feeling completely insecure. What had they missed?

They gathered some advice, sidestepping the professor they had been warned to avoid, and threw together a drawing set. But there was no catching up with their client. Sheila, it turned out, was what you might call a "self-starter." She had some vague background in architecture – landscape architecture or design of some sort, maybe – and by the time Jake and Erin had put together a set of plans, Sheila had left them behind.

When the time came for their next appointment, they arrived at her home to find that the concrete footers had already been poured. As she walked them over the site – it was already a site – they passed "a small project" Sheila had started in the meantime: she was building a massive wooden sauna. By hand.

Neither of them could think of a time when they had felt as ineffectual as they did in that moment.

But ineffectual wasn't the primary sensation, really. The main thing they felt was disoriented. The rug had been pulled out from beneath their feet. They had excelled in architecture school those first two years. Not all of the feedback had been sunshine and rainbows, but they knew they were very strong students. That was why their mentor had sent them on this job.

Shouldn't strong students make strong architects?
If the skills they were learning in school – from drawing
to digital modeling to presenting work – weren't enough
for Sheila, this kind and supportive woman who seemed
to want nothing more than their success in the project, how
would they ever be enough for their careers?

A few months later, Erin was in New York and Jake was in China when they each received calls from their mentor. Sheila had passed away unexpectedly. The teahouse had been very near completion, missing only a few windows and some other cosmetic finishing touches.

The building, it seemed at least for the moment, would remain unresolved. It was, in a way, a fitting tribute to their first "real life" gig as architects – an incomplete structure that could attest to the gaps they were beginning to identify in their training. The disconnect given form, embodied in a piece of unfinished architecture.

#

This was not the first inkling of the disconnect, of the misalignment between some aspects of architecture school and the way the business of architecture was actually practiced. You had heard a snide comment or two from a professional who had guest lectured in class, dismissive remarks about learning things on the job. The focus was so consistently on replicating the professors' perspectives. You had been asked to think outside the box, of course, but only in terms of new design concepts, never in the way you approached the work.

Perhaps your class had gone to visit a local firm, to tour the site and speak with an architect. She was an alumnus of the program who had now established a thriving career in the field. You all looked forward to hearing about her work, to seeing what architecture firms were really like, to learning about this career that allowed you to think conceptually for a living.

Conceptual had really always been the word of the day.

That is, until the moment you set foot in this firm. The alumnus walked you around the office, introducing you to the various players: a partner, the studio manager, an intern. All of them looked exhausted and seemed to have little time to speak with you. You wondered if they had a big deadline coming up. Although, it did seem strange that they would have invited you when they were up against a deadline. Why not wait for a slower time in the calendar?

You brushed that concern aside as you continued into the alumnus's office. She talked you through her current project. It was all much more technical than you expected, all schedules, consultants, and the building department. You kept waiting for the concept. She seemed to have gotten stuck in the minutiae of square footage, in thinking through which windows fit the needs of the clients at the specified price point, of considering the minimum number of units needed to maximize the use of bulk materials.

Until this point, your entire training had been conceptual, conceptual, conceptual.

Hearing architects talk about real architecture with a huge, looming, capital "A" was beyond disconcerting, not that you necessarily realized that what you were hearing about was capital-A Architecture.

You hadn't been trained to speak about architecture the way the alumnus did. You hadn't even been trained to think that way. Your stomach flipped and sank, and you hoped this was just an anomaly.

On the bus ride back, another student, a guy you didn't particularly like, made a derisive comment about those other architects. He called them the "have nots" of the field, who had settled on talking about price points and building permits and the durability of materials. He was glad you had gone to visit that firm. Now he knew what to avoid in his own job search. He would never sell out his art for the mundane business of builders.

He had always been kind of a jerk, so this wasn't surprising to you. But you were a little surprised at how comforting it felt, and how tempting it was to follow his lead, using snootiness to brush aside the discomfort of inadequacy.

His comment kicked around in your mind the rest of the night. You couldn't shake the sensation that it revealed something important, something that you desperately wanted to ignore, but that was nagging at you even more feverishly every time you tried to brush it off.

Why would an alumnus of our program understand the profession so differently from the way we see it? What changed for her in the years since she was in school?

You thought of other professionals who had visited: a friend of the program who had served as a guest critic, an architect who had gone to school with your professor and dropped in for a guest lecture, the local architect who called your project "under-cooked."

At the time, you felt enthusiastic about your project as you headed into that review. You were at least as confident as possible given the circumstances. You had pinned your drawing to the board – truly one of the most beautiful pieces you had done in school so far – and transferred your model to the pedestal with kid gloves. You were excited when you saw the guest critic. Sometimes you wondered whether your professors were overly harsh because they knew you. A fresh pair of eyes couldn't hurt, particularly on a project that you knew was especially strong.

And then came the review.

As you neared the end of your presentation, you saw the guest critic fold his arms across his chest. His forehead dipped slightly downward, and he seemed to be chuckling slightly as he shook his head back and forth.

You finished speaking, and he raised his head and drew a sharp breath in. The professors turned to him, but he just stood there for a moment, a pained expression on his face. "You know," he started, then seemed to falter a bit. He gave a cynical half laugh. "You honestly have no idea. If we tried – " An uncomfortable pause, while he shook his head, eyebrows raised. "Do you know how much this would cost? You would never be able to build a building like this."

"Well, first of all, fuck you," you said aggressively. Except, no, you obviously didn't say that out loud. But you certainly thought it. That's not what this is about, you wanted to shout.

You cleared your throat. "This isn't necessarily about the building, though," you said, glancing at your professors out of the corner of your eye. None of them jumped in to help. "This project is really about the design concept. I wanted to signal the dichotomy between the light space and the dark space. The way you feel as you move between these distinct – "

"Right, but it doesn't have doors."

If you could have rolled your eyes straight up into your head, you would have. You truly wondered whether anyone had ever missed a point so colossally.

Before they moved on to the next student, the critics all concluded that your project was "under-cooked, unfinished."

You had licked your wounds with snarky comments that weren't so different from those of the jerky kid on the bus ride back from the firm visit. Perhaps you weren't quite as elitist as he was, but you wondered whether you should question this trend of dismissing professionals who rejected the conceptual approach of your program a bit more.

Just get to thesis, you reminded yourself. You can figure out the career part later. And anyway, you could always learn a lot of this from your internship.

#

"We're not taking interns." The woman barely glanced up from her work as she pushed Jake's portfolio back across the reception desk. She had a rich, resonant voice and tortoise shell glasses, and she seemed not at all interested in the work of reception.

"Okay, I'll just leave a copy of my portfolio. If anything changes, please let me know." Jake pushed his portfolio back toward the woman. This time she didn't look up at all. He paused for a few seconds, waiting for an acknowledgement. Realizing none was coming, he thanked her and turned confidently to leave. He sensed that this was a bit of theatre. The firm was demonstrating its exclusivity by feigning disinterest. He knew they took unpaid interns regularly and suspected – or hoped – that part of the route to working there was demonstrating both tenacity and deference. He couldn't bring himself to grovel at the feet of reception, but he was more than willing to drop off a copy of his portfolio every day. He had brought plenty to spare.

Jake arrived in Rome two weeks before their six-month semester was scheduled to begin. He determined ahead of time to spend a period working for a firm there before he returned stateside. Sometimes students stayed behind in the city and took a semester off. That gave them a full semester to do an internship abroad without having to pay international airfare a second time. That approach was fairly typical in the recent history of the program.

But Jake had a habit of taking anything typical and dialing it up a few notches. He thought he might combine the study abroad semester with the internship semester. It would be difficult, since architecture school demanded a lot of its students. Early in the semester, they were expected to put in six- to eight-hour days. It would be more like ten or twelve during finals week. But

Europe had no shortage of espresso, and he felt reasonably confident he could make it work.

He set his eye on working for a prominent international architect based in Italy, and he had been dropping off portfolios there since his second day in Rome. The first day was primarily reserved for sleeping off his minor jet lag. Every day since, he had walked into the small, exclusive firm, sat down in the receiving area, and asked to speak to the lead architect himself. Every day he had been turned away with varying degrees of dismissal. They were undeniably beginning to recognize him, and that could only help his chances.

Then one day his request to speak with the architect did not receive the typical dismissal. Instead, he was directed to take a seat in reception. The person who emerged ten minutes later wasn't the architect, but he wasn't a security guard either.

The man introduced himself as the firm's studio manager, and as they walked back to his office, a small room off the shop floor, he stopped in a break room to refill his coffee. Jake used the time in transit to highlight particularly strong aspects of his portfolio, noting his skill with woodworking and particular interest in model-making and technology.

"We have strict limitations on our internship program," the studio manager said.

Jake nodded to demonstrate understanding and flexibility.

"So I would like to take you on to work in the model shop. But you should know that we only offer unpaid internships in that area to start."

This was not at all unexpected. From what Jake had heard at school, most students took unpaid internships. And surely it was worth taking an unpaid role at a prestigious firm. Working for free now was an investment in what would later become a wider range of career options because of this experience. Right?

The man continued, "After six months we can reevaluate and determine whether you would be eligible to stay on as a paid intern."

"Yes, that sounds amazing," Jake replied. "I'm a student, and we're just gearing up for the new semester. I would just love any opportunity to get some experience working here."

They talked more about the specific expectations of interns at the firm, and Jake noted that he could come in for a few hours a day after classes concluded in the afternoons.

On the first day of the internship, he did just that. The firm was on his way home from school, and Jake popped through the door of the firm, just as he had every day for the past few weeks. He noted that the chilly reception from the front desk remained consistent, even now that he had business there. He had a sense that he must prove himself, as though the assumption was that he would never measure up. He shrugged it off. Jake was happy to prove himself through the work.

The model shop was a dream come true for Jake. He was building models of incredible works of architecture. To be among the first to see pieces that would someday become hallmarks of contemporary architectural excellence was a new type of mind-blowing. He could feel his life beginning to transform from student to professional. After all, he was building these models for actual clients.

The internship was intense from day one. He would arrive at the firm when classes were over, generally around two or three in the afternoon. He would work there for six hours or so, then walk back to the studio to finish his own projects before heading home to catch a few hours of sleep. It was difficult, but certainly worth it.

Then as February turned to March, the expectations began to increase. He was now spending closer to eight hours per day at the firm, and soon that increased to ten-hour shifts. He found himself walking back to the studio, exhausted and anxious, in the early hours of the morning. If this had been the exception to the rule – one huge deadline, or a particularly taxing model, perhaps he could have made it work. But this pace showed no signs of slowing. The models he was working with were incredible, and he was truly grateful for the opportunity to be part of the firm's groundbreaking work. And yet, there were only so many hours in the day.

When finals came around, it was clear that this schedule was unsustainable. "I wrapped up the Armani project," Jake said, leaning against the doorframe of the studio manager's office. The man looked up from his paperwork, bleary eyed. "But I wanted to mention," he continued. "I can't come in next week. It's finals week, and there's just no way for me to do both."

The man blinked. "No," he said calmly, his eyes flashing behind the fatigue. "You'll have to find a way to come in."

This was not the response Jake was expecting. If anyone understood the demands of finals week in architecture school, it should be architects. "It's just not possible. There aren't enough hours in the day," he said regretfully.

"No. You must be here."

Jake was flummoxed. "You're not paying me," he said, the words leaving his mouth before he could filter them.

The man's demeanor was disconcertingly calm. "Do you want to be able to say that you worked here?"

"I did work here. I'm here now. Physically. I just finished a model for you." What was this guy's game?

"Well, at the end of your internship the firm signs a letter saying that you worked here. That's your pay. That's your proof."

Jake's mouth would have dropped open if his jaw weren't so tightly clenched. "Are you telling me," he said, mimicking the slow deliberate tone of the manager, "that if I leave now, I'm not going to get this letter?"

A small smirk surfaced on the man's face. "Yes. Absolutely."

Jake had tried to ignore the massive rift forming between the way work was discussed in school and the way labor functioned in the profession, at least at this one prestigious firm.

> *Work, in architecture school, placed a premium on concept and creativity. But labor – the kind that means working 16- to 20-hour days, every single day for the foreseeable future – that wasn't something they discussed.*

In the end, Jake would get that letter proving his hours of free labor donated to one of the most recognizable architects in the world. He had first used his determination to get the job, if you could call full-time unpaid work a job. Now he would use it to get that letter. The receptionist had warmed slightly to Jake over the weeks and now looked at him with a hint of pity in her eyes when he strolled through the door. He didn't care.

After sitting in the waiting room every day for the last two weeks of his time in Rome, he finally asked for an unsigned letter. "Could you just get me the standard letter on the letterhead?" he asked the woman.

She did that for him. At least he hadn't left Rome empty handed. He had the form letter certifying his internship hours, and he had pictures of the models he had painstakingly created.

In school, the focus was always on concept. Jake realized this wasn't only a distraction from the practicalities of the profession. It was also a refusal to recognize the real implications of sacrificing everything for your art. Or, in this case, for someone else's art.

That last part became clear enough a few weeks after Jake returned to the states.

In his resignation, Jake had asked permission to use images of the models he had created in his portfolio. That permission had been granted by his immediate supervisor, a kind man who had been generous in a way that broke with the firm as a whole. But one day, Jake awoke to an email from the firm's lawyer. It was a cease and desist letter, threatening a lawsuit if he didn't remove the work he had done for the firm from his website.

In discussing the incident with other students, he learned that his experience was not uncommon. In fact, firms like these routinely brought in interns with the promise of paid jobs after the first six months. They would be abruptly fired during their seventh or eighth month of work.

This type of manipulation was par for the course in professional architecture, part of "paying your dues," some professors said. Some students said it too. It was as though school was training them to see everything but the exploitation.

#

Perhaps you experienced the disconnect during your own unpaid internship, or maybe you felt it later, when you transitioned into the profession full time. Perhaps, like some of our clients, you found your first work experience out of school to be shockingly misaligned with your expectations. You eagerly sought out a job with a small but respectable architecture firm – one that was willing to work with you to gain the thousands of hours required for licensure, an issue of its own that we discuss later in this book. You cheerfully burst through the doors on your first day of work. Coffee in hand, you sat down with your supervisor who gave you your first project.

It was not at all what you thought it would be.

Of course, you knew you wouldn't be given huge design projects right out of the gate. But you hadn't expected to find yourself pricing window fittings and steel brackets. You didn't think you'd be hunched over paperwork for eight hours every day. In school, you had studied architecture. You talked in concepts and design. Now, you shuffled through the papers you'd gotten from your supervisor, and those abstract, artistic ideas were nowhere to be found.

You hung in there for a bit, hoping that this was just a matter of paying your dues. But at some point, it became clear that this was it. This was the job. Take it or leave it.

Maybe you, like our client Jody, refused to be broken by this realization, by the bait and switch you had built your life around. So you went home every day at five, if you were lucky, more often six or seven, and spent another seven or eight hours in the evening working on your own projects. Honing your design skills and building a portfolio that would, you hoped, eventually allow you to design your way out. To find, as Jody did, a fulfilling career working for a company like Adidas.

Or maybe you experienced the disconnect most intensely after you'd worked in the profession for quite some time. Your architecture program had leaned into the practical more, or perhaps you were just young enough to take the shift in stride. Either way, you worked with a firm for a several years before deciding it was time to earn your master's degree. You had always wanted to go back to school. Now you found yourself in a classroom full of 20-somethings who used the term "b-word" rather than talking about buildings. Our friend David had this experience, warning us as young graduate students that the world outside the program's walls was truly, and harshly, different from the lessons we were discussing in lectures and the projects we were constructing in studio.

In our work, we find that this disconnect is one of the common threads that ties all of our clients together. It's the sense that you were sold a bill of goods, that your training didn't match up with the expectations of the profession, and the profession couldn't live up to the vision you had for what it could be. This sense is deeper than disappointment. It's more than just paying your dues. It's a deeply embedded feeling that something is wrong.

Maybe, at this point, you decided to look around to see what else was out there. Or, if you were like many of our clients, you decided to soldier on in the hopes that things might turn around. And still, years later, the disconnect loomed large in your mind.

CHAPTER 4
WHEN THE DREAM BECOMES A NIGHTMARE

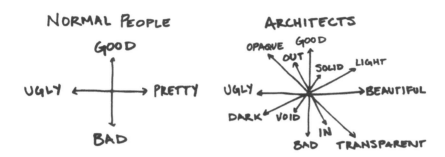

Nothing in school prepared you for the particulars of your first job. Well, not exactly nothing. You probably took one class, two or three if you were lucky, in Professional Practice, a curriculum crammed full of advice for junior architects embarking on their early careers. You heard a lot about passion in this course, about following your dreams. You got the sense that you were expected to find an architect you admired and follow in their footsteps. Maybe you could work at their firm or at the firm of someone they had trained. This was the path to building a career that was modeled after everything you loved about architecture in the first place.

You heard less about the particulars of the day-to-day operations of an architecture firm and how new architects fit into that complex web of activity.

This wasn't entirely your professor's fault. If they were members of the American Institute of Architects, they were limited by the professional code of ethics in terms of what they were allowed to share with you. Namely, they could not talk about their fees. They could not talk about fees at all. That meant, practically speaking, they couldn't really talk about your potential value either.

DOI: 10.4324/9781003300922-6

It would have been difficult to train you in Revit – the collaborative software used to coordinate between architects, builders, and contractors – because the program, by design, requires a team that is working through the technical challenges of constructing a building.

And things like licensure wouldn't come into play for at least another three to five years. Even if your professor mentioned the process, it remained abstract at best – out of date at worst – until you were ready to embark upon the huge time commitment and small fortune it would eventually take to earn your architecture license.

You tried to make the most of your professional practice course, but in the end, you were dropped into your first job teetering on the edge of insecurity and disorientation.

That first day, you were introduced to your Project Manager – your boss, you thought, and you aimed to make a strong first impression. Then you were introduced to your Project Architect. Your...other boss? It took you an embarrassingly long time to realize that, yes, you reported to both of these people but that they managed different aspects of the work. Scheduling questions went to the PM. Design questions to the PA. For all the questions in between, you'd just have to figure it out on your own.

But while you were figuring it out on your own, you were also supposed to be finding ways to make yourself useful. The job description, "Designer I," gave you few, if any, hints. So you simply did everything you were told. Things seemed to go okay when you did that, but the approach had the unfortunate side effect of zapping your sense of autonomy, agency, and self-determination.

"You're not really useful until you're five years or so out of school," a guest lecturer in Professional Practice had quipped, a hint of empathy in her voice that belied the wry grin spreading across her face. This was something of a field-specific axiom, something you earned the right to say after you'd spent your own five years of not-really-usefulness on the job. Something you said after you'd paid your dues, or at least the first installment.

What she hadn't mentioned was how difficult it was to do the things that would allow you to become useful. Nobody particularly wanted to train you. They just didn't have the time. This meant you struggled to even get that first job, let alone to ask for help once you got it. And then, whoever happened to help you not only became your mentor, but your model. Their skills became your skills, because you learned to do the job based on what they could teach you.

What they could teach you was, it turned out, totally different from what you'd learned in architecture school. That thing you loved doing – the design aspect of school – had kept you going through the all-nighters, the occasional disappointing reviews, the sometimes fierce competition from classmates, and the impossible work-life balance. Now that you'd begun your first job, the design agency that you had in school was nowhere to be found. And it soon became clear that it would be years before you would use those design skills again in a way that let you sink your teeth into a project.

You had trained for five years to do something that you probably wouldn't do again for twenty.

Oh, sure, there were touches of the familiar. When you'd interviewed for the job, you had shown them your portfolio. That felt just like school. You would talk about projects, the ethos, the way people circulate through space, and that felt familiar too. Maybe they gave you a diagram to work on, and you were a little embarrassed at how elated you felt at the opportunity to do something you had experience with.

But when you were faced with anything that was beyond the first ten percent of the process of conceptual ideation, you felt totally and completely lost. Now, as everyone told you, you just had to pay your dues.

#

Erin was already a year out of graduate school when she went to work for a very well-known firm. She had taken the Professional Practice advice to heart and brainstormed a list of the architects she admired. She chose one firm from the list and was thrilled to get her foot in the door. After six rounds of interviews with various people at the firm, she finally got the call.

She hadn't been taught to negotiate salaries at school – that AIA prohibition on discussions of pay saw to that – but she knew how important it was to fight for as much as you could – to get what you needed. Around the same time, Erin was teaching her first class at Cornell. This meant that she negotiated to spend one day per week away from the firm, the 40-hour workweek condensed into the other four weekdays. The schedule would be hard, but the pay was good. And she would be working at a firm whose work she loved, whose founding architect she truly admired.

It was a dream position.

Her first day corresponded with a major deadline at the firm. Though the high-pressure setting exacerbated her sense of uncertainty, Erin had always been a go-getter. She dove in, asked what she could do to help, and stayed until midnight contributing in any way she could.

She had learned in the Professional Practice course – as well as in her previous job and from other graduates in her cohort – that the only way to learn was to do what you were told. But she also wasn't afraid to ask for clarification.

Often, when she was asked to put together a piece of a current project, she would ask for the template. If she was given a CAD project, she requested clarification on how the model would be used.

With each request, she was told, "Look around the office. Figure it out."

"The amount of time I'm wasting! You wouldn't even believe it," she vented to her boyfriend one evening, a few weeks into the job. She was speaking literally when she said he wouldn't believe it. As someone who had spent a good deal of time working in corporate environments, he was often baffled by the behaviors of Erin's coworkers. "If they would just tell me what to do, I could – " she waved her hands emphatically to signal her frustration, the whiskey in her glass sloshing dangerously toward its brim. "And how can you tell someone to 'figure it out' when you don't have any reference materials – let alone stuff that's actually organized – for me to look at?"

"I don't know, love."

This became an evening ritual. She would return home and let loose all the pent-up frustration of the day. Once she got it all out, they could finally enjoy their time together. Sometimes, she had trouble letting go of the tension, but at least she knew someone else was on her side.

But by the end of the second month, the venting was losing some of its potency.

The relationship between Erin and the team leader was spiraling threateningly close to toxicity. It was becoming antagonistic.

In the first month, she found the issues nearly laughable. "Why don't they just set clear expectations? If they would just say what they wanted from me, I'll do it! I always do it!" Then, with an air of sarcastic humor and a swing of the arm reminiscent of a 1930s cartoon character, "I'm your go-to gal!"

Three months in, her outlook was dismal. "I'm running around in circles. There has to be some way to fix this. Right?"

By four months, the venting had devolved into full-on ranting: "I never know what's more important. Everything needs to be done by yesterday. It gets handed to me at seven o'clock at night and needs to be done by the morning. How is this sustainable?"

The next month, she invited the team leader for coffee. She was professional, but assertive, directly asking for guidance, for a clear set of expectations. Their course was unsustainable. He was the leader, so perhaps he should have initiated the conversation, but she would take on this bit of emotional management. She would clear the air.

During their coffee break, which was secretly a covert kind of personnel meeting, it quickly became obvious that the guy was overwhelmed. As a team leader on a huge tower project, he had found himself in over his head in an environment where that was the norm. The stress was exacerbating his behavior, she realized. She tried to empathize but was met with more of the same.

"Just figure this out. I don't have time to tell you what I need. I just need you to figure it out."

Okay, she thought. I guess this is what they mean when they tell you to "pay your dues." The dues were starting to seem exorbitantly expensive, but this is what architects did, right? They soldiered on.

At some point, the team realized that Erin was an excellent model maker. She was given an intern, and they set out to build a quarter-scale model of three stories of a skyscraper in just three days by hand. The timeline would be tight, but at least there were two of them.

The second day, the project manager took the intern away.

That night, Erin was adamant that she would not pull an all-nighter. She skipped her dinner break as a sort of motivation: the stick of hunger, the carrot of a relaxing dinner at home. She would eat when she went home, and she swore to all things holy that she was going home that night.

From across the workroom, she heard the team leader's voice, a crescendo against the backdrop of the night's electric hum.

"Can you imagine?" he chortled. "These people are trying to diet, and these chips, they gave them" – he did an empty-mouthed variation on a spit take – "anal leakage."

They burst into hysterical laughter.

"Like, you're at work, like" – he affected a cartoonish voice – "'oh God, my anus is leaking.'"

More laughter.

"And they had to say that phrase in court, which is like" – the laughter was more like wheezing at this point – "totally unheard of."

"Right, like this super serious judge is like, having to talk about anal leakage."

Erin had skipped her dinner break for this.

The second she finished her goal for that evening, she packed up her things as quickly as possible and made a beeline for the door.

"Where are you going?" the project manager said, his mouth full of chips. They were apparently the kind that don't cause anal leakage, but it was difficult to be sure, and Erin didn't particularly care.

"Home," she replied shortly.

"What do you mean?" he said, walking over to her workspace. "This isn't done."

"No. I'll have to do more tomorrow. I didn't take a dinner break." Then, after a pause, "I'm sorry, but I'm not going to sit here with you and joke about anal leakage." She hadn't meant to be petty, but it slipped out. She followed up with sincerity. "I want to go home."

"That's unacceptable."

She was stunned and exhausted and annoyed. So incredibly annoyed. "This isn't going to be done tonight. But it will be done tomorrow. Why is it unacceptable?"

"Whatever," he said, crushing a chip into his mouth. "I guess I can't stop you."

With that, she gave a tight smile that was perhaps more of a grimace, and she turned to leave.

What had typically been venting time was, that night, a serious talk about appropriate behaviors in professional environments.

"That's it! It's your smoking gun," Erin's partner exclaimed.

"Really?" she said. "He was just being a jerk. Like he always is."

"No. This is different though," he replied. "You have to go to HR." He knew plenty about the unprofessional behaviors endemic to architecture, but he knew even more about the legal liabilities of a hostile workplace. And if the team leader's behavior hadn't already crossed the line, this was explicit evidence of harm. It was the kind of thing that would be difficult to explain away if it was written up as formal documentation.

To Erin, this particular behavior seemed relatively mild compared to some of the other passive and direct aggressions she had experienced during her short stint working at the firm. The topic of anal leakage probably did cross a line, she could definitely see that. But what annoyed her more was the idea that she could work through dinner while these two jerks spent their time waxing scatological about nothing of any relevance, and even then, she apparently hadn't earned the right to sleep. Nothing was ever enough for this guy.

The next day, Erin drafted an email to HR explaining the situation, then got immediately back to work on her model. The lead architect was starting to pressure her for it, and she was being as reassuring as she could while working as quickly as she could. The air of irritation from the evening before circled like a swarm of gnats around her head. But they had a big deadline coming up, so she tried, as usual, to tune everything out but the work.

She sent another email a few days later. And another the next week. By this point, she was very near to begging someone – anyone – to take the issue seriously. Things were reaching a fever pitch, spiraling to a point of no return, and they had been for months. The team leader was increasingly aggressive toward Erin, and it was taking a toll on her mental well-being. She was determined not to let her work suffer, but she also knew that they could not keep going this way. Something bad was going to happen.

Then, something did.

Rushing to finish the model she'd been assigned – a project that was unreasonable in scope, particularly after her intern was reassigned – and frustrated to the depths of her soul by yet another thinly veiled criticism about her work hours, Erin's hand slipped. She had been working with a piece of chipboard and an Olfa knife with a brand-new blade. But her mind wasn't fully on the task. If you've ever been in a truly hostile work environment, you know that a situation like that takes a lot of mental energy. Finishing a project and burying your rage almost become a form of multitasking.

On that particular afternoon, she buried more than her rage. She buried the knife approximately an inch into her thigh.

She'd lost count of the emails to HR and the partner. The attempts to talk with the team leader about the work atmosphere. The times she'd tried a new approach to make the environment work. Nothing had worked. Now she had a massive – and growing – bloody circle near the hem of her white dress. A red flag to top them all.

Now, after all of her requests for support from the partners, she finally got a meeting with a partner. The partner, an entirely different person from the several she had been emailing for months, allocated one hour on the day that the skyscraper project was due. They would meet to discuss the work environment in the afternoon and Erin would stay until the early morning hours to work on the project. It was the cherry on top of the huge pile of dysfunction.

Erin had been keeping documentation. She calmly and methodically presented every email she had sent, she shared her many requests for clarification and feedback, and she went through the records she had kept of her hours worked, well above the firm's general expectations, not to mention fair labor practices.

"Frankly," she concluded, "the fact that they can joke about anal leakage but can't take the time to explain a file structure to me is ridiculous and unacceptable."

The partner nodded, a look of concern spreading across his face. "I see," he replied. If Erin were a less cynical person, she might have had hope. "You know," he continued, "I've seen this kind of thing before." He coughed awkwardly. "Mostly on all-male teams."

Erin felt her blood pressure rise instantaneously and swallowed the urge to throw her coffee across the table.

"I think the problem is that you're just a girl on a guy team," he said, as though that explained it. "They're just making guy jokes, and it's perfectly understandable if that's not your sense of humor."

It was as though he had not heard a single word she'd said.

"You know," Erin said evenly. "I'm not sure I want to work here anymore."

The partner looked shocked. He offered to move her to a different team, although of course that team would be working within 20 feet of her previous team leader. "We've invested a lot in you, Erin," he said, implying, as partners so often do, that they were entitled to her loyalty regardless of the horrendous working conditions.

Erin finished the project that night. The lead architect raved over the model and the intricacy of the detailing on the basswood furniture, which could be removed to show the installation sequencing. The client fell in love with the model.

That was the last project Erin did for the firm.

#

Unlike Erin, Rachel had landed in a firm with a relatively healthy team dynamic. Nobody likes paying their dues, but she was doing okay with that, too. Maybe the job didn't feel like a dream every day, but it didn't feel particularly nightmarish either.

But that's the thing about nightmares. Sometimes they seem like ordinary, everyday dreams until that little rustle under your bed leaps out and wraps a cold, slimy hand around your ankle. An unremarkable, day-to-day struggle could morph so quickly into an insurmountable barrier.

She knew that someday she would have to choose between having a family and advancing in her career. That was just the way that architecture worked. When the thought crossed her mind, Rachel reassured herself, "It wouldn't necessarily be the end of my career. Plenty of women have both. It's not the 1970s." She wasn't particularly convincing, even to herself.

Plenty of women in the general workforce balanced careers and families. Most architects did not.

She flipped through the mid-career women architects she knew and admired, landing with a sinking feeling on a mentor she deeply admired. Julia was an amazing designer, an up-and-coming star in the field known for her messy desk and her very late nights. Rachel had been struck by her kindness when she started at the firm. Julia had gone out of her way to take her under her wing. Over the years, they had shared many quick breakroom chats.

"I'll be gone next week," Julia had said one afternoon with a conspiratorial grin. "The whole week."

"Oh?" Rachel replied. "Tell me more!"

"It's that time of the year! Every year my husband and I try to spend a week together."

Rachel took a sip of her latte and nodded enthusiastically. "That's amazing!"

"I'm so excited," she gushed. "Typically we try to see each other on weekends. When we can." Then, in a voice that invited empathy, she added, "But you know how it is."

"Sure," Rachel answered. But she wasn't really.

"And during the week," Julia sighed performatively and shook her head. "Well, that's a lost cause!"

Rachel was still fairly new to her career when she had this conversation. Certainly, she was junior to this woman. If a non-work friend had confided in her that they only found one week per year to spend time with their husband, Rachel would have sat them down, explained the importance of balancing career and life, and encouraged them to take on less at work.

But this wasn't that kind of relationship. And architecture wasn't that kind of field.

Julia gave everything she had to her career, and people admired and respected that.

At that moment, Rachel nodded along with her. Outwardly, she returned the older woman's conspiratorial chuckle, the smile that said she was "in the club."

Inwardly, even then, Rachel had begun to develop serious concerns about the profession. It was becoming clear to her that this career path was a way of life, and the expectations of prioritizing work over family – over everything else she loved and enjoyed – certainly didn't end when you had finished "paying your dues."

Rachel had loved imagining herself as Julia someday. Her work was phenomenal. She was kind and fun. She'd found a way to balance being respected with being well-liked around the firm. In retrospect, as she remembered that casual, off-hand conversation with Julia, Rachel wondered whether the sacrifices could possibly be worth it in the end. It wasn't that she had always dreamed of children. But it hadn't really occurred to her how stark her choices were. How clear it was that, if she wanted this career, she didn't have the option of children. Architecture didn't care whether you wanted a family or you just wanted to leave that option open for the future. Architecture demanded everything.

#

It was as though the job posting had been written with Jake in mind. This wasn't the usual architecture job description – the kind that says you will "perform general architectural assignments." This was one of the rare jobs that provided a description – a defined set of expectations for the person who would take on the role. And the description was everything Jake loved. It was his dream job.

"Just listen to all this though," he exclaimed excitedly to Rachel. He had carried his laptop into the room where she was working and announced that he had found his job.

She grinned. His enthusiasm was contagious. "Okay, slow down. What does it say?"

He'd barely looked up from the screen, his eyes scanning back and forth across the ad. "Some of it's a little more standard," he rattled off, "well, 'standard,'" he cradled the laptop in the crook of his elbow and awkwardly curved his index fingers to signal the quotation marks. "It does mention Revit as being a positive" – he made a face to signal his feelings for the program. Jake thought of the Building Information Modeling software, or BIM as it was typically called, as the "software from hell." Rachel grinned at his exaggerated expression. "But it isn't listed as a requirement. And they also want computational design, virtual reality experience – which I have! How many people have that? – and," here he read directly from the screen, "'an intrigue and a willingness to innovate and try new things.'"

"Surely that's not just an Architect I position?" Rachel asked. Jake had seen many of those standard, incredibly vague jobs posted during his hunt.

"No, it's for a 'Digital Technology Director,'" he replied.

"Oh my God, it sounds perfect for you!" Rachel agreed. "Have you applied?"

"I just saw the post, and I wanted to come tell you about it," he said. "But I'm gonna submit my portfolio now."

Like clockwork, he applied and heard back the following week. With a Master in Design Studies, teaching experience at Northeastern, and a number of interviews already under his belt, he wasn't sure if he had ever felt more confident in his life.

When the interview finally arrived, Jake found himself seated at a long conference table opposite the firm's HR manager, a short man with a slightly oversized suit whose statements all sounded vaguely apologetic. As they waited for the partner to join them, the two men had made small talk about the weather and their weekend plans, and just when Jake feared they had run out of topics for the pre-interview chat, a harried woman in black pants and an asymmetrically cut black blazer flew into the room like a tornado of energy.

She smiled apologetically. "A client meeting ran long," she said with a shrug as she raced to the seat next to the HR officer and dropped a folder of papers and a legal pad onto the desk in front of her.

Without missing a beat, she asked Jake to describe his experience with Revit. He pulled his portfolio – the physical culmination of years of design work – back slightly from the middle of the long table. It wasn't necessarily how he had envisioned beginning the interview. He had explicitly stated on his resumé that he did not know the software. Maybe, he figured, she was frazzled and just started with a standard job interview question. Whatever the reason, she didn't seem concerned when he stated, honestly, that he did not have much experience with or interest in the software.

From here, the woman asked Jake to talk through his resumé. He perked up and slid his portfolio back towards her. As he narrated through his projects in augmented experience design for Italian cuisine, the multi-dimensional history of architecture he was exploring as part of his thesis, she nodded her head. Occasionally, she gave a slight raise of the eyebrows or a quiet, "great." She seemed genuinely impressed.

"So why are you interested in this job?" she asked. "What makes you think you'd be a good fit for the position?"

Jake had done enough interviews to know that this question was coming. He had practiced his answer extensively and launched into an explanation of his experience, taking care to connect the particular examples to the demands of the job as he understood them. He painted a picture of his love for digital fabrication and the way he blended technology with organic material. He discussed his vision of technological innovation that mimicked the common tech start-up approach of responding to – and seizing the opportunities of – digital disruption. He highlighted aspects of his portfolio that concretely demonstrated his skills in the area and emphasized his excitement at the opportunity to learn more as challenges presented themselves in the context of the firm. He was not only confident; he provided the evidence to back up his claims. He was the right person for the job.

By the time he had finished, the woman's whole posture had changed. It was strange, because Jake felt certain he had nailed his response and the interview as a whole, yet her movements were a radical departure from how he had imagined her response in his mind. At the very least, he thought she might thank him for his time and dismiss him cordially – the base expectation of professionalism during an interview.

Instead, she slouched down into her chair in a massive eye roll that began at her irises and swept down her entire body in a huge, ridiculous display of rejection.

Jake stared.

"That job," she scoffed, "does not exist."

Sometimes it's difficult to stay calm when someone criticizes or rejects you. But in this case, Jake's shock at this woman's behavior tempered the rejection.

"I'm sorry," he asked. "What do you mean by that?"

"We are really looking for more of a BIM Manager for this role. Someone who can handle model syncing, support the design team, you know," replied the partner.

The shock was wearing off. "Are you seriously telling me that you posted a role seeking innovative and open-minded creatives when all you're after is someone to babysit your 3D model? An IT manager?" He looked over to the HR manager who quickly diverted his gaze to the empty notepad in front of him and scribbled something nonsensical.

"Our BIM Director just left last month."

"Respectfully," he replied, "you can't go lying about the role to make it sound like something more exciting." He thought for another moment, then added, "But it seems clear that this job is not for me. Thank you for your time."

They were only halfway through the allotted time, but he rose calmly and strolled out the conference room door, down the hall, and into the parking lot. In mere seconds, his vision of working in the job had morphed from a dream to a nightmare.

That job does not exist, she had said.

"Well," Jake said into the warm spring air. "Now I've got to find it."

And eventually he did.

#

Architecture is, to some extent, an intuitive profession. Design requires us to trust our gut, to try a different solution if something doesn't feel right. It requires us to keep pushing forward, designing through the discomfort until we finally arrive on a product that speaks to us.

For some reason, that's not so easy when it comes to our careers.

Maybe you sense something is wrong but can't quite put words to the feelings. As Erin did, you bury the discomfort and soldier on until, one day, you can't do it anymore. Hopefully, it doesn't take stabbing yourself in the leg to realize that you need a change.

Maybe by that point, you've invested years into your career only to realize you are exhausted, broke, and miserable. Like many of our clients, you have seen colleagues, coworkers, and collaborators you admire sink into depression and burnout.

You're increasingly asked to work more and more hours with very little to show for it. You feel disrespected at work, or you just don't fit in with your team. You're not sure how much longer you can keep it up.

You begin to wonder whether membership is worth the price of the dues you painstakingly paid.

It's almost a joke among architects that the clock starts ticking the second you go to work for one of the big firms. In three years, maybe – five years, max – you'll either quit architecture completely or gradually transform into a zombie with an architecture license.

It's a foregone conclusion that your early career years are brutal. Nobody even bothers to talk about it. If you want to work for the best architects in the world, you have to abide by the established culture – of overwork, lack of boundaries, constant pressure and insecurity, hostile team dynamics, low to unlivable wages – if you want to work under a star architect, you will do it for as long as you can. That probably won't be beyond your early to mid-twenties.

To become an architect is to dedicate years of your life to the craft. Not only the years of college education but the additional years of internships, of work hours toward licensure, of junior-level employment and "paying your dues." Abandoning something like that can feel unimaginable, akin to abandoning your life's work. It's difficult to do. It's difficult to even talk about.

If, for you, the dream of becoming an architect has become a nightmare of fatigue, burnout, unclear or unfair expectations, and mountains of debt, you are not alone.

> *Client after client shares the same harrowing stories with us, of work cultures akin to abuse, of disillusionment and disappointment – of feeling like a failure and being afraid to quit, to "admit defeat."*

Of course, most people don't tell us directly that they want to quit. They say, "I'm burned out." They tell us, "I just can't do this anymore." They say, "I'm sorry I'm such a mess."

That last one always catches us off-guard – "I'm sorry, but I can't keep this up" – because leaving a career that makes you unhappy is nothing to apologize for. It's something to be celebrated. It's about the act of redefining yourself – difficult, but so incredibly rewarding. It's about examining your past and your present to figure out which parts you love and which have become a trap of toxicity.

> *So much of our training breeds a sense of inferiority, a devotion to a profession that is far beyond reasonable expectations or what other professions demand. Beyond what is even conducive to creativity and good design.*

So why do we continue to struggle, pressing onward as though nothing is wrong when, for many of us, we deeply feel the disconnect between our love of architecture and unsettling – or outright nightmarish – experiences in the field? Why do we apologize for demanding a better life for ourselves? Why do we feel shame when we seek out ways to carry the things we love about the field into other career paths?

The solution, we believe, lies in reconnecting the circuit between our passion and our true value as professionals. In identifying the moments of disconnect and understanding when – and why – they became part of how we think of ourselves as architects. And in asking why they prevent us from imagining a future out of architecture.

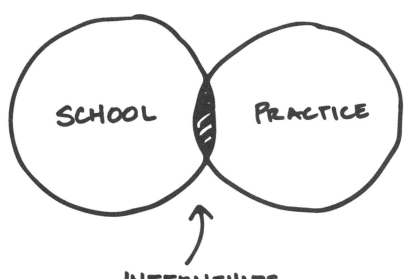

THE OVERLAP BETWEEN

SCHOOL

PRACTICE

INTERNSHIPS

PART TWO
WHY IS IT LIKE THIS?

It can be difficult to find a pathway out when we don't fully understand how we got here in the first place. The current models of architecture training mean that toxic lessons are often passed down through generations of architects from mentors to mentees, who then go on to become mentors themselves. While we appreciate the work of mentoring – strong mentors were instrumental in our development as designers – we simultaneously note that students and early career architects often internalize self-destructive habits that are baked into studio education and the profession more generally.

In Part Two: Why Is It Like This? we use our own narratives and those of clients to illustrate these harmful patterns and the ways they negatively shape our professional experiences, approaches, and cultures. Throughout the chapters in this section, we maintain an outlook of hopefulness – we believe that recognizing the toxic lessons that undergird professional practice allows us to unlearn self-destructive habits and reframe the way we approach the art form we love.

DOI: 10.4324/9781003300922-7

CHAPTER 5
WELCOME TO THE FAMILY

One dreary, overcast Tuesday morning as Erin made her way to work, she looked up to see a bicycle careening toward her. She felt the front tire slam into her knee as her instinctively outstretched hands connected with the bike's handlebars. The world seemed to spin for a moment before stopping suddenly – too suddenly – on a view of the sky from 7th Avenue. Blinking back the confusion, Erin gingerly touched her forehead. Her hand came away sticky with blood.

"Oh my God, are you okay?" a bystander emerged from the mass of people pretending not to notice (the cyclist included).

"Yeah, I – " Erin started, reflexively. "Actually, I don't know." Finally getting her bearings, Erin realized that her head must have slammed into the curb. She looked up at the bystander. At the bystanders. The identical triplets, or maybe quintuplets, who were staring down at her. "I think I hit my head."

But the bystanders were already flagging down a cab, and before she knew it, Erin was somehow piling herself onto the bench seat, bound for Urgent Care.

She shuffled around in her bag for her phone and opened the email app. All of the email apps. Or maybe none of them, it was difficult to say. With one eye closed, then both eyes squinting, then both eyes stretched wide, Erin tried to power through her concussion to email her firm. Obviously, she was going to be late, and she needed to let them know. Her eyes were not cooperating.

DOI: 10.4324/9781003300922-8

"Don't barf in my cab," the driver said supportively, eyeing her in the rearview mirror.

She nodded, or at least she thought she did. The world was spinning.

"Siri," she said, "call work."

She hadn't been working for Tod and Billie long, but she adored them. The architects were a married couple, and they truly cared for their employees. They were invested in nurturing a healthy workplace culture at the firm, and they took their roles as mentors very seriously. They almost felt like a second set of parents; the workplace, a second home.

The firm was competitive for big projects, so the work wasn't easy. But Tod and Billie made sure everyone had what they physically needed. If a team tried to pull an all-nighter, it wasn't unusual to hear Tod's voice echo through the workshop, "Alright. We're all going home. You've been here too long. We've been here too long. I don't want to see any of you here before noon."

Erin truly felt like she fit. Her coworkers all seemed very happy and confident that they belonged there: part of the family. It was clear that Tod and Billie had spent years working to break down some of the more toxic aspects of the architecture profession. They were highly invested in making sure the young architects they brought on board felt cared for, supported, and loved.

"Tod Williams Billie Tsien Architects," the receptionist's cheerful voice brought her back to the hazy, spinning reality of the cab. A wave of nausea threatened to deeply disappoint the cab driver, but she took a deep breath and, instead, spat out some muddled description of what had happened. She would try to be in later in the afternoon, she explained. She really didn't feel well, but she wanted to put on a brave face. Tod and Billie had given her so much, and she was determined to get her head together – literally – and get her work done. She owed it to them.

Once she reached the clinic, she hadn't been waiting long before she felt a hand on her shoulder. She turned her head, realizing too late what a terrible decision that was, and was surprised to see one of her coworkers.

Molly, another junior in the firm, slinked into the chair next to Erin. "Are you okay?" Molly asked. She didn't wait for an answer. "Tod said to tell you that you are on strict orders to take at least two weeks off."

"Oh," Erin said dumbly. Her head was really starting to hurt, and she hadn't expected to see anyone from work here. "Are you – " she started. "Did he seem upset?"

Molly's brow furrowed. "I mean – we're all worried about you, obviously!" She paused a moment, apparently processing what Erin had asked. Erin hoped the question had been in English, but she wasn't particularly sure anymore. Her head really hurt. "Are you asking if they're mad?" the woman asked, apparently aghast.

Even in Erin's foggy-headed state, she could make out her coworkers exaggerated expressions of emotion. Maybe that's why they sent Molly. Her poker face was abysmal, which, it turned out, was very useful when talking to a person whose brain had recently slammed against the inside of her skull. "I guess – I mean, I was working on the – "

"Of course nobody is mad, Erin," Molly cut her off. "Billie would have come herself, but they have client meetings all morning." Then, with a glowing smile, "You know we're like a family there."

Erin blinked. "Did you come all the way here to tell me that?"

Molly laughed, a bit too loudly for the space. "No," she said. "I'm here to wait with you. And I brought bagels!" she chirped, seeming to suddenly remember the small paper bag in her hand. "They just didn't want you to be out here on your own. I guess you didn't sound great on the phone."

Erin would have laughed, but she was pretty sure a reaction that animated might literally kill her – after her misguided head turn, she had resolved herself to stay as still as possible. She hadn't sounded great on the phone, that much was certain. But she hadn't expected the firm to send anyone to sit with her in the waiting room.

In the end, they had done much more than that.

As an hourly-rate, less-than-full-time employee, Erin hadn't been able to sign up for employee-provided health insurance. Like so many of her fellow millennials, she had been scraping by without insurance, hoping that her general good health would hold out until she could move up the ranks to a position that included benefits.

Following the bicycle incident, the firm offered her health insurance to help with her recovery. And she took the two weeks to recover and rest, something she wouldn't have been able to do at many of the firms where her friends worked. Erin felt truly lucky – and truly grateful – to have found a home with Tod and Billie. There was something comforting about feeling like your mentors were really looking out for you, especially in the overwhelming and incredibly taxing first few years out of school.

The firm truly felt like a family.

#

Architects who dream of working for a firm that feels "like a family" are in luck: if you can believe their advertising copy, most firms fit this bill. A quick Google search for architecture firms and "like a family" returns over 13 million results:

"We encourage our talented, creative and enthusiastic team to take time to play, volunteer and celebrate together – like a family."
"More like a family than your typical company."
"We're not too small or too large, it still feels like a family."
"Our highly collaborative team is like a family."

It reads like a Who's Who list of some of the most famous names in the world: Gensler, SOM, KPF, SHoP. Starchitects and small collectives, multi-site corporations and independent designers, innovative new studios and firms with decades of projects under their belts. These companies run the gamut of organizational structures and approaches, and yet what unites them all is their conceptual blending of business and family.

This can sound like a dream come true if you, like Erin, hit the jackpot with your first job out of school. Landing a job with a firm that lives up to the ideal implied by the "like a family" descriptor makes you feel truly cared for. Your workplace becomes the space of a nurturing, supportive childhood home, complete with two loving parents, cooperation, respectful guidance. Maybe you even feel the warm glow of platonic love.

Of course, not all families live up to that ideal. Homes can be abusive spaces, full of verbal or physical violence, emotional manipulation, impossibly high standards, and a variety of other dysfunctions that leave family members with lasting psychological scars and a skewed sense of what family should be. These are the families where toxicity passes through generations like an unnoticed inheritance. Abused children become parents who abuse until maltreatment becomes a natural extension of the family name. Perhaps your first job felt more like this type of family. You found yourself working harder than you'd ever worked, contributing underpaid or free labor to the firm, desperate for some sign of appreciation or, at the very least, performance feedback. It felt like begging for attention from an emotionally unavailable parent, jumping through hoops to show them you were worthy of their love, in fierce competition with your siblings for a few minuscule, infrequent crumbs of validation.

There are really great families and there are really abusive families. There are parents who inspire us to be better through their unconditional support and there are siblings who use our weaknesses to manipulate and exploit us. When they said their firm "felt like a family," they never promised it would be a healthy one.

We opened this chapter with Erin's positive experience working in a firm that felt very much like a healthy, well-adjusted family to demonstrate an important point. Many architecture firms who advertise themselves as feeling "like a family" are excellent places to work. The sense of being valued, of being seen as more than a worker, of general care in the workplace, is incredibly valuable.

But when architecture students are trained to expect a family dynamic first in their education and later in their careers, those expectations usher in a skewed understanding of the profession. Replicating a parental relationship with our mentors and bosses, in particular, can leave us feeling indebted to our companies and to the profession in general. A proportionate sense of gratitude for those who invested in us is natural. But when a distorted sense of loyalty prevents us from setting boundaries – from advocating for ourselves and building a better future for ourselves and our actual families – it's time to take a serious look at the damaging mental frameworks of the mentorship model.

#

Perhaps you were surprised, initially, by the casual atmosphere of architecture school. You were 18 years old and fresh out of high school. The college your teachers had prepared you for was rigid and impossibly professional. You had visions of absent-minded professors whose thumb and forefinger seemed glued to their chins as they wandered the halls, lost in thought. And yet, those same professors, you were told, would not allow talking during class. They would not tolerate a late arrival or a visible cellphone. Once you got to college, they said, you needed to be on your best behavior at all times. You needed to be the constant model of a professional.

Then, in strolled your professor. She didn't look at all like what your high school teachers had led you to believe. She was wearing high-waisted jeans and a loose-fitting top and she looked somehow both effortless and a little intimidating. Her hair was piled onto her head in a messy bun and you could see at least two pencils protruding from the mass of curls. She wasn't late, but she seemed as though she had just run from across campus, with the stack of papers in her hand getting mangled in the process. She came in and flopped a huge leather bag onto the work table. Then, seeming to suddenly remember where she was, she looked up and flashed a genuine, if harried, smile at the class.

"Hello," she said. Her voice was quiet, and she gave no sign of being the forceful, take-no-prisoners professors your high school teachers had told you to expect. "I'm Professor Stafford," she added. "But, please, call me Kate."

This was common, it turned out. All of your professors asked that you address them by their first names. That was the first, and perhaps the easiest, boundary to disregard. In high school, your teachers had been very obviously separate from the students. They dressed differently. They ate lunch separately. They would have been appalled if you had called them by their first names.

You remembered one evening during your senior year of high school, you'd seen your English teacher at Target, and you realized that you could not think of him as anything other than your teacher. The idea that Mr. McKinley had a life beyond the one, very segmented, regimented hour of your school day was simply baffling. The boundary between his work and his life was so obvious you never thought to question it. You would never have thought to call him by his first name. Come to think of it, you weren't even sure what Mr. McKinley's first name was.

Architecture school felt nothing like that. In fact, here, the boundaries were so flimsy – if they existed at all – that you might not have even noticed when they were missing.

Kate – because you very quickly stopped thinking of her as Professor Stafford – and your other studio professors would pop in at various times during the day. They weren't limited to the course's assigned noon-to-five schedule block. The lack of boundaries around time seemed helpful at first – even nurturing. You appreciated your mentor's availability and the knowledge that they might appear at any time kept you doing your best work.

Maybe they would pop in with a sandwich and join you in the studio as you ate dinner. It didn't feel particularly strange. You often kept working while you ate, so it made sense that your studio mentor was joining you for a meal, since they were also answering questions about your project. And anyway, you all ate together. You had to. You were staying in the studio for six, eight, ten hours at a stretch. Why would anyone question the lack of boundaries around something as essential as food?

Communication followed suit. If your school experience was relatively recent, you probably had your mentor's cell number. This meant you could send a text if you had a question, recognizing that your work extended past typical business hours, and so the work of mentoring likely did too. You could casually inquire about a particular struggle with a project, or, in some cases, maybe your mentor even took on an unspoken parental role, encouraging you to reach out in cases of emergencies. Maybe your mentor texted you sometimes, just to check in or offer a word of encouragement. You were so grateful for their total availability.

Mentors also shared their own, often uncensored, strategies for surviving the rigors of school and the field. They encouraged you to play heavy metal music or smooth jazz or Gregorian chants when you had to pull an all-nighter. "It really keeps your mind sharp when you start to get that hazy, up-for-twenty-hours-straight feeling," they said.

Or "if you're nervous before review, a shot of whiskey will do wonders." You ate it up, smiling that easy grin of the insider. The lack of boundaries felt a lot like a gift – like something that you wanted and needed desperately. It was a signal of acceptance in a field of competition that felt fiercer by the day. Mr. McKinley definitely would not have approved, but at this point in your life the idea of setting up arbitrary boundaries around time, space, and professional interaction seemed unnecessary at best, stodgy and out of touch at worst. You were there for the full immersive experience of architecture.

#

The full-on, mind-melding sense of total, intellectual immersion with your mentor is something that changes how you think forever. There is really nothing like the experience of diving deep into a project with a mentor you trust, who values your input. After several long days of pouring yourself into the concept, buoyed by a sense of support without limits, you find yourself completely conceptually intertwined with another person. It usually sneaks up on you. You're working along, totally engrossed in the flow, and you realize, suddenly and intensely, that you have lost all track of time, place, the boundaries between your thinking and your mentor's thinking. It is indescribably intimate.

That bond is hard won – it takes a lot of time and energy and vulnerability – but that kind of mentorship is what makes great architects. When you have mentors who support you, you work harder. When you feel valued – at school or on the job – you naturally want to do even better. You do your best, most creative, innovative, original work in a studio where you know it will be treated fairly, with kindness and respect. That kind of creativity requires us to let our guards down in a way that is only possible in a trusting environment. The casual nature of architecture school helps to support that type of relationship. Boundaries are softened or demolished to allow for this level of connection.

Connection doesn't mean total positivity, though. Good mentors still push you, sometimes harder than you think they should in the moment. That person you'd just been deeply connected to can turn into the "bad cop" at review or call you out for something they think – or know – you could have done better. And yet, a good mentor approaches criticism in a way that feels like an investment. A supportive mentor doesn't simply tell you to, "do more," or "try something else," or "figure it out."

A supportive mentor invests energy into the relationship. They take the time to tell you why something isn't working. They model for you how to efficiently spend your studio time. They hold your hand – not only literally as you hunch over your desk in those early drawing classes – but throughout the conceptual process. When final review comes, they don't tell you what you should have done. They stand next to you and respect your progress. They provide helpful criticism for how you can improve your work on this project and the next. They highlight your successes and point out the fruits of your intellectual labor. They value your work, and they say so.

When you have a mentor like that, you feel like you're part of something important. Through the mentorship model, you become "one of Kate's students." You become part of your mentor's pedigree. You share an unspoken bond with your mentor's other mentees, and you know you will always feel comfortable in your mentor's office. Your mentor is your mentor for life, and you are part of their intellectual lineage.

After school, many graduates decide where to work based on a similar model. They seek out their first career mentor based not only on whose work they admire but on how that work emerged from a particular line of architects. Maybe you really admire Bjarke Ingels, for example. Since Ingels's lineage is through Rem Koolhaas, you think, maybe you'll try to work for OMA. Your mentor may have even whispered in your ear about which firms would be a good fit, introducing you to their former mentee or partner or colleague. "Oh, you're one of Kate's," they say at first. Later, "Oh, I can see Koolhaas's influence here."

We are trained to think of ourselves as mentees in a long line of a particular architect's way of thinking. Welcome to the family.

This idea of lineage, of family ties, helps you to see who you are in the best possible way. It limits the myriad choices that exist in terms of artistic identity, precise skillset, and professional goals. This is an incredibly valuable gift.

Without it, it would be nearly impossible to hone your skill to the highest levels of innovation in the field. Being part of a lineage you admire is an identity-defining experience.

> *But defining your identity through an architectural lineage – through an architectural family tree – can be powerfully constraining. If your entire professional identity – your lens for understanding your vision, your skills, and your goals for your career – is built on your mentor's lineage, it can be nearly impossible to define what it is that you value. Who you are.*

The idea of setting boundaries becomes unthinkable, to both you and your mentor. After all, neither of you was trained to draw the line anywhere but on the page. They trained you the way they were trained, and the family dynamic – healthy or toxic or, most likely, a little of both – passed down through the generations.

The mentorship model is the backbone of architectural training. We are incredibly grateful for the supportive mentors we had in school and in our early careers. Those mentors lifted us up with their enthusiasm. They were positive about our work while giving us the space to grow. Most architects have some experience with a supportive mentor – otherwise, it is nearly impossible to get through the grind of studio training. And because we all know how central that mentorship was to our success, it's natural to feel some sense of loyalty, even indebtedness, to our mentors. It's understandable to feel we owe them something.

But that sense of owing someone else more than you owe yourself is a distorted sense of value. It opens us up to manipulation and abuse. And, as our clients demonstrate, it makes it nearly impossible for us to leave.

#

"You know, it's amazing that this service exists. It's just so nice to have someone in your corner!" Sophia's eyes welled up a bit, and she blinked pointedly, before giving a cynical laugh. "It's interesting. I've had so many mentors in my life, but I had to come outside of architecture to really feel like someone totally had my back."

Jake and Erin grinned. They had only been working with this client for a few weeks, but already, they had seen her mood shift markedly. Sophia was a 30-something architect who had found a home at a big, international, multi-office firm right out of school. After Sophia had invested nearly a decade into the company, her father had been diagnosed with a rare form of cancer. He would need chemotherapy and radiation treatments and would be homebound and quite ill for at least a year. That year could quite possibly be the rest of his life. With no other living family in the area, Sophia knew she needed to care for him. She needed to spend as much time as possible with her father while she still could.

"I honestly didn't know what to do," she had explained to Erin and Jake on their first call. "And the fact that I didn't know what to do – whether to choose my family or my work – made me feel so," she paused, contemplating, and her eyes seemed fixed in the distance for a moment, "So sad."

On one hand, this was her father. He had no other family except her. Her mother had passed away years ago. Wasn't the choice to care for him obvious? What other options could she possibly have?

On the other, she had been taken under the wing of a major architect, a mentee of a Pritzker Prize winner who was well on his way to the top echelon of the field himself. He, too, had been like a father to her, and she felt incredibly privileged to work under him. She had spent years at this firm, and they had poured so much into her. They had truly invested in her success, and she felt both appreciative and incredibly guilty. She couldn't shake the sense that she owed them her loyalty and that she was being ungrateful to those who had mentored her along the way.

In the end, she had decided to ask for more remote assignments. It was standard practice to call or Skype into meetings, she reasoned. She could take her laptop along with her to her dad's chemo treatments and log in to meetings using the hospital Wi-Fi. The firm would hardly notice the difference.

Her mentor had begrudgingly agreed to the arrangement, but as the months went by, Sophia noticed a shift in what she had long seen as her second family. She made sure to email all of the relevant players with updates about her work hours. First, she received chilly responses, one or two words of acknowledgement. Later, her emails weren't acknowledged at all.

She realized how much of the family nature had been manufactured from the constant time together, from how often they had all eaten together, drank together, stayed in the office together through the night and into the early morning hours. She hadn't thought much of this – it mirrored her experience in school and mapped easily onto her career as a junior architect – but now that she was spending more and more time way from the office with her father, she realized that the lack of personal boundaries was more than just a norm. It was an expectation. The more she asserted her needs, the less she felt part of the firm.

Her priorities were changing and, as a result, so were her boundaries.

Then, she started to notice her professional role in the firm was shifting. The easy relationship she'd had with the lead architect now ranged from strained to nonexistent. She was suddenly being passed over – not even considered – for projects and roles that would have been earmarked for her before. She was working just as many hours and just as hard as she had before, but she now found herself creatively demoted and emotionally drained.

She had believed that her firm was "like a family," that her mentor was a second father. Now that she had chosen to prioritize her time with her actual father, she found that her loyalty to the company was not being returned.

The issue wasn't with the work itself. Sophia still loved architecture. She still found many aspects of her job to be fulfilling. She still enjoyed design and working with her hands to bring an idea to life in material form.

The issue was that, like so many of our clients, Sophia found herself utterly disillusioned with the patterns of the profession. She was grateful to her mentors – in school and in her early career – for giving her the chance to work on innovative, exciting, beautiful projects. She'd had great experiences in school, she'd learned a lot in her internships and in her early career. Sophia realized that she couldn't have learned the profession without mentors investing in her, encouraging her, supporting her as she honed her skills in the field. She had benefitted immensely from the generosity of her mentors. They had given her the gift of experience that allowed her to learn and grow in the field.

But that gift wasn't just a gift. It was also work. And she couldn't just forget the stark difference in how she had approached her mentor – the sense of unexamined loyalty she had held for all of those years – and how her mentor apparently saw her.

Mentorship will always be central to architecture. And that's not necessarily bad. The sense of deep connection with another person, the opportunity to learn from a mentor's skill and vision, and the intimacy of working closely to create something new are invaluable aspects of any craft.

In fact, we began this chapter with a positive story to illustrate our belief in the supportive aspects of mentorship. We think it is crucial to recognize those mentors and firms who have invested energy into building a healthier profession. A firm that is "like a family" can be a truly rewarding place to work if that family focuses on the well-being of employees.

And yet, the idea of lead architects and managers who prioritize healthy work-life balance, mutual respect, and supportive mentorship doesn't need to rely on the inherent power dynamics of parent and child. This type of relationship is perhaps understandable between a professor and an 18-year-old, but as it carries on through school and our early careers, the reliance on a single, all-powerful mentor can encourage an intensely skewed sense of our own value. It can inhibit our willingness to set boundaries for ourselves, to build full, well-rounded lives that balance work with outside interests. And it can leave us with a sense of indebtedness that makes it nearly impossible to leave.

In the end, Sophia decided to take a drastic step – a leap, really. She left her position at the firm to become a full-time caretaker. She planned to use that time to reevaluate her goals and values. She didn't know what she would do next – we would help her figure that out over the coming months – but she knew that she couldn't return to her old job or her old way of seeing the world.

She submitted her letter of resignation with a request for a meeting with her mentor. She had grown somewhat resentful of the guilt she felt for leaving – it was her life, after all – but she truly valued his investment in her. The next day, she received an email from HR notifying her that her resignation had been accepted. After two team meetings in which her mentor had made no mention of her resignation, Sophia emailed him one last time. "I would really like to speak with you, to thank you for all you've done for me. Today is my last day, so if you have a few minutes, please let me know."

She never received a reply.

CHAPTER 6

PERFECT GENTLEMEN

It was a highly sought-after government contract. Rachel's firm had been tasked with designing a new embassy training center. It had begun with an already demanding multi-story complex and had morphed to include complex landscaping in the lot surrounding the structure, an indoor hanging garden, and a partially bilevel underground parking garage that allowed cars to enter at the rear of the building and visitors could take an elevator up to reception. The project had expanded a bit. The budget had, too.

This wasn't entirely uncommon in Rachel's experience with the firm. The lead architect was the son of a well-known mid-century designer, and perhaps as a result, he seemed to believe that money was no object. He had shot up in the profession right out of school, designing a home for a family friend that quickly caught the eye of architectural tastemakers across the east coast. He was known to be somewhat solitary. A brooding figure who worked late into the night. His wife had to remind him to eat, people said, because he routinely got lost in the tiniest details of his work. He was brilliant. A true master. His career had been launched in a matter of years, leading him to open the firm at which Rachel was now employed.

She had been thrilled for the opportunity to work at the firm, considered one of the "big names" of the contemporary field. And she was loving the embassy project.

DOI: 10.4324/9781003300922-9

With a mid-project deadline approaching, she and her colleague Bradley had been working a string of late nights. That Tuesday, they popped out of the firm to stretch their legs and make a quick Starbucks run. The caffeine would help fuel them through the evening's marathon work session. They'd grabbed their coffees and were heading back to the office, enjoying the crispness of an early spring afternoon.

"Were you in the meeting with the client?" Bradley asked. He and Rachel had started at the firm around the same time, and he was known for his delightful sense of snark.

"I wasn't, but I heard it went pretty well," she replied, taking a sip of her iced coffee.

"Hmmm, okay, because, listen. Why is our boss spending the entire day working on texture samples for the freaking garage mural?" The pitch of his voice was rising steadily as they made their way down the sidewalk, and Rachel glanced around for any unwanted eavesdroppers. Bradley continued, "did somebody ask him to do that? No, you know what? No. I already know. Nobody asked him to do that."

Rachel knew what Bradley was referring to. The lead architect had grown somewhat fixated on the garage portion, a section of the building that seemed to demand a straightforward, concrete structure but that now involved a textured mural of sorts, its curvature and finish mimicking the arc of the building's upper stories away from the street below.

Bradley had started to giggle, and Rachel was laughing now, too, the absurdity of the situation meshing with their escalating exhaustion. "Oh, it's probably a 'nice to have,'" she said with a sly half-smile. They were venting a bit and certainly teasing, but the project would no doubt be beautiful. She was actually very curious to see what the partner would come up with.

"Whatever gets us paid, I guess," Bradley said as they approached their office building. He grabbed the exterior handle, a long bronze bar mounted on an exaggeratedly narrow plate. It looked custom, and Rachel wondered whether the lead architect had pored over that detail too. Another "nice to have," no doubt, a component of a project that was almost entirely extraneous but that helped to fit the ideal of the artist-architect. The firm's lead architect fancied himself famous for these extra touches, bits of a tiny detail that signaled perfection to other architects, but that the vast majority of visitors would never notice.

As much respect and admiration as Rachel had for the partner's taste, she often wondered about the business practicalities of his approach. No project could ever be called "complete" under this model. There were always more "nice to haves." And while the lead architect would never dream of asking an Architect I to complete something so artisanal – he always took on the details that bordered on obsessive – his tendency to spiral into increasingly intricate details meant that the junior architects at the firm were left picking up the major pieces of project presentations.

Rachel and Bradley were always happy to do as they were asked – Bradley meant it when he said "whatever gets us paid" – but the truth was, their boss's attention to the texture of the garage mural was almost certainly not the thing that would get them paid, at least not on its own. His attention to the cosmetic detail that would greet visiting cars might help encourage the client to fork over more money. At least he seemed to believe that was the case. But it couldn't stand apart from the labor of the lower-level members of the team.

In fact, after the meeting earlier that afternoon, Rachel had been asked to complete a set of ten renderings by early the next week. It was a lot to ask, on top of the other components of the project she'd already been assigned, but she felt sure she could make it work. At least she hoped.

A few days later, Bradley swooped into her workspace and leaned conspiratorially against the doorframe. "Oh my God, did you hear?"

"What? No," Rachel said. "I just got here. What happened?"

"They ran out of money!" he paused for a reaction. Rachel hadn't even finished her first cup of coffee, so Bradley was visibly disappointed by her lack of enthusiasm for this gossip. "Well. Not exactly, I guess. They said they have to 'stop and track our budget.'"

"Nobody told me," Rachel said, glancing down at the half-completed rendering. "Are we supposed to work on something else then?" She wondered whether the project manager had just happened to see Bradley in the hallway. She hadn't seen an email or any other sign that this rumor was true.

"No!" Bradley said. "That's the most ridiculous part! We're just gonna keep on going. I guess the idea is that we can deliver this amazing, perfect project – his vision – and it'll convince them to fork over more money. It's nuts!"

It *was* nuts. But it turned out to be true. The lead architect was too far down the design rabbit hole. The project had become more about realizing his vision for the project than it was about a sustainable financial business model, for either the firm or the client. In truth, that was fairly standard for the firm and, as Rachel had learned over the past several years, for architecture in general.

The entire project team – all eight full-time, salaried employees – continued working their unpaid overtime in hopes that funding for the embassy project might eventually come through. In hopes, but under no guarantee, that the firm would eventually be paid for the work.

It underscored an assumption that was endemic to the architecture profession:

everything hinged on the brilliance of the lead architect.
And it was this brilliance, never the money, that drove
the work.

After all, they were artists, not tradespeople. Or, at least, that was what their lead architect seemed to believe.

#

In a painting that is, for architects, as iconic as it is illustrative, Michelangelo stands at the right edge of the frame gesturing authoritatively toward a model of St. Peter's Cathedral. Several men are gathered around the model, including Pope Paul IV, as the great Renaissance artist regales the group with his presentation of the now-famous cathedral's design. The model itself is impressive. Set on a short platform on the floor, the model stands as tall as Michelangelo himself, and the artist has taken care to dress all in black, ensuring that the focus of the moment will be on the design – never on him.

Yet, the artist *is* central to the painting meaningfully entitled, *Michelangelo che da il modellino di San Pietro a Paolo IV* or, roughly translated to English, *Michelangelo Presents the Model of St. Peter's Cathedral Dome to Pope Paul IV*. Despite all apparent attempts to remain peripheral to the art, Michelangelo remains the central figure of interest in the scene and the name most associated with the basilica's iconic dome. And while perhaps Domenico Cresti and his painting can't be blamed for omitting the full context of an enormous architectural project like St. Peter's Cathedral, the painting does seem to imply that the project was Michelangelo's alone. It is as though the idea, perhaps even the model itself, sprung fully formed from the sculptor's brilliant mind.

No unpaid interns were harmed in the making of this model.

Michelangelo almost certainly did not complete the model on his own. Nor was he even trained in the practical skills required to see a building through from design to structure. It was the very distinction between artist and builder that granted Michelangelo the use of the title "architect" in the first place. As Mary N. Woods writes, the use of this title by men like Michelangelo was, at the time, meant as a foil to builders.[1] Builders constructed buildings. Artists dreamed. The former was a long-established, often unionized trade. It was clearly and explicitly a labor of the practical and material world. The latter was elevated in a way that gave the architect an air of artistic brilliance. The isolated individual, pouring his heart and soul into the project, unsatisfied with any result that fell short of creative genius.

This image, of the singular artist, is one of the most persistent in the history of architecture. Nearly 500 years after Michelangelo was commissioned to design the basilica, the celebration of a lone, brilliant artist lives on through the Pritzker Prize. Forty years of laureates captured in the simplicity of black and white portraits. All but four of the award winners stand alone. Artists, recognized for their attention to every detail and their indulgent dedication to flawless, beautiful design. These men have no concern for paltry material things like money, food, rest, a social life. They subsist on art alone, which they create in the still, echoing isolation of their studios.

The idea is as romantic as it is ludicrous. People need money. They need food. They need rest. And, above all, they could not create much of anything without the contributions of others. Architecture has long privileged creators who had no real need for a salary, whose social position allowed them to work in incredibly inefficient ways, with underpaid peasants picking up the laborious, less glamorous tasks while the artist obsessed over the signature details. These architects had access to relationships, often through family, that fast-tracked their success. And once they reached the top of the field – often relatively quickly thanks to a letter of reference or a simple phone call from a powerful family friend – they leaned on others' hidden labor to help them materialize their brilliant ideas. The ideas were their own and they were very often field-changing. But the work was never theirs alone.

Architecture is commonly referred to as a "gentlemen's profession." The work of design was perfect for men of noble birth, who were enabled by family wealth to indulge in years of study and projects that cost more to create than they could ever return. Woods writes, "As a gentleman, the professional was a man of chivalrous instincts and refined feelings. His principal considerations, unlike those of merchants or tradesmen, were never financial. Honor guided his actions, and authority was his due."[2]

Woe betide the lowly craftspeople who couldn't subsist on honor alone, their contributions relegated to a footnote of history, if they were ever acknowledged at all.

\#

As architecture students, you probably were not so independently wealthy that you could build a career on the promise of honor or authority. And yet, your sense of dedication to your craft, your artistic vision, and your drive to create were likely instilled with a sense of honor. They were likely the reason you chose to attend architecture school in the first place. As the years passed and you grew more immersed in the training, your determination to innovate and imagine new concepts and ideas probably only intensified. Nobody imagines that they will be the next Michelangelo, but maybe you aspired to be the next Oscar Niemeyer. The next Kenzo Tange.

There was no shortage of architects to emulate. The contributions of these great men and a few great women were built into the very fabric of architecture school. The parti diagrams you copied in drawing class originated from major architectural works. The history you learned centered on the pioneers of the field. The sites you visited were designed by the famous architects of history. These were the field-changing architects. These were your role models.

You were in awe of their incredible attention to detail. How everything – from the concept to the design to the finished structure – was absolutely perfect. Their eye for nuance was as indulgent as it was inspiring. You could imagine the hours spent poring over subtleties of design that you hadn't even noticed until you were in architecture school. Those details weren't for clients; they were for the love of the craft. Those details encapsulated what it meant to practice architecture with honor.

To practice in that way meant to embrace perfection. And as you moved through school, it became increasingly clear how important it was to work and rework every concept, detail, and project component until it was perfect. Or, more often, until you ran out of time. Because as your eye for design sharpened, so did your ability to self-critique. There was always something that could be better. As long as there was still time, you could always do more.

This wasn't just a student issue. After graduation, you quickly learned that this was how architecture worked. It was up to you to present something the client would love. It was up to you to convince them to invest in you, often in competition with other architects. Your clients gave you parameters, and you delivered them beauty, innovation, aesthetic perfection.

You weren't always aware of the ways this drive for perfection sent you spiraling. How you would forget to eat because you'd slipped into the infinite possibilities of editing a model in Rhino. How you had sunk into a deep depression after you sat staring at six months' worth of work on a project that you now found utterly underwhelming. How you had worked enough unpaid overtime to effectively reduce your hourly rate below the poverty line because it meant you could construct the impossible details of intricately carved, movable furniture in the model for the client presentation, for a client who would never even hear your name.

You weren't given a benchmark for when to stop working – what was good enough – but that wasn't the point. The point was to indulge in the limits of the beauty your hands could craft.

Michelangelo hadn't been given a benchmark either. This was part of emulating the masters.

#

Unfortunately, as much as you tried to learn from their eye for perfection, there were other aspects of their lives that you could never emulate. You couldn't magically recreate yourself as the child of a famous architect. If your family didn't have powerful political connections with government officials, there was nothing you could do to change that. Technically, you probably could have sought out a romantic or sexual relationship with a wealthy investor, but that didn't seem particularly desirable, even if it were possible. If you didn't have the connections by birth or marriage – if you weren't part of the gentry – you'd have to make do with what you had.

And when you dug deep into architectural history – including famous architects from the not-so-distant past and current big names in the field – the role of family wealth and personal connections glared back at you with contempt. The "gentleman's profession," an idea that seemed so antiquated, was very much alive and well. If you thought too hard about this, you realized how truly difficult making do without connections might be.

You read, for example, about the wunderkind who exploded onto the architecture scene while still in school. His name was synonymous with edgy, high-demand housing complexes across the city.

A bit more digging revealed the enormous wealth that had funded his education. That family inheritance meant he would never have to work a day in his life if he didn't want to. Surely that was irrelevant, though, you thought. He had won a major competition. And he was undeniably talented.

He was talented, that was true. But then a snarky comment from one of your more controversial professors put things into context.

"You know he was sleeping with the client's daughter at the time, right?" The professor paused, waiting for your reaction. "But if we're being honest, that's not the *least* traditional way of winning a competition."

As was often the case, one big competition early in your career could be leveraged into others down the line, and the rest was history.

This was the pattern, too, for the famous architect commissioned by his family. Actually, there were several of these cases, you learned. Perhaps the most famous was a Pritzker Prize winner who had uniquely contributed to the understanding of architecture in the American context, specifically. His work was beautiful. His theory was mind-blowing. His family was wealthy, and they had been his first clients, investing in his potential through a commission to build them a home.

Many years later, when he'd been awarded the top prize for architecture, it was as a solo artist, differentiated through the award from the team of architects at his firm, including his partner. A lone genius, until you started to read more about him. Until you heard the inside scoop from professors and professionals in the field.

Story after story seemed to chafe uncomfortably against your assumptions about these role models. About the sense that they had risen to the top through the sheer perfection of their designs alone. That they'd risen to the top alone at all.

And not only were their teams often totally erased. You learned, too, that their teams were sometimes abused. There were the horror stories, of course, of students like Jake, whose internships were wielded against them as a way to extract more unpaid labor. Who weren't allowed to use projects in their portfolios. Whose work was totally, invisibly swallowed up into the famous names of the field.

There were also the architects to fear. The ones your professors had suggested you intern for, but always in pairs – the buddy system, but grown up in the worst possible way. You were told this with a raise of the eyebrow or a whispered warning behind the closed door of an office. "Just be sure you're never alone with him." "If he calls you into his office, keep the door open." For years, even generations, this quiet backchannel circulated the dark stories behind the "starchitects" whose genius still meant they commanded the authority and respect of their station at the top of the "gentlemen's profession." When the lid was blown off of one architect's history of sexual harassment, you nodded. Maybe even shrugged, disgusted but unsurprised. Your classmates and professors had known about this for years. But what could be done? He

Why Is It Like This?

was a pioneer in the field. A member of the gentry. What use was a peasant's word against nobility?

What made this so hard to wrap your mind around was that these architects were undeniably talented. It would have been so much easier if their work was shoddy or sloppy or derivative, but these were truly geniuses of the field. The fact that their social position had played such a heavy role in catapulting them to stardom certainly didn't diminish the value of their work to architecture. You had chosen to pursue this education because you loved the art form. And their art was amazing.

But as you moved forward into the profession, it became impossible to ignore the advantages of your classmates with well-connected families. The incredible edge provided by financial support. In Michelangelo's time, gentlemen embarked on the "grand tour" to become well-rounded members of the gentry. Now, family wealth propped up unpaid internships, facilitated travel abroad, and offered the ability to focus on passion projects on which every detail was polished to perfection. Family connections facilitated projects completed under one's own name. The gentry never had to labor, completing the invisible grunt work of one famous architect or another.

Being able to participate fully in the "gentleman's profession" didn't diminish anyone's talent. But it helped to make time and space for that talent to develop, and it certainly helped to make that talent visible. Meanwhile, talented classmates without the same social status were struggling for artistic recognition and minimum wage.

#

It was always the architects and students struggling for minimum wage who came to Out of Architecture for guidance. One of Erin's former students, Caty, had taken the Professional Practice course the previous year. Erin remembered the group of students vividly. She had brought in a young professor to do a guest lecture for the class. He was a practicing architect and had immigrated to the US, giving him a unique perspective on the financial aspect of the profession. Studying in America had been incredibly expensive for him, and he was open with students about the costs, financial and otherwise.

"Well, architecture's always been the gentleman's profession," he told the class. "You're not supposed to think about money." He gave a soft chuckle belied by his clear sense of disillusionment. "Of course, that's not so easy when you're staring down hundreds of thousands of dollars in debt. You've got this idea of the profession, but then the actual jobs barely cover your student loan payments."

Caty had lingered after class and thanked the speaker for his candor. Erin was surprised to see the student approaching the podium – she was very quiet and rarely spoke up in class, although she always smiled and nodded along with Erin's lectures. She seemed shy. Even a bit deferential. That day, Caty had seemed nervous to approach the speaker but seemed to relax once they started chatting. The student had shared, then, that she came from a lower-middle-class family in West Virginia. Her father was a house painter and her mother was an elementary school teacher. She'd gotten an education in the "gentleman's profession" during her first few years in school when so many other students seemed to have a very different perspective on money than she did. Caty knew about hard work, and she understood well how much a few hundred dollars could mean if you were teetering on the edge of making ends meet.

Now, in her final year of the program, she had asked Erin for a private meeting as an extension of both the professorship and Out of Architecture. Caty explained that she had been given the opportunity to participate in a project with one of her professors. The professor, a relatively well-known architect on the East Coast, was working on a competition and had approached her about contributing a series of renderings.

"I was so excited because they were going to pay me," Caty explained. Erin noticed that her drawl had gotten less pronounced since they had first met. Caty, it seemed, was not only cognizant of the quality of her work, she was also incredibly aware of the things that made her stand out from other students.

"What did you charge them?" Erin asked, masking her sense of dread. Students never asked for the amount of money they were worth.

"Ten dollars an hour," Caty replied. "I didn't charge for materials or anything like that," she said, "because I didn't want to seem greedy. I'm grateful just to have the opportunity."

The student went on to explain that she had completed the renderings and submitted the invoice. The total came to $600. It had been her first invoice; she borrowed a template from a friend and was so proud to submit it to her professor. She'd thought the professor would be impressed. Instead, he had countered with an offer to pay her $250.

"I know $600 is a lot of money," she said, a trace of disbelief in her voice. "But I thought that's what we agreed on."

Erin nodded sympathetically, then drew in a sharp breath. "Okay, well, the first thing I would say is that I know people who charge $2,000 per image."

The student's eyes grew wide. "That's ten grand. So if you're feeling like you overcharged, let me just put that to rest."

Erin felt herself growing angrier and angrier on the student's behalf. It was clear that the professor had entered a competition, and, realizing the possibility that he wouldn't win the job, he had leveraged cheap student work under his own name. No doubt the professor was indulging himself with the fine details of design while his student completed hours of labor for the honor of working under him. The amount Caty had requested was already a dramatic underpayment for the student's time and talent. To undercut that invoice by half was shockingly unethical behavior.

"I probably would have just let it go," Caty continued, "but then he published the design, and he spelled my entire name wrong. First *and* last." Tears welled up in her eyes, but she blinked them away. Erin was glad to see a flash of indignation behind the woman's quiet demeanor. "I won't even get searchability from that."

We wish we could say that Caty's experience was isolated. That it was a result of one bad apple in the profession. But, sadly,

the use of underpaid or unpaid laborers to prop up the elite names in architecture is baked into the history of the profession.

The professor didn't worry about whether Caty's name was spelled correctly because, to him, the project had very little to do with her. The project was always about him. His authority and honor.

When Michelangelo pointed his long, thin finger toward that model of St. Peter's dome, he gestured toward the work of an indefinable group of unnamed others. Omissions that, like the misspelling of Caty's name, render invisible so much of the labor of architecture. We do not believe that recognizing the contributions of others to Michelangelo's iconic work diminishes its prestige. We certainly don't mean to dismiss his beautiful, paradigm-shifting architectural perfection. There is no doubt that the artist was a genius and that his vision changed the future of Western aesthetics.

And yet, Michelangelo himself must have known that vision and genius alone would never have been enough. That his family's land ownership positioned him as a member of the gentry and allowed him to enter the honor of the architect rather than the hard labor of the tradesman. The world is fortunate for that accident of birth. Had Michelangelo been born to a family of servants or laborers, perhaps our contemporary notion of architecture would look very different. It would have suffered without his influence.

That is precisely our point.

> *If we believe in the power of architecture – of art, design, beauty, and innovative uses of material and space – to change our lives for the better, then we must believe in a way of practicing those ideals outside the modern-day gentry.*

As long as being an architect requires some level of independent wealth, we are dedicated to helping our clients find spaces to practice the skills they love outside of the "gentleman's profession."

Caty had found her work on the professor's project to be exciting and fulfilling. Yet when Erin asked her to reflect on whether she would be willing to continue working for him if the wages remained well below the minimum wage, Caty ultimately found the courage to say "no." She drafted an email to the professor, and Erin was thrilled to see that the student had communicated her needs and boundaries clearly, professionally, and without a hint of deference. The email courteously asked to be paid at the previously agreed-upon rate and requested that the misspelling of her name be corrected on the publication.

Weeks passed with no reply. Caty followed up first via email, then by phone message. Finally, she received a reply, which she shared with Erin.

In the email, the professor mused at his disappointment. He did not believe that Caty had written the email herself. The tone simply did not sound like her. "In other words, 'we never thought someone so pleasant would stand up for herself,'" Erin translated wryly. The email went on to note that the misspelling of her name was not his fault, as "Katie" is the more common spelling.

The professor was a jerk. That much was obvious. But that wasn't really the point, in the end. Because, while the lesson was hard-learned, Caty had ultimately realized that her work had never really been valued as *her* work. As a lower-middle-class student trying to work her way through college, Caty hadn't been aware of the traditions of the gentry. But now her eyes were open. She had unwittingly taken on the role of Michelangelo's apprentice, contributing countless hours of talent and labor toward the professor's honor and authority.

She doubted Sallie Mae would accept honor and authority as her monthly minimum payment. She determined to work her way forward, unwilling to donate her time, talent, and labor to prop up the legacy of architecture's top names.

NOTES

1   Mary N. Woods. *From Craft to Profession: The Practice of Architecture in Nineteenth-Century America.* Berkeley, CA: University of California Press, 1999.
2   Ibid., p. 6.

CHAPTER 7
THE INSECURE OVERACHIEVER

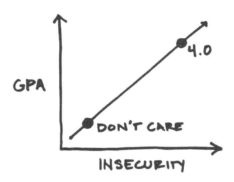

Now that he had several years' worth of emotional distance and experience under his belt, Jake found it hard to believe that he had ever questioned the project. It was easy to put it at the very top of his portfolio, this set of structures that blended his passions for nature, technology, and beautiful, functional design. The imaginary clients conjured by their madcap British professor required a studio space that would allow them to house themselves and their frequent guests during the annual flood season. "The spitting image of antidiluvian architecture," the team had subtitled the project. It was a play on the biblical term "antediluvian," before the flood, which signaled the structure's practical answer to life on a flood plain. When he looked back on the project, he could clearly see its innovative vision. The approach to building from bioplastics and recycled materials made use of every scrap of waste in a 50-mile radius of the site. The layout of the space encouraged community gathering, with the circular rooms and haphazard stick construction reminiscent of the birds' nests studied as precedents in the first portion of the studio. The whole project, from design to presentation, was just cool.

DOI: 10.4324/9781003300922-10

He hadn't seen that at the time, though. Before review, he'd been scrambling as usual. Not that the project was behind schedule – it definitely wasn't. But he had his eye on going above and beyond. With every "nice to have" he completed, there were eight, twelve, twenty more ideas he had brainstormed with his studio professor leading up to the review. "Wouldn't it be cool if – " "What if we were able to – " "Do you think you could – " These were the kinds of questions that pushed the envelope. They were the questions that facilitated innovation and transformative thinking. They were the questions of overachievers.

And everyone in the studio was an overachiever. They had all over-performed, presenting projects that far exceeded the expectations of their imaginary clients. The work had even received an enthusiastic review from notoriously tough faculty members.

"I get a very clear sense of where you're headed with the spit-joint construction," one reviewer remarked. "But the concept – this play on 'expectorant' – I guess I see what you're doing there, but I think it could be clearer. I want to be salivating just looking at it."

"It's very visceral though, isn't it?" a second reviewer mused.

"Right. What if you adjusted the density of the joints in certain places?" another replied, pointing to the model. "In other words, you could use the viscosity to reflect the origins of the idea. Take inspiration directly from these incredible birds' nests."

There was more enthusiastic chatter between reviewers. That was always a good sign, when you felt a little like they'd forgotten you were even in the room.

"Or the way you have the platform hovering just above the fifty-year flood line," the first reviewer said, drawing Jake back into the conversation, "I would love to see if this could influence the heights of the various pods."

"Build up gradually to emphasize the height," a third reviewer interjected.

The review had gone on this way, with all reviewers excited about the project. It was, as reviews go, quite a congratulatory conversation. They commented on the graphic design, a digital collage-style presentation that captured the collision of technology and nature that threaded throughout the project. The reviewers loved this element so much, in fact, that they had encouraged him to push the drawings further. The same was true for the materials overview. Jake had proposed a bioplastic made from corn – polylactic acid, or PLA – that was biodegradable and designed to reduce greenhouse gasses. The reviewers had been so excited about the idea that one had offered up other fabrication options, encouraging him to explore a greater variety of mold-making processes.

Every suggestion was enthusiastic, yet each one opened up another series of possibilities that he hadn't considered. Every new idea seemed to multiply before his eyes until it became impossible to determine which solutions were best – or even which ones were "good enough."

When Jake left review that afternoon, he showered, ate a sandwich, made a pot of coffee, and sat down to rework one of the project's centerpiece drawings. He hadn't slept more than a few hours for the past several nights, and his eyes were beginning to cross from fatigue. And yet, he couldn't stop himself. The critique had been encouraging, but it had also been focused on the possibilities for improving the design. They had primarily discussed the things he could do if only he had more time in the semester. There was no room for celebration – to congratulate himself on a project he truly felt proud of. If the piece was to be included in his portfolio, portions of it needed to be retooled. If he was going to claim that this was his best work, he knew he needed to continue.

This type of critique had made him a noticeably better designer over his years in architecture school. But somehow, he still couldn't shake the idea that there was more to do.

Years later, Jake looked back at the project and was baffled by the memory of his bleary-eyed post-review work session. The project was gorgeous. If he were pressed, he could probably find a handful of elements that could be improved, but no reasonable person would have supported his choice to continue working rather than take time for the sleep, socialization, and celebration he had been depriving himself of for weeks.

The whole project had been incredibly ambitious, and somehow he had found a way to produce this innovative and strikingly complete design. He had gone above and beyond.

So why did he still feel so uncertain of himself?

#

The answer may lie in the structure of architecture school itself.

According to a policy brief commissioned by Complete College America, more than half of all full-time college students in the US enroll in fewer than 15 credit hours per semester.[1] In stark contrast, many architecture students find themselves enrolled in more than 18 hours. Architecture students enroll in six hours of studio credit per semester, a course that overflows to fill as many daily hours as students can give, in addition to a full-time course schedule.

Credit hours aren't the only difference.

Architecture students also accrue, on average, 33% more student loan debt than college students across other majors.[2] Architecture supplies often cost anywhere from 500 to several thousand dollars per semester on top of the cost of books, whereas students in other majors typically don't need many supplies beyond standard notebooks, pens, planners, and laptops.

And then there are the demands. Whereas performance expectations might show up on rubrics for typical college students across the country, these tend to go largely unwritten in architecture school, the uncertainty functioning as a way to push architecture students to innovate, reimagine, and carve out space for themselves within a competitive artistic field.

Architecture students learn attention to detail, project organization, effective communication and presentation skills, and team management. Architecture school demands problem-solving skills, the ability to give and take critique, a sense of flexibility and adaptivity, and a drive toward entrepreneurship. And of course the prerequisites of hard work and passion.

All of these expectations produce two, seemingly contradictory approaches to work. On one hand, architecture students emerge from schools with more than a bachelor's degree. We also graduate with a reasonable facsimile of nine out of the ten skills essential for success in business. These skills, compiled by Harvard Business School, include things like discipline. No architecture student makes it beyond the first semester without discipline. Success in studio requires hours of work beyond the bare minimum. It requires you to show up when you're tired, hungry, and in desperate need of a shower. Harvard lists creativity and an open mind as two of the quintessential skills. These are the backbone of architecture school. Faculty could push all they wanted, but without an innate sense of creativity and open-mindedness, the level of creativity required in architecture school simply wouldn't happen. The list goes on, demanding strong people skills, a solid work ethic, and a self-starter attitude. Not to mention passion and determination, skills architecture students have in spades.

We are overachievers at heart, and through our need to please faculty, clients, and our own design aesthetic, we grow into the type of worker that is always in demand. We graduate with the ability to adapt to a variety of markets and industries. We leave school poised to find the careers of our dreams – or to design a new job that fits our unique skills, abilities, and desires.

But we pay a high price for the type of pedagogy that allows us to become innovators in the field. This type of teaching and mentorship means that we are constantly pushed to do more, to reimagine, to dismantle or redesign or think outside the box. Nothing is ever really finished. There is always something that could be tweaked, always something that could be better. In fact, most of us only stop working when we run out of time.

Perhaps we don't always love this type of push when it's happening, but we emerge as better designers because of it. This is the type of training that creates thought leaders. It's the type of training that gives us nine out of ten of the skills on Harvard's list.

But the second skill on that list is confidence. And here is where so many architecture graduates fall short. We've learned so many marketable skills without realizing it, and these skills become so embedded into our approach to work that it becomes nearly impossible to identify our value.

On one hand, we are ideal employees.
On the other hand, we don't know it.

We look back at our projects, and all we can see are the aspects we could improve. Our hindsight is skewed by our tendency to look forward. We can't see the ways we've grown or the skills we've developed through our rigorous education because we can only see the ways we should be doing more.

In other words, we are insecure overachievers.[3]

#

For insecure overachievers, the goal is always to please the client. At the end of the day, architecture is, after all, a service industry. All of your conceptualizing – the art of your work – feels as though it is for nothing if the client isn't happy.

In school, your client was your professor. Maybe you even had your first real client for a side project or picked up an internship or small commission during school. In those cases, you worked hard to please your *actual*, non-professor clients. As a chronic overachiever, you were compelled to please your professors and devastated if they seemed disappointed in your work. But even beyond your professors, there was always someone to please. Your team leader, your project manager, your lead architect. You had a huge array of people depending on you. Sometimes it seemed impossible to make them all happy, but you tried. And when you failed, even in the tiniest of ways, you deeply felt the rift between your enormous effort and your inability to achieve perfection in others' eyes.

By any reasonable metric, you didn't fail. But it still stung like failure.

Tears streaming down her face, Erin's student Camile recounted the layers upon layers of responsibility she had been assigned that semester. As a fourth-year student, she had the usual challenging class schedule. She was pushing herself in studio, realizing the increasingly stressful stakes involved as projects became potential work samples for her portfolio. She had taken on a role as part of a professor's commission.

And now she had been nominated by the department to apply for a prestigious fellowship. Only two students in the program could apply, so her nomination alone signaled her outstanding talent. The good news was that she had the support of the faculty, who, by selecting her to apply, demonstrated their faith in her ability to represent the program well. That bad news was that all that faith translated into pressure. Camile had painstakingly compiled a portfolio for the fellowship competition and, as the very model of the insecure overachiever, had asked a faculty member to look over the portfolio to give her feedback before she submitted it to the fellowship committee.

It wasn't that the critique was particularly harsh. It certainly wasn't mean or rude. But it was a critique, and given everything else on Camile's plate, it had pushed her to the brink.

Her previous success in the program had won her new opportunities, which led to offers for more outside projects. This ultimately culminated in an overwhelming cascade of work, all of which Camile expected herself to perform to perfection. No new opportunity was really seen as the honor it was. She could only see it as a task that, once again, demanded that she prove her worthiness.

Now, what should have been relatively reasonable portfolio revisions became the proverbial last straw. Erin saw the woman break before her eyes.

"I know it's not perfect," she sniffled, "but I worked really hard on it, and I guess I went in the total wrong direction. I don't know when I'm gonna have time to redo this whole section, and I just feel like I let everyone down."

All Erin could think about was how this immensely talented student felt that she had "let everyone down," when, in reality, her performance had been so exemplary that she had been chosen as one of the top two students in the entire program. "Camile," she asked. "What do you want?"

The woman's brows furrowed as she searched for the answer on Erin's face. "What do you mean?" she asked.

"I mean, what do you want?" Erin repeated. "Do you want this fellowship? Do you want to work on the terrace project? Do you want to do the extra work on this portfolio? What do you want?"

Camile paused and glanced down at the floor. "It seems like everybody wants me to – "

"Okay, but what do _you_ want?" Erin interrupted, unwilling to watch this bright, talented woman continue to spiral into unwarranted self-doubt.

Camile looked up at her, confused, and Erin could almost see the wheels turning behind her eyes. They sat in silence for several moments as she contemplated the simple question. "I guess I hadn't really thought about that," she finally said sheepishly.

"It doesn't matter what everybody else wants. If you don't want to do all of this, then give yourself permission to just stop. Let something drop."

This was easier said than done, of course, but thinking about the prospects of deciding one's own fate was an important part of the process. When Camile left Erin's office that day, she had resolved to think about the question of what she wanted. When you're so entrenched in toxic perfectionism, it can feel impossible to suddenly let a ball drop. If you're used to pleasing everyone, then saying "no" can feel like a failure.

In the end, Camile thanked the professor for his feedback on her portfolio, but graciously declined to make the revisions. She felt unnecessarily guilty, but by clearing just one thing from her plate, she gave herself room to breathe, room she badly needed in order to think about what she wanted from her career and from her life.

Why Is It Like This?

Several months later, Erin was unsurprised to learn that Camile had received the prestigious fellowship even without making the revisions. It turned out there was no need for insecurity at all.

#

Erin had seen students like Camile before. In fact, the insecure overachiever made up a significant proportion of the Out of Architecture client base. While some of the issues that prompted students like Camile to break down under the weight of toxic perfectionism seemed to be school-based, the problem was that, by the time your education was finished, the insecure overachiever identity was difficult to shake.

Within this model, toxic perfectionism became a cycle that carried you through school and into the profession. It became the only thing you knew.

This mentality probably took root before you even realized it. Perhaps during childhood, but certainly by the time you finished high school, you were already an overachiever. Your teachers earmarked you as one of the students who was destined for great things, pushing you to apply for the best universities and the top scholarships. You chose to study architecture, and, as a certified overachiever, you obviously chose to apply to the top programs in the field.

You probably celebrated a bit when the acceptance letter came in the mail, but it didn't take long for the insecurity to set in. You'd succeeded so far, but would you be able to overachieve in this new world? With all of these people so excited for your acceptance into the program, how could you avoid letting them down? And what if you got there in the fall and they realized they'd made a mistake? That you weren't who they thought you were – you weren't nearly as talented, smart, or driven as they'd assumed. You probably weren't used to failing. Now the realization that you were about to embark on something exceptionally challenging – the prospect that you might fail – loomed large.

Throughout architecture school, the threat of failure became a crushing weight on your shoulders. You found that a sense of insecurity could even be useful at times, your determination to prove yourself adding to your passion for the craft. Often you weren't the best in the class – most of your classmates were overachievers too – but you fought hard to perform above expectations. In those moments, you were grateful for the recognition. You might not have been able to keep going without it.

At the same time, acknowledgement of your talent meant one more thing to live up to. Every achievement raised the hurdle a little higher until you reached the ultimate accomplishment: graduation.

Except that graduation, it turned out, was just one more raised bar. Nothing magically changed when you started your first job. You were still desperate to prove yourself – maybe now more than ever – and you still aspired to a toxic level of perfectionism because it was the only way you knew how to design. You'd learned a lot of things in school, and many of them made you a talented architect and designer. But you'd also learned to associate your value as a person with your ability to please every potential client and stakeholder. You had internalized an impossible vision of who you should be as a designer.

In that first role, you were probably paid by the hour. That meant that your tendency toward over-performing was at least financially rewarded on some level. Your paycheck was tangible evidence of the extra hours you put in to help make sure your portion of the project was perfect, or at least as close as possible given the time constraints. But, once again, good work was rewarded with ever-higher expectations. After years of hard work, late hours, and compulsive – and sometimes compulsory – perfectionism, you finally got the news you'd been waiting for. You had been promoted to a salaried position.

The news of the promotion was emotionally satisfying. You may have even rewarded yourself with a Saturday evening celebratory dinner with family and friends once you'd finished your weekend work at the office. But it quickly became clear that the promotion carried with it even higher expectations and an even less frequent system of rewards. The shift from an hourly rate to annual pay scale meant that you would actually be taking a cut in pay. And yet, you were not only expected to maintain the same amount and quality of work – the promotion seemed to demand even more of you. The structure of the profession fed both your insecurity and your habit of overachieving.

As you moved from school to early career to mid-level status at your firm, the systems of rewards continued to function as a paradox. You desperately needed validation. The physical and emotional stress of the job demanded some kind of praise, because that was the only way to sustain this level of expectations. It had always been the only way you kept going. Conversely, though, with every bit of tangible praise – graduation, hiring, promotion – the expectations imperceptibly raised until the bits of affirmation weren't enough.

You'd landed squarely in the cycle of toxic perfectionism, your insecurity feeding your need to overachieve and your overachievement feeding your insecurity. The problem is that, by the time you realized you were embedded in this dangerous cycle, it seemed impossible to escape.

#

Erin and Jake were all too aware that they would be addressing a group of talented, bright, engaged, insecure overachievers, and as the Zoom windows began to populate, the nervous energy in the room was almost palpable. 2020 had not been a good year for job searching, given the raging pandemic, and the group of students they were speaking with were all near graduation.

"Let's think of this as a live counseling session," Jake had joked early in their presentation. While the line drew a few chuckles, as the talk progressed, it became clear that this really was a form of therapy. Jake and Erin didn't think of themselves as career therapists, but client after client told them that their meetings were cathartic. For many, this was the first time they were allowed to – even requested to – vent about their frustrations with people who intimately understood their complaints. Usually, clients left feeling much more positive, armed with actionable ideas to pursue and the reassurance that there was no shame in leaving architecture, that they were under no obligation to continue pursuing the career they'd imagined five years ago when they first read *The Fountainhead*.

The presentation had primarily involved a brief discussion of the company. They focused on the goals of Out of Architecture and the various ways they approached client support.

"Our process is very much personalized, depending on things like career stage, values – " Erin noted.

"We basically help people prioritize their physical, mental, and family health over everything else," Jake added.

Several of the students attending the talk seemed perplexed. Jake and Erin noticed slow head nods and furrowed brows on the videos tiled across the screen. They weren't particularly surprised. This idea of putting your own needs first was always a tough sell for people who were used to pleasing everyone else first, people who have been trained to see others' happiness as their own top priority.

Erin and Jake continued, offering a few examples of previous clients, touching on the role of various skills that students take away from architecture school – technology, project management, graphic design – and ultimately asking, "what is your ideal day?" This was the question they used to guide every client toward a career that best suited their skills and life goals. As the presentation concluded, the Zoom room fell quiet.

"We'd love to answer any questions you might have," Erin noted. This was the core of the presentation, the opportunity for students to chime in, and in so doing, to demonstrate that curiosity about non-traditional careers was okay. That it was perfectly normal not to have everything figured out.

Finally, one student tentatively raised his hand. "I was just wondering," he said hesitantly before interrupting himself. "I'm sorry. I should have asked first. Can I ask a question?"

"Yes! Of course!" Jake said, doing everything he could to nonverbally encourage the student. "What have you got for us?"

"Okay," the student smiled apologetically, "I was just wondering. I'm curious to know what you think from the employer's standpoint are the most valuable qualities from people with our design backgrounds. And, like, why is that useful for most employers?"

It was telling that the question itself was posed from the employer's standpoint. Even in a casual question and answer portion, the student had scanned the various stakeholders – Erin, Jake, the presentation host, as his potential future employers – and was taking a demonstrated care to please everyone. And in his need to appeal to these various stakeholders, he was ultimately undercutting the confidence he should have had as a soon-to-be graduate of one of the country's top architecture programs.

The question was a practical one, so Jake began by offering a few of the marketable skills clients had brought to bear on their careers. Erin followed up with a few of her own. But then they brought the question back around to the issue implicitly raised by the posing of this question.

"But Cade," Jake added firmly. "You need a healthy confidence. You've gotta present yourself in a way that shows employers your value."

"No more over-apologizing," Erin scolded with a hint of good-natured humor. The student grinned sheepishly. She smiled back. "But honestly, I totally get it. Confidence can be really difficult." She had once been an insecure overachiever, too. The term was never meant to be pejorative as much as it was instructive. It was simply a descriptor of a condition they saw over and over in their business.

At the heart of the insecure overachiever is a failure to recognize one's own value as intrinsic. The insecure overachiever sees their value as arising from

Why Is It Like This?

others' praise. As long as the gold stars and the A pluses and the attaboys hold out, the insecure overachiever can maintain their confidence. But, of course, that kind of praise becomes increasingly sparse after the formal mechanisms of school. And once we are dependent upon others' implicit opinions of our work to build our self-worth, we have set ourselves up for failure. We have relinquished control of our lives to the fickle assessments of our bosses, teammates, and clients.

Of course, there are obvious benefits – perhaps even necessities – to the system of rewards set up throughout our educational lives. We need feedback to improve. We need the possibility of praise and acceptance to keep ourselves motivated. And we need honest assessments from our teachers and professors of the skills we require to be competitive in the job market.

We also need to understand that we have inherent value.

Our sense of self-esteem should not be tied entirely to the arbitrary system of praise and reward set up in school and adopted within the profession.

Once our clients begin to separate their value as individuals from their value as workers, honoring and exploring both in turn, they often find that they become more confident in their abilities and less compelled to overachieve. There is simply no need to constantly please others if you have a solid sense of self-worth. And once you have a solid sense of self-worth beyond your career, the possibilities for your future begin to open up in a way they haven't before. No longer are you beholden to the career visions of your mentors and professors. Suddenly, you are free to pursue your own best life.

In reality, this is a life-long process, full of ups and downs, victories and setbacks. Erin and Jake were always open about that with their clients. But at the same time, they insisted on pushing people not simply to overachieve but to own their value as people and as highly trained professionals.

They left the students on this note, emphasizing their ability to navigate the challenges of the future. "You are entering a very uncertain time," Erin told them. "One of the most important things you can do is to remember the difference between risk and uncertainty." This was a talk Erin frequently had with her classes, and she pushed forward, modeling the confidence they both wished for the students in the room.

"Not having a job is taking a risk. You're taking a risk if you're not doing the things you need to do to be competitive when you apply for jobs. You can understand risk. You can wrap your head around it and take steps to mitigate it.

"That other part – the thing you can't measure or solve or even wrap your head around – that part is the uncertainty. And the uncertainty is always going to be there."

The nervous tension in the room had lingered throughout the presentation, and now it felt heightened.

"But do not have anxiety about the risk," Erin said definitively. "You can manage the risk. You can handle this process, even though it's going to be a little bit different than maybe you thought it was going to be. You can do this. Trust me."

"We're here to help, too." Jake added.

Erin nodded enthusiastically. "Absolutely. The uncertainty is very difficult, we understand that. However – " She paused for effect. "You are a designer. Every time you start a project, every time you have undertaken a new relationship with a professor or a client or a stakeholder, you have actively managed their uncertainty. You have taken charge of it."

"Exactly," Jake said, punctuating the point. "You have more experience than you think with all of this."

They left the group on one final note of reassurance. This group of aspiring architects and designers already had the skills they needed to succeed. All they needed now was to own it.

NOTES

1   Postsecondary Analytics, "How Full-Time are 'Full-Time' Students," *Complete College America*, October 2013, Retrieved from https://completecollege.org/wp-content/uploads/2017/11/2013-10-14-how-full-time.pdf.
2   Nicholas Korody, "The State of Debt and the Price of Architecture," *Archinect,* November 2014, Retrieved from https://archinect.com/features/article/112509888/the-state-of-debt-and-the-price-of-architecture.
3   Credit for this term belongs to Tom Wisniewski, a guest invited to Erin's Professional Practice course to lecture on "Value and the Young Professional."

CHAPTER 8
IMPLODING TEAMS

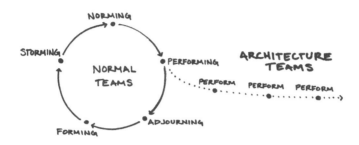

"Okay, so I'd say we have a rough idea of the concept, if everybody's cool with this direction. What do you guys think?" Erin asked, raising the heavy mug to take a sip of her beer.

"Totally. I think that's a good starting point," Katie replied.

Jake nodded, "there's definitely room to polish, and we'll refine some of these things later, but yes. A good, rough idea."

"Cheers, then!" Erin said, extending her glass to the middle of the table. Even though they were rapidly approaching finals week, the group of four – Jake and Erin and their classmates Katie and Mikhail – had agreed to put together a submission for the Design Miami competition. The winner of the competition would design the entry pavilion for the event, a massive, multi-day gathering of designers, collectors, curators, artists, and architects.

Their entry was called "Pitch," a title that signaled the angle of the pavilion roof, the act of selling someone on a concept, and, at the heart of the project, the process of erecting a tent. The entryway would take an active role in selling the event from the outside. But the project also needed to account for the event's hurricane-prone site. The team had tentatively decided to bridge these competing goals with an origami-inspired tent. Giving the appearance of folded paper, the structure would function as an anamorphic projection: it would read "Design Miami," but only from a particular angle. When a viewer

DOI: 10.4324/9781003300922-11

approached the pavilion from the designated point, the pitch would become clear, inviting attendees into the space. And in the end, the tent could be broken down in under an hour. The concept was sleek and cool, and it blended the team's aesthetics. The group was formed around a vision for a highly efficient team, necessary given the fact that they were all running on fumes by this point in the semester.

"So, what's next?" Mikhail asked, squishing a sample of the memory foam the team hoped to incorporate into their design. There was something so energizing about the tactility of project materials. And who could resist pressing their fingers into memory foam? Nobody. And the team was counting on that to give their project submission an extra touch of interest.

Jake responded, "We'll all be in studio together anyway, right? Can we just – "

"Actually, I would really rather not work in studio," Katie cut in, smiling apologetically. "I get kind of cranky in that space," she laughed, "so I'd honestly rather work at home. But we can touch base at school?"

"Yeah, honestly," Mikhail said tentatively, looking up over the table as he crouched to slide his notebook into the messenger bag he had propped against the leg of his chair. He'd pocketed the memory foam sample, too. It was like a stress ball – very appropriate for their end-of-semester anxieties. "I'd rather work at home, too. Just to separate studio from this project."

Erin shrugged. She knew that Katie and Mikhail preferred to work at home, and she tended to be pretty easy going about that kind of thing. "In that case, let's go ahead and divide out tasks right now, before we head out. Then it won't matter so much where we're working."

"Sure," Jake responded. "Erin, you're doing the model, right?" In other groups, this presumption might have been trouble, but everyone at the table agreed that Erin was an amazing model-builder. Jake planned to help once he had finished up with the Rhino model, one of his specialties.

"We were thinking we would work on the renderings," Katie said glancing at Mikhail. "Is that kind of what you had in mind?"

"Yeah, and Katie, if you can take the lead on those, I can work on the packaging and just polishing all the linework and text at the end." Mikhail leaned back in his chair, the fatigue of finals week showing under his eyes. They were all feeling the exhaustion, doing the best they could to power through and finish their projects strong.

"Sure, sure," Katie said smiling. "You guys, this is gonna be an awesome project!"

The team enthusiastically agreed. They had a relatively short time period to put together an entry, but they felt confident in the team's ability to complete a competitive project. And now, only a few days into planning, they had already solidified their various roles and worked together to complete a rough outline of the concept. When they left the basement bar across from studio that evening, they were humming with excitement about the work ahead. They felt like they belonged. They were valued members of a team.

That sense of community – of working together toward a shared goal in a mutually supportive environment – was even more intoxicating than their pints of beer. Every team has its ups and downs, and the Design Miami project was no different. They had to develop a sense of trust in one another and in the team and navigate one another's boundaries. As with any team, there were conflicts. How should they align the layout of the design with the specifications of the competition? When could they get together one last time to go over the final submission? Why couldn't they meet in this place or that? Wasn't it possible that the renderings were overly stylized compared to the other project components?

They weren't a perfect team, and the project wasn't always easy. Still, the Design Miami team discussed their issues, made compromises and affordances, and moved forward together.

By the time they reached the deadline, the project was strong. There was always more that could be done, and this submission was no exception. At the same time, the team was proud of what they had put together. They had settled into their roles and found a relative state of flow, each person contributing to the best of their abilities in the areas where they most excelled.

When all was said and done, they didn't win. And yet, they found themselves back at the Queen's Head Pub anyway, once again clinking glasses together to toast a job well done. Win or lose, they knew the project – and another semester in the books – was something to celebrate.

#

It wasn't intentional, and they didn't realize it then, but the team had almost perfectly progressed through the stages of Tuckman's group formation model.[1] Based on a meta-analysis of 50 previous studies, Bruce Tuckman determined that there are behavioral patterns common to most groups. His 1965 model included four stages, including forming, storming, norming, and performing. The rate of progression through the steps is often a reflection of the overall structural health of a team, with a slow rate of progression – or failure to progress through the stages at all – signaling a misstep in team strategy.

Tuckman's first stage, *forming*, involves the process of orientation. During this stage, group members feel out one another's boundaries, preferences, personalities, and task orientations. The Design Miami team modeled this behavior in their initial assignment of tasks, structuring the group around each individual's strengths and weaknesses, while demonstrating assertive communication of workspace boundaries.

Compared to forming, Tuckman's next stage feels less upbeat. The central characteristic of *storming* is conflict. The forming process brings disagreements to the surface, and these conflicts are expressed and resolved during the storming stage. While it isn't heathy to linger in the storming phase for too long, this stage is a natural part of group formation. Open discussion of compromise and consensus – focused on workspaces, rendering style, and scheduling within the Design Miami team – allow the storming phase to strengthen teams as they move into the third stage of group formation.

The process of resolving conflict is, itself, a bonding experience. In the third stage, *norming*, team members begin to view their contributions as something larger than themselves. During this stage, groups settle into their interpersonal and task-related roles. Conflicts still arise, but during this phase, team members feel bolstered by their ability to navigate disagreements.

This leads to Tuckman's final stage: *performing*. Key to this stage is the acceptance of individual roles. Since the crucial but often conflict-laden work of assigning tasks and responsibilities has already been accomplished, the group can move forward, focusing its energy on work tasks rather than interpersonal issues. The Design Miami team seamlessly moved from norming into performing due to their clear outlining of individual responsibilities early in the work process as well as their years of friendship. By defining roles from the outset, the team was well-poised to move forward, with each individual's work contributing to a greater whole.

Just over a decade after Tuckman published his original theory, he and co-author Mary Ann Jensen added a fifth stage: *adjourning*. Included as a way to recognize how group membership seems to manifest after a "life cycle model," this final step of adjourning allows for both celebration and mourning.[2] It recognizes that healthy group membership is a cyclical process that is deeply personal and often tied to important individual issues like self-esteem and identity within a group.

Describing the iteration of the adjourning stage that involves celebration, Tuckman and Jensen noted in their work that it was important for groups to pause from the work at key points to assess their progress and celebrate their wins. They observed that the healthiest groups tended to take time to step back, congratulate themselves as a team, and give one another – and the group as a whole – closure on a particular task. Doing this allows us to feel positive about our role in the group and to find warm feelings about the group in general. It gives us a sense of being supported by a community and of supporting one another.

This process isn't only revelatory, though. Through the process of celebrating our wins, we also provide supportive feedback for individuals within the group. Team celebrations tend to involve communication about aspects of the work that were particularly compelling, inspiring, or labor-intensive. We show newer group members, through positive reinforcement, where their time is best spent. We communicate our gratitude for others and often acknowledge, then brush off, the things that didn't go well, thus preparing to perform more effectively on future tasks.

In Tuckman's original study, and in his follow-up with Jensen, this process isn't a matter of explicitly or systematically marking a checklist of stages. The entire process, of progressing gradually through each stage of group development, should flow naturally as groups get to know one another, their responsibilities on each project, and the tasks that make up that project.

But architecture, for the most part, never got the memo.

So often, the groups we find ourselves a part of in architecture school and later in the workplace fail to allow for the vulnerability required to move from forming into the necessary stages of storming and norming.

The enormous pressures that are built into educational and professional architecture – to work quickly, to indulge in minute details of design, and to be, already, the best in the group – mean that we often skip even the most basic stage, failing to take the time to define formal and informal roles and orient new members to the group.

Instead, teams are expected to acclimate, immediately, to the performing stage. There is no time for dipping one's toe into the water. New group members are tossed straight into the deep end, where the water is icy and often full of sharks.

Not only do our groups attempt to begin at the performing stage, but we also refuse to move out of this stage. An adjourning stage that goes beyond the odd team dinner to actually acknowledge the completion of a task can do wonders for helping new group members to acclimate and grow and orient to the group's culture. Instead, the emphasis is constantly brought back to performing. Nothing is ever finished – no one can ever be accepted as good enough. It's always back to the drawing board, back to the constant expectation of performing, with no room for working through interpersonal conflicts, orienting oneself to the team's cultural norms, or taking a moment to breathe between projects.

#

Tuckman would have been appalled to see the ways most architecture firms have been organized, or perhaps the ways they have been disorganized. The central role of the leader was totally convoluted in so many firms. Either there was a single, very overloaded person whose job it was to perform every possible management duty as well as their own design work. Or there were two managers – a project manager and a project architect – two bosses who were rarely explicitly introduced to new people as such and who split the responsibilities of management in a way that made sense to them and to the firm but that was totally indecipherable to any new group members. That, or some mix of the above.

Perhaps before you entered your new work environment, you'd felt confident that you knew how teams functioned in architecture. You'd done plenty of work in groups as an architecture student, even taking on leadership roles on a number of projects in your last couple of years. And yet, nothing could prepare you for the utter sense of helplessness you felt when you entered the professional realm and realized that there was no orientation week. There wasn't even an orientation day. Maybe you got a tour, if you were lucky, but otherwise you were left to figure things out on your own. You'd learned early in architecture school that this was the norm for learning the ropes of design. Now you found that it was the norm when it came to group function as well.

Not only were you completely unsure of who your boss was – in fact, you'd spent the first day trying to endear yourself to the guy you *thought* was your boss, only to realize that he wasn't actually responsible for anything other than collating timesheets and documenting sick leave – you were also incredibly uncertain of how you fit into the team structure.

You and two other Designer I's had all been hired together, and you were all given tasks within an apparently newly formed team. Others in the team seemed to know one another, but you weren't really invited into their conversations or relationships, and there hadn't been time to get to know the other new hires either. You were asked to put together some renderings, and you went to your desk and got to work. It was incredibly isolating to realize you'd been plopped into the center of a team but to have no real way of incorporating yourself into the group dynamic.

As time went on, the three of you who had been hired at the same time became old hat at the firm's work. Newer new hires came in, and now you weren't the new people anymore. Even as you settled in, you still found yourself without any real sense of team roles. If the firm had a hierarchical structure, it was muddy at best. There were the partners at the very top, and below them, everybody else seemed to fend for themselves. Otherwise, the guiding question was, "How long have you been at the firm?" There was no time for figuring out the group dynamics, for working through team conflicts – interpersonal or work-related – or for building a sense of trust and vulnerability within the group. There was too much work to do and no clear structure for how to do it.

In moments of visceral frustration with a task dropped here or a project component botched there, you wondered why the project manager didn't sit down and make a plan that actually considered team members' individual skills in the process of assigning tasks. Things could have gone ahead so much more fluidly if you each had clear direction on how your role fit in with others in the group. But you also realized that the project manager didn't have time for that any more than you did. Everyone was simply maxed out and there was nothing to do but scramble to get the job done.

Everything was a constant struggle, moving you from one frantic, overloaded project to the next. Sometimes you were even pulled off of one project and reassigned to another – or your intern was moved to another team or the only person you really trusted left to join another firm. You could never really get your feet underneath yourself.

And all of that scrambling set the team's nerves on edge. So, of course, there was bickering. Not the healthy kind of conflict, where the push and pull of individual work dynamics were brought into the group's shared workspace and processed for the good of the team. That would have taken time and energy that nobody had. Instead, it was a constant, low-grade dissatisfaction that bubbled under the surface of the workplace culture. Maybe you brought it to your mentor or the project manager. If so, you were likely told that this type of conflict is common. It's fine. Just focus on the work.

But more likely, you wouldn't have even known who to talk to about this kind of thing. It was obvious that everybody was completely in over their heads. You barely had time to do the work that was required of you. You certainly didn't have time to work on your interpersonal team dynamics.

Just like the work itself, you were expected to figure it out on your own. You never got the benefit of the "forming" stage – orientation and the definition of roles. Neither did the "storming" or "norming" phases happen in any productive way. Sure, people complained about one another, but those complaints never had the benefit of being aired out; they were always brushed aside to make room for the next project deadline. There was only performing. The constant pressure to be "on," pushing ahead to the next item on the list. An endless cycle of pressure with no end in sight.

#

Maybe you cognitively realized it, or maybe you just absorbed it through osmosis: you would never be finished. There was always something else hanging over your head, one or two or a hundred more things you could do. The next deadline was always looming. And, you suspected, even if you finished all of those tasks, more would materialize – if not on that project, then on another.

There was no chance to breathe, let alone process any critical feedback on your work beyond redlines. And while your team often went to happy hours and dinners together, they never felt truly celebratory. After all, there was always more to do. What was there to celebrate?

Perhaps if there had been well-defined roles, you would have been able to mark a point of completion, or at least assert autonomy over your own aspects of the project. Instead, work was always fungible. You hadn't gone through the "forming" process of group formation – where roles and positions might have been assigned based on group members' interests and talents – so you were all responsible for this endless dance of performing.

You desperately longed for the days of your later years in architecture school. Sure, you weren't totally confident in your projects then either. There was always more to be done. But, at the same time, your celebrations had felt genuine. You could actually bond over work well done. You could take a bit of time for yourselves between semesters, these marked periods of beginning and end that you had so taken for granted back in school.

Now, there was less and less delineation between the end of one project and the beginning of another. In most cases, projects overlapped. That meant you were never really able to take time to process, to get feedback, to improve or readjust your approach.

And the lack of clear group structure meant that there were consequences if you tried to take a day – even an hour or two – to catch your breath. When someone had to leave the office early, it seemed to send a message that someone else should pick up their work. "Oh, are you not planning to finish this, then?" someone might say. Or "are you too busy today? You must have a lot of things going on outside of work, I guess. Must be nice." There were plenty of ways to remind other team members that nothing was supposed to be more important than work. Nothing took precedence over the project.

You'd all been thrown into the pool together, and you were all supposed to keep yourselves – and others – from drowning. Thinking of it as drowning didn't feel like an exaggeration most days. The work-without-end approach to team projects felt as though you were always just a few inches above the surface, wearily treading water, with no real hope of ever reaching the shore.

#

Burnout takes many forms. Perhaps the most annoying of these is the "bullshit burnout." Bullshit burnout is a type of relentless fatigue caused not by overwork – or at least not solely by overwork – but by the day-to-day bullshit of toxic team dynamics. This process of burnout is a race to the bottom in that it seems to take Tuckman's process of group formation and obstruct it – even pervert it – at every turn.

Where there should be organized formation, there is only uncertainty. Where there should be healthy conflict, there is only gossip. Where there should be a sense of settling into the expectations, tasks, and strengths and weaknesses of group members, there is only bullshit. Like a fruit fly caught in a relentless, buzzing orbit around your head, this type of group dynamic is a constant, underlying hum of annoyance, chipping away at the joy and satisfaction you once found in doing good work and contributing to your firm's progress.

Lisa knew about the buzzing annoyance of bullshit burnout. With eight years of experience under her belt, she was right at the cusp of mid-career, and she had spent a significant portion of her professional life thus far at one, very well-known corporate architecture firm. She found herself working on a small project team with a relentlessly irritating fruit fly named Cal serving as her team leader.

Lisa kept hoping things would get better, but the more she tried to prove herself through her work, the more threatened Cal seemed to feel. Lisa's complaint would prove common in Jake and Erin's work, showing up in clients again and again.

Fresh out of college, Lisa had taken a job with a lead architect she highly respected. Overall, she had been pleased with the types of projects she was assigned, and there were plenty of team members she liked. But, as Lisa learned, the rewards system on the job was very different from the rewards system in school. She had come to the firm straight from architecture school, expecting that a project review every few weeks could keep her motivated and working. Now that she worked at the firm, opportunities to get feedback on her performance were few and far between.

And then there was the uncertainty surrounding group roles. She had come in at the same time as another architect, but Cal had more experience than she did. No problem, Lisa had originally thought. She wasn't an overly competitive person. Except that Cal seemed intent on competing with her, constantly trying to one-up her, especially when Lisa tried to disengage from the toxic relationship. Cal constantly took credit for the team's work and asserted his own leadership among the group members.

As in so many architecture firms, Lisa never felt there was time or energy to raise the issue of group dynamics. All of this was compounded by the fact that she knew talking to the partner wouldn't get her anywhere. She had been there for years, so even though she might have appreciated a sense of caring for a long-term employee, she'd also seen over the years that the partner was not interested in the team's interpersonal issues.

And then things escalated. Lisa knew Cal didn't like her. She wasn't particularly sure why, but she suspected that Cal didn't like her tendency to offer suggestions when she noticed errors in others' – particularly Cal's – work. Cal was not the kind of person who appreciated feedback. Yet even though Lisa knew he didn't like her, she still expected some degree of professionalism.

Then, one day at happy hour, she overheard Cal describing her as "the kind of person who shoots up the office." She felt her heart skip a beat, a sense of disbelief and hurt flooding her body. She stuck it out through the rest of happy hour. She was a light-hearted person. Easy going and likable. She didn't like to make waves.

She had known Cal regularly gossiped about her, but suggesting that she might be a mass murderer seemed a bridge too far. Finally, she decided to speak with a HR representative.

The HR representative had listened to her complaint, but by the end of their meeting, Lisa had a sinking feeling that she had made a mistake by coming to her. It was clear that this woman was not empowered in any way to make things better and she feared that things might even get worse.

She was right to be afraid. The HR representative had reported the conversation to the firm's lead architect who immediately took the report personally. At the heart of the issue was the partner's contention that Lisa should have come directly to him. But, of course, even after he heard about it, nothing really happened. There was some sense around the workplace that the partner had called a meeting with Cal and told him not to say things like that. The meeting only increased Cal's animosity toward her.

In some ways, Lisa's experience is extreme. In others, it is all too common. It is a natural outgrowth of the standard system of hiring and promoting architects based on their years of experience, then setting the group loose to figure out their own team structure.

There are no designated roles. There are no designated tasks. There are very few leaders who are trained and experienced with leadership, as workers tend to be promoted not for their leadership abilities, but for their design skills, their years of experience, or both.

What's worse, those who might actually bring leadership skills – or even people skills in general – to an architecture work environment are saddled with the same overwhelming workload as others on the team. There is simply no room for problem solving, for adequately and thoughtfully assigning tasks, or for working through the standard conflicts that arise in any workplace.

All of the elements of effective teamwork – the building blocks of a healthy, happy workplace – are put aside and pushed to the back until they ultimately, finally come to a head. If not through an egregious example like Lisa's, then through the burnout that brings so many people to Out of Architecture.

Cal's behavior had helped Lisa to see that her work environment was untenable before she found herself completely burned out. She still felt deeply compelled to pursue a career in architecture, but she now knew, beyond any doubt, that she could not continue at her current firm.

Lisa worked through all of the conflicting feelings in her early meetings with Erin and Jake. After identifying Lisa's skills, goals, and work style, Out of Architecture presented her with a number of possibilities for a career pivot. In addition to an option that included a part-time architecture job, Jake and Erin suggested potential career paths in the fields of design research, design education, and product design.

In the end, Lisa's easy-going attitude combined with her attention to detail — the very trait that had made her a target for Cal's bullying — made her a perfect candidate for an opening at one of the top design agencies in the city. While Cal was the furthest thing from Lisa's mind, it certainly didn't hurt her feelings to know that he was still languishing in the same dead-end job at the same disorganized firm. Meanwhile, she had scored a better title with higher pay. To her surprise, the new job also came with a benefits package that included more vacation days than she had accrued after years at the old firm — and, here, employees were actually encouraged to use them.

Like the cherry on top of it all, it turned out that adjusting to a new job didn't have to be so difficult. Within a few weeks, she felt confident that she understood most of the contours of her new role, thanks, in part, to the new company's dedicated orientation modules. She commented to Jake and Erin, with just a hint of playful sarcasm, that she had never realized how useful it would be to walk into a job with a clearly defined role.

Bruce Tuckman would approve. Lisa, Jake, and Erin did too.

NOTES

1   Bruce W. Tuckman, "Developmental Sequence in Small Groups," *Psychological Bulletin 63*, no. 6 (1965): 384–399.
2   Bruce W. Tuckman and Mary Ann Jensen, "Stages of Small-Group Development Revised," *Group and Organizational Studies 2*, no. 4 (1977): 425.

CHAPTER 9
THE FALSE DICHOTOMY OF PAY AND PASSION

At the client's request, Jake arrived at the site early in the morning. Ron was already outside, leaning against the exterior wall of the house. As Jake approached him, the client flashed him a toothy grin that raised his self-tinting glasses slightly off the bridge of his nose. He stretched out his hand assertively toward Jake, and Jake took it, hoping his handshake felt as solid to Ron as Ron's felt to him. Jake felt a little skip in his stomach – excitement or some minor nerves. This job was big.

He'd seen the house before, on a site visit in his first or second year of school. Richard Meier had designed it at a very young age, and it had morphed from an apartment on top of a chicken coop to a striking, art-filled home at the southern edge of Ithaca. The current owners, Ron and Shelley Cooper, were converting a space on the ground floor from tractor storage to a public gallery. They had specifically wanted a Cornell architect to do the work, and they found Jake through a mutual contact. Other well-known Cornell

DOI: 10.4324/9781003300922-12

architects had worked on the house over the years, and Jake, Erin, and Rachel were incredibly excited about the prospect of contributing to the update.

"Let me take you around the place, and I'll tell you what we're looking for," Ron said, starting toward the large open space to their left.

Jake followed him, adding, "Mr. Cooper, I'm – "

"Oh, call me Ron." He glanced back with a grin.

"Ron," Jake corrected, "I'm just so honored to be able to talk with you about this. This house is legendary. It's an unbelievable opportunity."

They had reached a garage of sorts, which opened out into an incredible view of the somewhat irregular tree line that flanked the house. "We love this house," Ron said. "And you come very highly recommended. Glad to have another Cornellian on the project."

Ron went on to explain their vision for renovating the garage space, then continued with a tour of the property. He and his wife had only lived there a couple of years at that point, but they were very community minded. Not only were they careful to involve the Cornell architecture community – even requesting an architecture student, Jake assumed, to give a young designer some applied experience – but they also wanted to share the space with others in the Ithaca community. They envisioned lively gallery openings featuring the artwork of Cindy Tower, a Cornell graduate who had become quite well-known in the art world since her early exhibitions in the 1980s.

As the client talked, Jake felt himself getting more and more enthusiastic about the project. Even the opportunity to be here, speaking with Ron and learning about the past and present visions of this iconic Ithaca home, was humbling. This project was right up his alley, and he knew Erin and Rachel would be enthralled with the concept, too. This was exactly the type of work they all loved. It was the kind of project that had inspired them to go into architecture in the first place.

Just to the west of the home, a crew was moving a load of sizable rocks from the truck to the space where a stone half-wall was beginning to take shape. Ron stopped to eye the growing structure, folding his arms across his chest and nodding. Behind them a crew of painters were working on the back of the house, and the property was buzzing with architectural activity. It was inspiring to see the work being done to update the building while still maintaining its soul and place in the community.

Just then, Ron turned back to Jake and said, "Okay. Let's do this. What do you think is a fair rate?"

Why Is It Like This?

Jake's heart skipped a beat. Seeing the site, walking around the house with Ron and hearing the stories of the property from his perspective, Jake had felt things were going well. He had only grown more hopeful for the opportunity to work on the project as Ron had talked, but he hadn't prepared to be offered the job on the spot.

"Oh," Jake stammered. "Great!" He felt humbled to have this opportunity. As a fourth-year student, he had hoped for the chance to work with clients, but he hadn't dreamed he would be working on the Meier house. As he saw it, the project would be a chance for him to learn and grow. He could put the project in his portfolio, and that, alone, would be worth quite a few credibility points on future job interviews. Payment hadn't even crossed his mind. He would have done the job for the experience alone without a second thought.

"Well?" Ron asked, pulling Jake back to the conversation.

Jake had been working a job on campus for a few years. It paid minimum wage: $7.25 per hour. In what felt like an enormously bold move, Jake took a swing at pricing his services. "Would you think $10 an hour would make sense?"

Ron's eyebrows shot up behind his dark glasses, and he let out a jovial chuckle. Placing his hand on Jake's shoulder and grinning ear to ear, Ron replied, "I'm going to pay you $20."

"Oh," Jake said, not expecting this turn of events.

"And I'm gonna tell you why," Ron continued. His hand shifting to Jake's back, Ron turned them to face the crew stacking stones along the crest of the small hill. "If any other tradesman came to my house to do work – any of these guys, the painters back there – I wouldn't blink an eye if they asked for $20 an hour."

Jake did a cartwheel in his mind, feeling suddenly wealthy. Trying to tamp down his excitement at this unexpected pay bump, Jake smiled back at Ron. "I really appreciate it. Just the experience of working on this place is so valuable to me, for my portfolio, and I just appreciate the opportunity."

Now Ron turned serious. He stopped and looked Jake in the eye.

"Remember," he said. "I'm getting value out of your work. You need to learn to value it, too. Don't sell yourself short."

#

The three of them learned a lot from Ron Cooper over the next year. Most architecture students could have. Ron and his wife had been quite successful businesspeople before their retirement led them to the Meier house. They were passionate about that house, passionate about building a community around beautiful art and design, passionate about living the good life.

They were passionate.

And they also understood business.

This is where architecture students – and architects in general – could learn from Ron's approach.

> ### *When business and passion intermingle, it becomes very easy to lose track of the value of your labor. It becomes very easy to sell yourself short.*

Most architecture students are incredibly passionate. It's this passion that helps drive students through the long nights, the physical and mental fatigue, the disappointment of a bad review, the stress of investing so much into a project that it keeps you up at night. Passion is key to any artistic endeavor.

Professional architecture is about passion, too. But it's also a business. And here is where things often go astray.

Erin is fond of pointing out the definition of "profession" as a way of illustrating the roots of the problems in the business of architecture. Webster tells us that a profession is first, "the taking of vows of a religious community." Second, a profession is "the act of openly declaring or publicly claiming that belief." And third, a profession is "a devout religious faith."

Architects often joke about bowing at the altar of architecture. You eat, sleep, and breathe architecture, professing your faith to the field. Perhaps it's not so strange to think of the religious undertones of the word "profession" when put that way.

Of course, the word has other definitions: "a calling requiring specialized knowledge and often long and intensive preparation" and "a principal calling,

Why Is It Like This?

vocation or employment." While it's easy to say that the first three definitions – definitions that are clearly related to the idea of professing one's faith – are less applicable than the final two, we find that the idea of a "calling" comes troublingly close to the idea of a faith profession. It should be ludicrous to expect architects to profess our faith to the field in the way clergy profess their faith to God. And it should be equally as troubling to understand our choice of career as a divine calling.

So often when we understand our profession as something we profess to – something we are called to do by a divine, higher power – we fail to maintain a healthy balance between passion and business. We don't see our job as something that should pay our bills, help us build a retirement fund, allow us to take family vacations, and pay off our student loans. When we internalize this idea that architecture is our calling, we simply cannot see things that way. Instead, we see architecture as something we are devoted to, regardless of the economic, physical, and psychological toll it may take on us. When we understand our profession not as a career but as a calling, it becomes easy to lose sight of the benefits a career should provide, distracted endlessly by elements better left to a religious or spiritual faith. We forget the fact that our career can – and should – include both passion and fair pay.

We are not the first to raise this point, of course. Marisa Cortwright's widely circulated article, "Death to the Calling," examines these issues, noting that, "the myth of the calling…encourages architects to surrender their workers' rights."[1] Cortwright's article notes that the idea of a professional calling positions our jobs as central to our identities in a way that feels intrinsic. It puts architecture at the very core of our beings. If we believe we are "*meant* to be an architect," she writes, then we happily "rationalize the experience of enduring the mental, emotional and physical stresses of years of design studios." This is true of architectural students and easily applies to the professional traumas of architects in the field. But Cortwright's argument that suffering is an intrinsic part of a career calling goes beyond just experiences of abuse and neglect. This idea of suffering for your calling means that we are also willing to suffer financially because, from the perspective of the calling, the reward for our work comes in the currency of identity.

This calling is only one of the religious aspects of architectural training that works hand in hand with the deification of both the art form and, more perversely, the major names in the field. We make mythical creatures of "starchitects," all but worshipping them throughout school. By the time we go to work for them, we have thoroughly internalized the idea that they are inherently good, not only as architects, but as people. Those who are "lucky" enough to work for them often end up working 80 hours per week for a 20,000 dollar salary, if they are paid at all. Because these are gods on earth – because we have professed our loyalty to the discipline they represent – we grind on in service of their sacred vision.

Architects should become more comfortable at articulating the meaning of that grind as labor. We love our work – but it is still work. To borrow Adjustments Agency's poetic phrasing, "architecture is a form of labor that masquerades as a labor of love."[2] That masquerade – that dishonesty – isn't inherent to architecture.

But it is inherent to the concept of the "calling," a devotion that requires us to convince ourselves that we owe a degree of misery and a level of suffering before we can count ourselves as true artists. And, as a result, so many of us begin to see discussions of salary as sacrilegious, or vulgar – antithetical to passion or the true devotion to the craft.

So we endeavor to suffer as architecture students. We commit to never asking for salary details, never questioning an unpaid internship with a starchitect. We move into the field and accept an unlivable salary. All because we have committed ourselves to the idea of suffering for our art to such a degree that we forget that our art is actually our job.

And if there is any question of whether this type of religious imagery is used to the benefit of those architects on high – the deified starchitects – for the purpose of exploitation, look no further than Bjarke Ingels' interview with Jessica Mairs of *de zeen*, in which he responds to questions of architecture's inhumane work schedules by noting, "That's the price you pay, but the reward you get is that you do something incredibly meaningful."[3]

We believe exploitation is too high a price to pay for doing meaningful work.

#

The thing about this type of exploitation is that it begins so innocently. Everyone wants to love their profession, and when we begin our time in architecture school, enthusiastic and full of ideas, we know we love the work.

Why Is It Like This?

Every new project is like an obsession. We attack our assignments with passion and care, and we incorporate them into who we are. It's difficult to think of a more incredible experience than watching a project you really believe in take shape. It truly is a labor of love.

But every so often it becomes clear that a labor of love is still labor.

As undergraduate students in their professional practice course, Erin and Jake had been tasked with designing a case for a flash drive. The idea was to create a beautiful and functional vessel that could be manufactured in bulk and given away in a corporate promotion. They had been asked to create a prototype as well as a timeline, a contract, and a budget for completing the work, including a breakdown of the pricing calculations.

The pair was happy with their completed flash drive holder. It was sleek without being flashy and minimal without being overly simple. Practical for mass production without seeming generic. By this point, they were old hat at combining their individual design aesthetics and skills into cohesive project designs, and they felt happy with the flash drive case they produced.

Fortunately, they also had some experience with pricing and contracting. They had worked on other projects before – Sheila Kingbury's tea house, the Cooper-Meier house, a furniture project here and there – so they had learned some of the pitfalls of pricing a project through trial and error. They knew that, even if you were passionate about the craft, even if it were your dream task and you loved every minute of the work, it was still work. You still deserved to be compensated fairly. A custom design didn't cost the same amount as a mass-produced piece, shipped overnight from Amazon to your doorstep – even if that meant that some potential clients might be priced out of your business.

Jake and Erin priced their proposal accordingly, accounting not only for materials, but for their design expertise. The creation of something out of nothing. The process of invention. For a project like a promotional flash drive holder, this cost would be absorbed into the product through a bulk sale – an hourly charge for design would be a one-time fee, so the more pieces the company ordered, the less impact that fee would have on each individual holder.

Most non-architecture companies intuitively understand this process – at the very least, they are aware that the cost-per-object for five objects will be proportionately higher than the cost-per-object for 100. And Jake and Erin trusted that a professional model of custom design should trust that the client valued their design sensibilities – the time spent inventing the perfect promotional item. When they figured in the precision cutting, which demanded time and expertise on a CNC machine, and the actual physical materials in addition to the hourly rate for design – by far the largest line item for a single flash drive prototype – the total charge came to around $400.

The winning project, on the other hand, came in at $85. The first-place project was chosen on the basis of form, aesthetics and function – aspects that the winning team had apparently decided were worth doing pro bono. The professor commended Jake and Erin on their pricing, noting that theirs was the only project that reasonably estimated the value of their labor and time.

And yet, Erin and Jake wondered at the fact that no other students had considered the value of their time. That every other project in the class estimated the cost of the flash drive case as an object. Every other project ignored, disregarded, or flat out forgot that the object could not exist without someone to make it. Someone who had already accrued years of training, the consequent student loans, and experience in design. It could not exist, in fact, without a passionate creator who was willing to spend time and mental energy dreaming and crafting it into existence.

As the pair exited the building into a freezing blast of winter wind, they marveled at the experience. Perhaps the incident had been colored by the fact that they were currently struggling to come up with the money to refill the oil tank that fueled their apartment's heater. The 50-degree indoor temperature put a lot of things into perspective. It was undoubtedly influenced by their interest in learning about financial planning – a degree of obsession with credit scores and APRs that prompted Rachel to jokingly call them "money nerds."

But it was also more than that. The experience had made clear that passion and pay were never actually separate. In fact, they fueled one another. Workers deserved to be fairly compensated for their labor. And they knew that the passion they brought to design made their work valuable. It was certainly worth more than $85 in materials.

#

If you ever heard discussion of money – of really valuing your labor as a student, intern, early career professional, or even as an advanced architect – you were lucky. Although, maybe lucky isn't the best word, since you typically had to force this discussion for it to happen at all. If you were brave, you pressed your professors on the point of average starting salaries. Or maybe you openly questioned the ethics of unpaid internships. Maybe you had a rogue professor who was honest with you about the prospects of payment, or a friend who graduated ahead of you in the program and returned with stories of living paycheck to paycheck. But for the most part, the discussion of money was not an organic point of conversation.

Maybe you remember talking about where you might intern. You sat in the Professional Practice classroom or in studio or at a bar, and you dreamed about where you might apply. The questions were always about aesthetics. Who fits my style? Who do I want to learn from? Whose practices seem to fit with my vision of my future practice? Where is my personality or design sensibility going to fit? The answers to these questions floated into the ether – all dreams with no grounding in practicality. This was a conversation about the great masters, those towering idols of architecture, and whether any of them might find you worthy enough to serve them. It was all about opportunities and passions and how much you were willing to sacrifice for your art.

What it was not about was the very real issue of your survival after school. It was not about the cost of living in Manhattan or San Francisco or Seattle. It was not about the student loans, which loomed over your head, demanding repayment in only a year or two, even as they expanded with each new semester.

It was not about the ways the dichotomy of pay and passion worked to talk you out of a financially stable life after school. In fact, for many of your fellow students, there was a very distinct inverse relationship between the conceptual level of a particular firm and the amount that firm was willing to pay. Those firms whose work was rejected by students as being overly generic or generally more boring than trendy, those were the firms that paid well. Not that you fully realized that when you were a student. After all, you didn't talk about pay.

But there was also a very simple reason that money was never discussed in architecture school. In the Code of Ethics of the American Institute of Architects, members of the massive national organization are explicitly prohibited from discussing their fees with one another.

The architects you spoke with on firm visits couldn't talk about fees. Even in those visits to more practical organizations, the focus was always on the process of the work. The projects at hand were understood from a very conceptual, abstract perspective. Architects who visited Professional Practice, too, were usually muzzled by the AIA rule, even if they had wanted to talk about money. And, frankly, they probably didn't. They came up in the same tradition you did, after all, so they tended to be more interested in talking about their passion and dedication to the craft. Your professors didn't talk about money, either. Many of them were AIA members, no doubt, and likely chose the educational track because they wanted to focus on the conceptual rather than what they thought of as the dry, dull business side of things.

So you all did the best you could with what you had. You were trained to think conceptually, so you conceptualized your future career prospects in terms of your passion for design. You developed your aesthetic and swooned over the famous architects whose work it was to take these beautiful structures from concept to reality. You modeled yourself after them and determined that you would join their world one day. And at some point you found yourself fully immersed in the idea that architecture was your one, true calling. You'd made the profession, and you were willing to make the sacrifice.

#

"Don't buy the Ferrari!" Erin and Tyler said in unison, the moment of revelry giving the call a sense of ease.

"Exactly!" Tyler laughed. He had found Jake and Erin through a friend, a former client of Out of Architecture. Tyler's friend had been considering graduate school when he became a client, expressing a common sentiment to Erin and Jake – he'd seen some things about the profession of architecture through his internships, and he hoped he could bypass the more unsavory components of the field by getting a master's degree. Erin had shared a favorite piece of advice with him: graduate school is like buying a really fancy sports car. If you already know you don't like the air conditioner in the car, you're probably going to hate driving it – so don't spend hundreds of thousands of dollars on it just because you see other people buying fancy sports cars. In other words, if you don't want to work in architecture, don't get an advanced degree in it. This piece of advice had now been passed along from one of Erin's mentors to Erin to numerous clients and finally to Tyler. "It made so much sense to me to hear it that way. I think I had thought maybe I could avoid some of the 'paying your dues' bullshit if I went to grad school."

Jake nodded. He and Erin had often talked about this issue. She saw it all the time in her teaching, and they had started to see an influx of students with similar stories. Students who believed that they could sidestep issues of meager pay and exploitative hours if they had an advanced degree. They were passionate about the craft, the thinking went, so they knew they could make it through a few more years of school at the graduate level. And maybe then, they could do work they loved for a fair price. Jake and Erin had both found graduate school beneficial, but they also realized that a master's degree didn't allow a person to skip past the financial difficulties of a field that didn't value labor. In fact, it only added a Ferrari's worth of student loans to the mix.

"I've thought about leaving the field," Tyler said, his voice suddenly quiet, "but I feel so embarrassed. Like I failed."

This was a common sentiment among clients. They had seen clients who chose to remain in the field because they were afraid of the fallout from their former mentors and coworkers. They had spoken with students who saw their choice to pursue a law degree or real estate license as a shameful secret that they guarded with their life. They had worked with clients who found fulfilling work outside of architecture but who still felt guilty about their choice to leave the profession. People often joked about Catholic guilt. It had nothing on the guilt of leaving architecture.

"You're never a failure for wanting to be happy in your career," Erin said. "Why did you want to be an architect in the first place?"

"Because I love design," Tyler quickly replied, "and I love working with my hands. Building something out of nothing."

Erin and Jake had worked with many clients who shared Tyler's passion for creating. They knew from their own experience that the problem-solving skills required for making things – from models to furniture to 3-D printed artwork – made architecture graduates infinitely employable.

"Those skills are more marketable than you think," Erin said. "You can still follow that passion, just in a different field. Even in a related field, if that's what you want. Furniture design and other interior design is a strong option."

"Yeah," Tyler replied, "but I've heard what some of the professors say: 'Oh, you want to do interiors? You want to be an inferior desecrator?'" Tyler's voice took on an appropriately silly voice at the pun on "interior decorator" – it was an ugly joke that was very common in many architecture programs.

Erin and Jake had heard these disparaging comments too. Designing and building furniture – designing and building plenty of other things besides structures – require many of the same skills at the core of architecture. But for many of the true believers, this type of work simply wasn't seen as the full religious experience of the art form.

Tyler was experiencing the fallout from the cult-like devotion to architecture. He was feeling the consequences of the type of devotion that includes overwork and underpayment, justified by the idea of a "calling."

That makes architects feel trapped in the field, even as their professional experience drains them of the passion they once felt for the craft. Still a student, Tyler was ahead of the curve, recognizing that the path he was expected to take by his mentors and fellow students was untenable for him. Graduate school would only prolong the inevitable. Taking on a poorly paying first job seemed undesirable, and leaving the field threatened to rob him of so many of the relationships that had gotten him through the difficult years of architecture school.

A decision had to be made, but none of the options seemed good. And years of understanding pay and passion as incompatible only made this decision more difficult.

Being an architect can feel like being in a codependent relationship. The profession demands everything from us, so we feed it and feed it, only to find that, for all of the work and passion and time we've invested, it only wants more from us. Like Tyler, so many of us are encouraged to use our passion for creating beautiful things to justify this toxic relationship.

Bjarke Ingels recently argued that, in other professions, a reasonable work week at a reasonable wage is expected, "but in the creative profession where you are designing something or…taking something that doesn't exist and you're making it exist, there those rules don't apply."[4]

We could not disagree more. In fact, we believe reasonable work hours – not to mention fair pay – are crucial to truly accessing your creativity in the long run. In a review of the scholarship on overwork, *Harvard Business Review* noted that working too many hours actually makes us worse at our jobs.[5] Overworked employees experience more accidents, require more healthcare support, and struggle more to effectively communicate on the job. To add insult to injury, some research also suggests that, over the long run, overworked employees produce similar work – in terms of quality and quantity – when compared to employees with a reasonable work schedule.

A few weeks after their initial call with Tyler, Erin and Jake presented him with a portfolio of options. Among them was the role of Product Designer, a career track that allowed him to maintain the communal feeling of studio that was so important to Tyler during his years in school. The track would give him an outlet for his interest in furniture and interior design. And it allowed him to work from a variety of locations, which appealed to Tyler's desire to move to a large coastal city.

Tyler would still have to deal with the stigma of leaving the field, but he felt happy to have some concrete options moving forward, whether it was in product design or one of the other tracks Out of Architecture had presented to him.

"You know," he said. "I've only told a few people that I was talking with you guys. I was afraid of what people might say."

This is the problem with treating one's job – one's profession – as a calling. It leaves us open to all kinds of exploitation and makes the idea of leaving the field unthinkable. It hides the fact that there are plenty of amazing, fulfilling, and exciting jobs available beyond the cloister of architecture.

"But I think I realized that it's not really about what other people say," he continued. "It's about my love of design and my passion for creating – for making things. Product design has that in spades. I'm really excited about design again!"

Jake and Erin were glad to hear that. And they knew that Tyler's choice to expect fair pay and reasonable work hours channeled him into a career field that would once again stoke his passion for design.

NOTES

1   Marisa Cortwright, "Death to the Calling: A Job in Architecture is Still a Job," *Failed Architecture*, August 15, 2019. Retrieved from https://failedarchitecture.com/death-to-the-calling-a-job-in -architecture-is-still-a-job/.
2   Adjustments Agency, "Refusal After Refusal," *Harvard Design Magazine*, no. 45 (2018). Retrieved from www.harvarddesignmagazine.org/issues/46/refusal-after-refusal.
3   Jessica Mairs, "'If I was Misogynist, Would I Hire a Woman as My CEO?' Says Bjarke Ingels," *de zeen*, June 16, 2017. Retrieved from www.dezeen.com/2017/06/16/bjarke-ingels-hits-back-claims-sexism -big-interview/.
4   Ibid.
5   Sarah Green Carmichael, "The Research is Clear: Long Hours Backfire for People and Companies," *Harvard Business Review*, August 19, 2015. Retrieved from https://hbr.org/2015/08/the-research-is -clear-long-hours-backfire-for-people-and-for-companies.

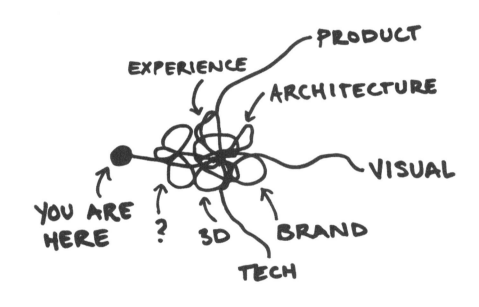

PRODUCT

EXPERIENCE

ARCHITECTURE

VISUAL

YOU ARE
HERE

?

3D

BRAND

TECH

PART THREE

PART THREE
YOUR CAREER IS A DESIGN PROBLEM

Part Three: Your Career Is a Design Problem unfolds as a series of case studies. With each chapter, we explore both an archetypical client type, including a variety of interest areas and personalities, and a particular career stage, from current architecture student to seasoned industry veteran.

These client case studies are based on our years of experience working with clients from all walks of life, although none of the case studies are based on a single individual. Rather, to maintain anonymity and offer the broadest range of professional insights, each case study represents a composite client designed to highlight the variety of challenges our clients face.

The chapters in this final section present solution-based case studies, in which the particular wants, needs, skills, and goals of five composite clients take center stage. Each client's career is, as the title indicates, a design problem – complete with design parameters, site limitations, assets, and an elegant, functional solution.

DOI: 10.4324/9781003300922-13

CHAPTER 10
THE NEWBIE

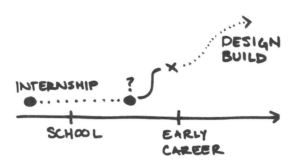

"Any job prospects on the horizon?" It was his grandfather's first question after he'd pulled Brian in for one of his signature hugs, the kind of committed embrace that began by actively knocking the wind from your lungs. Just when you caught your breath, he followed up the squeeze with a series of slaps on the back that felt like they might leave a bruise. The hugs were part of his grandfather's charm. The constant questions about potential jobs? Not so much.

The holiday season had been particularly brutal on that front, not only from Brian's grandfather but from the entire extended family. He was just coming out of an entire semester of experiencing this type of pressure at school. Now that he was home for the break, everywhere he looked, someone wanted to hear about his nonexistent plans. Family seemed to be lurking around corners or behind seasonal decor, ready to jump out at a moment's notice: *Any interviews? Almost done with that thesis? What's in store for next year?* Brian had hoped to just enjoy some cranberry sauce without confronting a parade of well-meaning questions, but it seemed that a little peace was too much to ask for.

"Not quite yet, Grandpa," he replied sheepishly.

"Somebody's gotta be hiring." His grandfather's voice carried a mix of encouragement and consternation. Brian typically loved asking his grandfather for advice, but he suspected his grandpa had shared all he knew by this point.

DOI: 10.4324/9781003300922-14

And it was becoming increasingly clear that his grandfather had finished school in a very different economy. "A bright kid like you? You'll find something," he continued. "Just keep getting those applications in. Did you follow up with your uncle Jerry? His firm might have something."

"I just got busy, Grandpa," Brian said, growing impatient. Then, instantly regretting his sharp tone, "I'll ask, though. That's a good idea." There was something buried inside him that was keeping him from beginning his search in earnest, but he simply didn't want to think about it at that moment.

"Don't wait too long," his grandfather chided. "You know what – "

Brian's aunt Julie burst through the door, and he had never been happier to see her. She trekked in, stomping her boots on the mat and calling out to the pair of toddlers who ran ahead of her into the living room. Her timing couldn't have been better.

Brian turned to Julie and welcomed her inside with a sincere sense of gratitude.

The holidays were supposed to be a time for getting away from the stress of life, but this entire conversation – thesis, career preparation, job prospects – was exactly the type of pressure he'd been living with every day at school. Layered on top of the typical studio and coursework stress was the fact that many of his fellow students were now beginning to find jobs. Just the week before the break had officially begun, one of Brian's frenemies had secured a Designer I job with a highly sought-after firm. You would have thought she had cured cancer, the way everyone fawned over her. He wanted to be a nice person, so he had congratulated her too, but inside, he almost felt sorry for her. He had seen people go through the ringer of a Designer I job and come out mangled on the other side. He had seen how entry-level employees were treated on his internships. If that was the type of life she wanted, good for her. But he couldn't quite wrap his head around the prospect.

Not that he could explain his feelings either. This had become entirely clear when his mentor responded to the announcement by offering to put Brian in touch with a hiring manager at an infamous Manhattan firm. This was the seventh or eighth such offer – honestly, he'd lost count. And this one was the worst of them all. The firm his fellow classmates had interned at in previous years and returned with true horror stories. He had politely declined, wishing he could explain all of the contours of what he was thinking and feeling. His mentor was amazing, but when he looked into her expectant face, all he could say was, "I'm working on a couple of possibilities, but I don't know if I'm ready to talk about them yet." At her confused glance, he followed up with a cheerful, "I'm on it though!"

The truth was, Brian wasn't "on it" at all. He didn't have a single job prospect, mostly because he hadn't really looked. Of course, he knew he *should* look. He'd definitely *thought about* looking. It would have been impossible not to, with the stream of fellow students bragging constantly about their amazing job offers, trying so hard to hide the fact that they were more invested in one-upping each other than in actually finding a job that made them happy. Sometimes he even got as far the search bar in Chrome. In those moments, he usually found himself staring blankly at the screen. A few seconds would pass before he sighed heavily and gave up. Or sometimes he would be struck with the inspiration to Google something other than job openings – the price of some materials he wanted for his thesis, perhaps, or a font family he wanted to download for the project, or maybe that new art installation he'd been meaning to check out. It wasn't a lack of interest in architecture that kept him from the job hunt. In fact, he still deeply loved architecture as an art form. But after his experiences as an intern and the stories his predecessors brought back from the field, he just wasn't particularly enthusiastic about the business of architecture.

How could he find a job that kept him doing only the things he loved in architecture?

Brian had always imagined himself as the type of architect who moved seamlessly between meeting with clients, drafting a new concept, visiting a construction site, and a host of other tasks that would each be completed with the energy and passion he felt about his craft. The sense of exciting, new opportunities on the horizon was a big part of why Brian loved architecture. The appeal of jumping from task to task fit beautifully with his general approach to life. As a student, he loved starting the day by learning about the history of a Roman basilica, before walking over to the university quad to sketch the crisp lines of the central pavilion, then having lunch with friends in the philosophy department, heading into studio to squeeze in a few hours on an ongoing project, and ending the day chatting with his favorite professor. The next day could be totally different – and the next different from that, always full of new possibilities. New things to learn. Interesting people to meet.

Brian loved learning new things. But learning how to get a job was not one of them.

To be fair, his uncle Jerry had warned him. The field of architecture had changed over the years. As a kid, he'd often spent summers at his uncle's firm. His mother was an elementary school teacher, and his father was a shift manager at the local lumberyard, so pricey summer camps or daycare options were typically off the table. And anyway, Brian had a knack for picking up new skills — even as a 12-year-old, he'd been surprisingly useful around the office of his uncle's small firm. These summer experiences had profoundly shaped who he was as a young adult. His passion for the craft had been clear from the very beginning.

Brian was surprised when his uncle had discouraged him from pursuing architecture as a career. As a high school senior, he had gotten into the top program in the country. His impressive portfolio had even earned him a small scholarship.

"It's not about whether you're good enough, Bry," Jerry had told him. "But these jobs aren't what you think. School is expensive, and the pay isn't great. A lot of firms like mine have had to shift gears. It takes a lot of years before you get to do the stuff you love. You really gotta pay your dues in architecture."

Brian had shrugged it off at the time. Most 18-year-olds would have. It's the folly of youth to assume your elders don't know what they're talking about. And as he'd moved through architecture school, he had loved it. Well, the actual architecture part, that is.

The internships, on the other hand, not so much. The practicalities and logistics and business aspects seemed irreconcilably distant from the work he had imagined was at the center of architecture. Brian had done three internships, and he had hated each one more than the last. All the things he loved about architecture seemed completely absent from the clusters of pre-fab, generic desks, and the sad-looking middle-aged people staring bleary-eyed into their computers.

Now, he looked across the table at his father, his uncle, his grandfather. How could he tell them that he had no idea what he was doing? That more and more he suspected that he actually hated the business of architecture, even as he loved the art? He had pushed so hard for this degree, first resisting his uncle's advice, then struggling through the gamut of architecture school, submitting to all of those horrendous internships, and winding up with a mountain of student loans. It was too much to process, and as a result, he found himself repeatedly pushing the thoughts aside. Kicking the can down the road, his grandfather might have said. He knew he would have to face it eventually, but he just couldn't bear to squeeze himself into a Designer I job — with its hours of staring into a computer screen and working on other people's designs — when he knew he would hate it. And at the same time, he had invested so much in the field. He felt like he was free-falling, and instead of enjoying what should have been a nice family dinner, he felt himself consumed by his dread of the future.

#

"Need some advice. Txt me back," Brian typed into the screen. He had managed to survive the holiday dinner and had spent the evening retreating into himself, soul searching, figuring things out. It was what introverts did best, and Brian was nothing if not an introvert.

He'd found a career test online, which basically told him what he already knew. He needed a dynamic job that would allow him to learn and try new things. He valued deep relationships built over time. He liked artistic pursuits and enjoyed opportunities to express himself visually.

None of this was news to Brian. In many ways, he just thought of himself as an average architecture student. He worked hard and was passionate about that work. He was always willing to take risks. He brought a natural curiosity to every situation and that served him well – he had even included other departments as he delivered core samples from trees at his site to the dendrology lab or partnered with a research assistant in the computer science department to develop an innovative visual presentation. But he didn't feel he had mastered any one thing.

Just then, Sarah's face flashed onto the screen and he swiped to accept the FaceTime call.

"Sorry I'm calling instead of texting," she said, "but I'm driving home. My mom wanted me to stay with her, but I'm gonna put in a few hours on this project, and then I need to do a little more studying."

"No, it's fine," Brian sighed. He'd met Sarah during his first internship. She was a few years out of school at that point, but they shared an alma mater and had hit it off right away. "You have to work on Christmas Eve?" he asked, feigning surprise.

"You know me," she replied dryly. "And the worst part is that everybody else is over there working already. I snuck off for dinner with the family."

Brian was troubled by the way Sarah talked about her experiences as an early-career architect, but he wasn't particularly surprised by it. Not anymore. Over the past year or two, Sarah had seemed to age before his eyes. "My eye bags have eye bags," she often joked. He didn't find it particularly funny.

"That sucks," Brian said. Not wanting to immediately bombard her with what was really on his mind, he asked, "What have you been up to today?"

"You know, super exciting stuff. Reviewing paint submittals for that university project in California." She pointedly turned her eyes from the road to the phone to say, sarcastically, "It's thrilling."

"Again?" Brian recalled her doing this exact task before and, frankly, assumed the entire project was at least close to wrapping up. "Haven't you been on this project for like a year?"

"Welcome to architecture," she said. "And actually, I've been on this project for almost a year and a half now. No end in sight."

He'd learned a lot through his friendship with Sarah. She had graduated school with student loan debt in the six-figure range, and now she was taking out new credit cards to pay for licensure study materials. He had once dreamed of achieving licensure himself, finally earning the right to call himself an architect. But after watching her go through the process – both in terms of hours of studying and the thousands of dollars of additional debt she was racking up – he wasn't so sure the title was worth the trouble.

"Sarah," he asked, turning the tone of the conversation instantly earnest. "Why are you doing this to yourself?" He feigned a playful tone, hoping to hide his growing reticence about the profession. "Please reassure your architecture student friend that all the hours and stress are worth it in the end."

Sarah didn't even hesitate, repeating the mantra he had heard so often in the past. "You gotta pay your dues, ya know?" As she drove, the streetlights shone onto her face through the car window, grotesquely emphasizing her physical signs of fatigue.

"Sure, but aren't there other jobs that aren't like this?" Brian knew he was grasping at straws, but it couldn't hurt to ask. "You're so talented. There has to be somewhere that would appreciate you. Why don't you look for a different firm where you could really flex your design skills?"

A bitter guffaw escaped Sarah's lips. "No, I'm sorry. I didn't mean to laugh," she apologized. "But Brian, you know as well as I do. This is just how it is. I've still got quite a few years before I get to run my own project. Sometimes I wonder what life might be like if I went into a different field."

Sarah paused for several seconds, long enough that Brian wondered whether the connection had gone dead. "But then I think that's just the tired talking. There's so much I love about architecture. I just couldn't imagine doing anything else."

Brian knew that feeling well. He had been determined to be an architect for as long as he could remember. At least 13 of his 23 years had been spent working toward that goal. And he had once loved the idea of carrying on his uncle's legacy – of making architecture a sort of family trade. But as every day passed, he grew more and more certain that the life of an architect was not the life he wanted. He loved the art. He loved his friend. He loved his uncle. But he did not want their lives.

"I don't think I want to be an architect," he blurted out.

There it was. He had said it. That phrase that had been hanging behind his eyes, that had danced in the back of his brain, that took up residence in his chest at night, tightening around his lungs until he could barely breathe. He hadn't wanted to admit it, even to himself, but now that he had said it, it was out there. It was like a break-up conversation – once you said the words aloud, there was no going back.

Sarah was quiet, and Brian immediately regretted saying the words out loud. He didn't want to offend his friend, and he knew that so many people were expecting him to follow through on his plans to become an architect, but all of the pressure of the recent months had told him one thing: he simply could not go the traditional route with a traditional firm.

"You still there?" he asked tentatively.

"I'm still here," she said. "I just – you kinda caught me off guard," she laughed.

He chuckled a little too, the sound of her acceptance deflating the lump in his chest just a little.

"Have you told anybody in studio?"

This, truly, was the problem that had held him back, kept him from exploring options, or even contemplating the idea of exploring options. It was what prevented him from taking on the job search with his usual zeal for new experiences.

She rambled on, "because I don't think you should. Tell them, I mean. Not until you're done with your thesis and everything."

"Yeah," Brian sighed. "I was thinking the same thing."

"But hey, I gotta go. I'm walking up to the office. Will you be okay?"

"Yeah," he told her. "I'll be okay."

She ended the call and Brian lowered the phone, staring at the wall. After a few minutes, he lifted the phone again, tapped to open Google, and typed a simple query: *How do you get out of architecture?* He didn't really expect to be told how to get out of architecture. The question seemed too big even for Google.

The results were a comfort of sorts. Others had written about why they chose to leave the field. He slid his thumb up the screen, then stopped. One of the search results was a site literally titled "Out of Architecture," nearly the exact search parameter he'd entered. He tapped the screen to reveal a rectangular button that read, "Book your free consultation."

He did just that, feeling the tension slip from his chest. He knew there was no going back, now that he had said the words aloud. He had to get out of this career path, and he needed to do it now, before he got so entrenched in architecture that he could never leave. He loved Sarah dearly, but he had to get out before it did to him what it had done to her…before it drained him of his energy, enthusiasm, and passion for the craft.

#

"What's your ideal day?" Erin asked.

Brian was 15 minutes into his consultation with Out of Architecture, and he was already feeling better. He'd vented to Jake and Erin about his concerns about overwork, the state of the economy, and even his more intangible fears. The first time he'd said aloud that he wanted out of the field, that night on the phone to Sarah, it had been difficult to get the words out. Now, the more he said it, the more it felt right.

"I think the main thing for me," Brian replied, "is I don't want to be behind a desk. I like to be able to talk to new people and collaborate on an idea, then come back to my desk and figure out a solution for something I'm working on, then maybe go outside and take a walk and look for inspiration or think about new projects."

"Like you do in school, right?" Jake added. "That is absolutely relatable. And you're right that a lot of architecture jobs won't offer you that. Do you think, for you, is it about being able to learn and explore new things?"

"Yes!" Brian exclaimed. "That is exactly it! I know that's what school is for, though. Not as much part of a job."

"I think you'd be surprised," Erin chimed in.

"Architecture students tend to be really strong learners. Excellent at identifying problems and then figuring out ways to solve them," Jake noted. "Even though you might not see that in yourself yet, it's a real asset for architecture students just out of school. You're not overspecialized, but you're a strong generalist with the ability to learn quickly."

Jake was describing his concept of the "tree-shaped employee," a model that fit Brian perfectly. Jake proposed the idea of the tree-shaped employee in 2015 in response to the trending concept of the T-shaped employee. The T-shaped employee was characterized by the ability to bring a well-rounded approach to a company while also offering exceptional command of a particular specialty area. The vertical line of the T represented the employee's primary specialty area. The horizontal line contained a number of adjacent tasks that the employee was qualified to support but not lead. This type of employee was usually hired in response to a problem or gap that had emerged within the company previously, with that gap filled by the vertical line of the T-shaped employee's specialty. The T-shaped employee was, essentially, a reactive hire.

Jake argued, though, that

companies should focus on tree-shaped employees, defined as applicants with a variety of experiences that produce a truly well-rounded candidate.

This person's core experience – represented by the trunk of the tree – is supplemented by a strong background in more than one field. Those fields serve as the employee's roots, and they help the worker to stay grounded. Tree-shaped employees also bring a variety of skills from previous experiences, and they are characterized by their ability to translate those disparate experiences and skills into value for their company.[1]

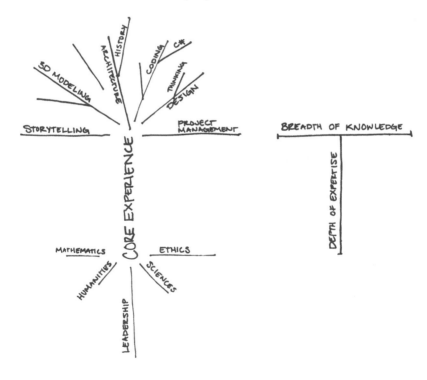

This was exactly what Brian brought to the table: skills in design, team and project management, problem-solving, creative thinking, and a genuine enthusiasm and aptitude for learning new things. Brian was a maker to his core, and even though he couldn't see himself as an ideal employee at first – he was truly an insecure overachiever – that type of tactile intelligence was easily marketable to a variety of fields.

"It feels so good to talk to someone about this," Brian told Erin and Jake. After so much criticism, not to mention his own self-criticisms, Brian was relieved to truly open up to someone. "But I don't know how to – I don't know what to do from here. Do I send you my resumé to critique, or…?"

"Typically, where we can be most useful," Jake said, "is in terms of helping you think about potential career paths. We call them tracks. Erin, do you wanna – "

"Sure," Erin said, picking up where Jake left off. She presented a variety of options – from industrial design to furniture design to design-make companies. "We want to make sure you leave this call with an action item. Since you're really still exploring at this point – you've got a few months before graduation – we can send you a handful of potential jobs. Why don't you take a couple of weeks and brainstorm what you like about each of them? We can do a Zoom follow-up at the end of January, if that seems like enough time?"

It did, and within a couple of days, Out of Architecture had sent over a document with a variety of jobs. They listed animation, small fabrication shops, firms with big model shops, and materials research. Brian felt overwhelmed in that way that often accompanies too many very good choices. He felt at once relieved to have concrete suggestions, insecure about his ability to actually do these jobs, and betrayed by the fact that these options had been hidden from him throughout his time in school.

Still, he was a good student, and he had been given a task. He was determined to complete it to the best of his ability. He reformatted the document to include two columns for each job suggestion – a pro side, and a con side – and began searching the web for details on the positions. Then, because Brian was nothing if not an overachiever, he created a box underneath with a list of advertised jobs and their requirements.

Required: five years of experience in fabrication.
Suggested candidates will have prior experience as professional model-builders.
Applicants should attach portfolio including professional experience with materials research.

With each new line he typed, Brian's heart sank a little lower.

Brian's experience was common among current architecture students looking to transition out of the field. It felt so daunting to think about leaving the field, and just when you felt you had a grasp on what it might mean to work out of architecture, you were struck with the realization that this new direction meant venturing out into spaces where you had no experience, all at a moment when the stakes couldn't have been any higher.

The ambivalence Brian felt about the job search was entirely unfamiliar to him. Learning new things had always been exciting to him. He was very good at identifying problems and finding solutions. And yet, when it came to this new task – of searching for a job outside of architecture – he felt his lack of training acutely.

The document had ballooned to several times its original length, and Brian felt more and more like it was a total mess. *I got a little lost and off track*, Brian wrote to Jake and Erin. *But here's what I came up with.*

Within a few hours, he had a reply back: *You did great! This gives us a lot to talk about. We look forward to talking about this during our call next week.*

Maybe he didn't need formal training in finding a job. Maybe he just needed the support of like-minded coaches.

#

"Remember what we talked about last time, though," Jake reminded Brian. "If you think of yourself as a tree-shaped employee, it's not a detriment that you don't have a single, well-defined specialty. That can actually be an asset," Jake explained.

"And from there, we can think about the types of jobs that will value you for your sense of curiosity and your passion for problem-solving," Erin added. "Looking at what you wrote, it looks like you are clearly wanting to get your hands dirty – to follow projects from start to finish rather than just sitting at a computer staring at Revit all day."

"I hate Revit," Brian said.

Jake chuckled and nodded emphatically, "Me too. It's the worst."

"The worst!" Brian exclaimed.

"So have you thought about jobs in smaller-scale or custom design? Things like custom furniture, or even tiny homes?" Erin asked.

Brian nodded. Of the potential tracks listed on the document Jake and Erin had put together for him, that was probably the most exciting. He loved building models, but even more, he just loved building *things*. The satisfaction of seeing something go from concept to an actual, useful object was incredibly exciting to him. "Yeah, I saw that option on there. Do you know – in that kind of job, what kinds of things do you do?"

"You'd be doing a variety of things, and honestly, most of them are probably things you've done before in school," Erin said. "Things like meeting with clients, reviewing mockups, leading small teams. That kind of thing."

"That all sounds great, but – " Brian trailed off, feeling his self-doubt edging into the conversation. "I'm just not sure how to even go about applying for these jobs, or how to get them."

"That's definitely something we can help with," Jake replied.

The next couple of months were packed, but Brian was used to that. On top of his typical schoolwork, he was completing his thesis and, now, searching for jobs far outside the box of what he had initially expected. Erin and Jake showed Brian how to conduct targeted searches, and they coached him in how to market his skills in this new world beyond the typical architecture firms his fellow students were talking about. He took an inventory of all of his skills – not just those that fit traditional firms but additional experiences he'd had by virtue of his curiosity – and found himself seeing his own value more and more. When he added up his interactions with the biology lab, sectioning and analyzing the chemistry of various natural materials; his brief forays into the service industry, serving customers and mentally inventorying their needs; and his other experiments in writing for popular audiences, exploring the competing philosophies of ethics, and dabbling in coding, Brian began to see himself the way hiring managers might see him: as a great investment for their companies. He even started calling himself an "expert generalist."

He still felt nervous about the transition, but the more he committed to exploring roles beyond the traditional expectations of the field, the more confident he felt that he'd made the right choice. And once he started sending out applications and taking interviews, that confidence made all the difference in the world.

Brian, like so many architecture students, needed support not simply in finding a job but in discovering his true value. As an insecure overachiever, he had spent years developing the skills he needed to position himself in the workforce but less time learning to identify and articulate those talents. While Brian was good at many things, he didn't have any one particular specialty – and Out of Architecture helped him to see that as a marketable trait.

Fortunately, Brian was able to overcome his initial insecurity and fear about the market, and after a couple of months of searching and a few interviews, he finally found a company that clicked with his unique set of skills and that felt like a good fit for his personality, values, and career ideals. Brian was set to begin his new job right after graduation.

He wrote to Jake and Erin to thank them, sharing the news that he had landed a role with a small design-build company with specialties in tiny homes, ADUs, and custom furniture. *I'm really excited about this job,* he told them. *It seems like it's going to be all the things I love about architecture. More like what I remember my uncle doing when I was interning at his firm. A variety of tasks, and the ability to see a bunch of projects through from start to finish. I can't thank you enough!*

Erin and Jake appreciated the update, and they weren't the only ones. That evening, Brian called his parents, his uncle Jerry, his friend Sarah, and finally, his grandparents.

"I've got some pretty big news," Brian told them.

"Oh?" his grandmother asked expectantly.

"I got a job offer today!"

His grandparents' enthusiasm was clear, and even though Brian had already shared the details of the job with several other important people in his life, he enjoyed sharing the news just as much the fifth time as he had the first.

"That's great, Brian," his grandmother said. "We always knew you'd make a great architect."

"Well, the job isn't exactly in archi – " he started, realizing then that the training he'd gotten in architecture school had actually led him precisely to this moment. Sure, this job wasn't with a big-name firm, and it wasn't the type of job his mentors might envision for him. But the job involved everything he loved about architecture, and he realized then that there was no need to apologize for his chosen path. He felt happy, and that was what mattered. "Thanks, Grandma," Brian said.

"Really proud of you, Brian," his grandfather said.

So much had changed in the past few months. He'd gone from an insecure overachiever, consistently undervaluing his own skills and worth, to a slightly more self-assured employee, aware of the assets he brought to his new company.

More than that, he'd gone from looking for a job to finding a career. He'd come a long way, and it meant a lot to him to hear the pride in his grandfather's voice. And somehow it meant just as much to Brian that he finally felt proud of himself, too.

NOTE

1   Jake Rudin, "Why Tree-Shaped Employees are Worth 10 T-Shaped Employees," *LinkedIn,* October 16, 2015. Retrieved from www.linkedin.com/pulse/why-tree-shaped-employees-worth-10-t-shaped-jake -rudin/.

CHAPTER 11
THE TECHIE

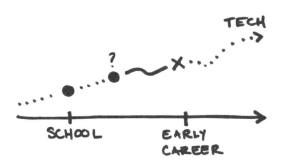

The click-clack of keyboards, rhythmic and steady like a gentle rain, was the default background noise in Najee and Milo's apartment. Not that they would know, necessarily. Both of them spent most of their free time hunkered down in computer chairs with oversized headsets covering their ears, the glow of the screen dancing on their glasses.

"Hey, do you – " Najee sighed, and rolled his chair around the massive desk, sliding his headset down to his neck to rest on his shoulders. "Hey, Milo?" He waved his hand at his roommate as he wheeled his chair around the corner, pulling his body into Milo's line of sight.

"Hold on," Milo replied, under his breath. His fingers moved feverishly over the keyboard then stopped abruptly. His brow unfurled, and he scanned the screen one more time, his eyes zigzagging across the monitor for a few seconds. Finally, he turned his attention to his roommate. "What's up?"

"I'm working on the responsiveness for this redesign. The smallest mobile size keeps cutting off the right edge of the title."

Milo stood from his chair and stretched, letting out a grunt. "I was gonna take a break anyway. Let me come look."

Najee needed a break, too. His back had started to ache from the hours spent hunched over the screen – even ergonomically designed chairs weren't

DOI: 10.4324/9781003300922-15

built for marathon coding sessions – and he could feel his senses dulling. But he had never been one to quit. And now that graduation had come and gone and he was starting to apply for jobs in earnest, he needed his website clean and polished. After all, the tech aspect of architecture was his superpower.

But there was more to it than that. The truth was that he was dreading applying for conventional architecture jobs. He'd never seen himself as a traditional architect in the first place, and now that the time had come to position himself within a firm, he was beginning to see more and more that the jobs in the field were exactly as exciting as a bowl of oatmeal. The idea of trading in his passion for coding for eight yawn-inducing hours of technical detailing – every single day – was something like his personal hell.

"Yeah," Milo said, dryly, conjuring Najee back to the space of their living room-turned-coding lab. "Were you trying to do something with the page's CSS?" He didn't wait for a response. "Never mind, something is off with your style setup for the title. I would go through and comment out pieces of your code until you figure out what's making it do that."

Najee sighed. "Seriously?"

"Sorry, dude."

The answer was frustrating, but Najee was grateful for his roommate. While most of his architecture school cohort was focused on building relationships with one another – architects had a habit of only hanging out with other architects – Najee had jumped at any opportunity to connect with Computer Science students – techies like himself and, of course, Milo. It had been a blessing and a curse. While Najee loved having Milo on hand as a reference for his experiments in web design, he hated admitting when he needed help. He much preferred being the person who helped others, which was often the case among his less technically minded architecture friends.

"Don't take this the wrong way," Milo said, cracking the tab on a can of Coke. "But aren't you supposed to be working on job apps?"

Najee couldn't take it the wrong way because he knew it was true. "I just wanted to finish this up so it looks good. It's part of the application." He didn't sound very convincing, even to himself. The truth was that working on his website was as much about procrastination as it was about his job search. "But yeah," Najee said. "I better work on applications, too. At some point."

"You better work on it pretty soon, dude," Milo quipped. "Rent's not gonna pay itself."

"Hilarious." Najee took a deep breath and flicked his screen over to the cover letter he had been working on. It was a computational job, but he'd been warned that it probably wouldn't be as exciting as it might have sounded. "Computational" conjured visions of complex 3D modeling and cutting-edge design technologies. But a surprising number of firms just needed a technically minded employee to run their BIM tools. Even though he had never actually worked with the software, he still felt somehow overqualified. Why did firms call those positions "computational" roles when they were barely more computational than "other architecture roles"?

Najee quickly read over the cover letter, correcting a typo in the second sentence, then uploaded the document and pressed "submit." He felt like he should have been nervous, but somehow he wasn't. Instead, what he really wanted to do was get back to his website. It wasn't that he particularly *liked* sorting through a whole mess of code trying to figure out where he'd messed up, but there was something about it that he found incredibly addictive.

This wasn't a new experience for Najee. Throughout architecture school, he'd taken every opportunity to push the boundaries. Most architects prided themselves on their ability to work with their hands, to create renderings that nodded back to the tradition of hand drawing. One man, one hand. It was eye roll-inducing. It wasn't that Najee hated it so much – he just found it incredibly boring. He wanted to be an innovator, someone who imagined what architecture could be, someone who wasn't afraid to take what worked about the systems approach to architecture and re-energize it, remaking dated technologies into something that could change the field.

And he hadn't been shy about that in school. On every project team, he'd been the one to bring the new, experimental technology component. Sometimes professors didn't like it. They'd say it was "half baked," or that he was innovating where no innovation was needed. He didn't care. Honestly, he secretly loved getting that kind of feedback. He'd carved out space for himself as a rebel – an avant-garde designer – and there was nowhere he'd rather be.

Chipping away at his website these last couple of months, he had realized that this – digital design – was actually what he loved about architecture. Sure, building websites didn't fit the traditional view of a career after architecture school. But from Najee's perspective, design technology incorporated all the things he loved about the field. It included problem solving. It used digital space to push the boundaries of possibility. It allowed him to build something from nothing, not with paper and wood, but with numbers and commands and the clean, sharp lines of purposefully arranged pixels. It was architecture, modernized. It was what he loved. And it had an uncanny ability to totally suck him in.

And so, a week or so later when his phone buzzed, notifying him that he'd landed an interview – specifically the firm wanted him to "be prepared to talk about BIM experience" – he grimaced for a moment, then deleted the email and went back to coding.

#

"Dude, you just deleted it?" Milo exclaimed. He shook his head, chuckling in disbelief. "Bold move for somebody without another job lined up."

This was not the response Najee had anticipated. Usually Milo was just as enthusiastic about rebelling against the system as he was. And this hadn't even been a rebellion. He'd just gotten caught up in a new coding project and decided the interview wasn't worth his time.

"It's a BIM role," Najee said dryly. "Do you even know what Revit is?"

"I do not."

Actually, Najee wasn't entirely sure either, not that he would ever admit it. He had heard about the program, and he knew that other techies despised it – it was about as dry an application as Microsoft Excel and a thousand times as complicated – but he'd never actually used Revit. It wasn't something you could really practice apart from actually working as part of an architectural project team.

Feeling a little startled by Milo's reaction to his revelation, Najee rose from the couch and headed toward the kitchen. All of a sudden, he wanted nothing more than to put some distance between himself and this conversation. "Well, it's basically a program designed to suck the creativity and life force out of you," Najee elucidated, excusing himself.

"Like, that's its literal purpose," Milo smirked. "To be anti-creative? You sure it's not just you? User error?"

"Shut up," Najee said, as good-naturedly as he could muster. "I swear to you, if the place where dreams go to die was a computer program, it would be Revit." He ducked into the kitchen and grabbed a glass from the cabinet. But now, away from the conversation – the conversation he'd thought would validate his choice but had actually made him feel something like shame in the pit of his stomach – he leaned against the counter, wondering whether he had made the right choice.

He knew his own value. He was talented – he'd designed a handful of websites for friends and family, and people always raved about his sleek, functional layouts. And he knew how rare it was for architects to be truly talented in the tech arena. In school, he'd been a highly sought-after team member because he could always be counted on to bring a futuristic spin to projects.

He dreamed of reinventing the way architects used tech, and he felt sure he could do it, too, if he were given the space, money, and opportunity. People like him were wasted sitting in front of a computer, drafting up someone else's ideas all day in a documentation tool. He wanted to design the system, not just use it. He would have loved a "computational specialist position" if it really involved specializing in computation – in reinventing, reimagining, and redesigning computation in architecture. But what was the point of any of this – of his experimentation, of his risk-taking and intermittent scolding, of his hours and hours spent learning new digital tools while others just used the same old techniques over and over – if all it got him was the most boring job in the field?

Was this job – or any job, for that matter – worth sacrificing his passion?

However, he had to find work. As much as he loved sitting around tinkering with his website, it wasn't actual employment. And while he knew he was about as capable as some of the Computer Science graduates he hung out with, he doubted that a degree in Architecture would get him through the door at the types of places Milo had once applied. In fact, when he'd asked Milo for a referral to his company, he'd gotten a non-committal response, and their other friends hadn't even been that helpful. It didn't take much persuading for him to drop the conversation entirely. He hated it when they compared his skills with theirs. They simply weren't the same. Sure, Milo was a better coder than he was – the guy had a whole degree in Computer Science – but Najee also knew that his own eye for any kind of interface design was head and shoulders above Milo's. He had a better eye than anybody he knew. He just had to find a place that valued his skill.

That place wasn't going to be somewhere that was looking for a Revit administrator. In fact, the very thought of that job made him involuntarily roll his eyes. There was no way he could have gone through with that interview, let alone gone to work there.

He filled his glass, then replaced the carton of orange juice in the fridge, more confident than ever that deleting the email had been the best choice.

Now he just needed to find the job he actually wanted. He plopped down in his well-loved computer chair determined to search, in earnest, for non-architecture jobs.

But where to begin? In the search bar, he entered "design tech." Two results appeared, one with a software company that specialized in BIM. Clearly, the universe was playing a cruel joke on him. He cleared out the search bar, this time entering, "digital design." Thousands of jobs appeared. The first one was an internship. Not super appealing. He'd pass on this one.

He kept searching. Halfway down the page, "Digital Designer" caught his eye. He clicked on the ad. They wanted eight years of experience. This was always the thing. You needed experience to get the job, but you needed a job to get experience. Next job.

A similar ad caught his eye. This one required less experience but had a similar salary. The experience requirement was significantly less, and he felt pretty sure he could fudge his internships to come pretty close to what they were asking for. They wanted a UX portfolio. He didn't have that, but he could probably tailor his design portfolio to fit. It would at least be a place to start.

Then he read the third requirement – "High proficiency in Adobe Creative Suite (specifically Adobe XD, Photoshop, Illustrator, and InDesign)" – and immediately clicked the back button on his browser.

"Nope," he said aloud to himself.

He had a strong grasp of Photoshop, Illustrator, and InDesign from school, but he'd never touched XD. Milo talked about it all the time, but nobody in architecture had ever brought it up, and he hadn't even seen it. There was no way he could get that job if he hadn't even seen the software, right? But as he kept scrolling and reading, searching and scrolling, his optimism began to wane.

Frustrated, he pushed his chair back and grabbed his phone. He checked his Twitter notifications – nothing particularly interesting. As he scrolled, a post caught his eye. His friend Trina had graduated a couple of years ahead of him. She'd been the person in her year who everyone went to for questions on Grasshopper and coding. When she landed at Google nobody was surprised. It just seemed like the right fit for the "techie" person in the year. He didn't know much about the types of roles people had at Google, so he wasn't sure what she was doing exactly. But whatever it was, it definitely seemed better than the prospects he was seeing in architecture.

Unfortunately, he had no idea how to go about finding a job like that. He wasn't typically the kind of person who asked for help, at least not formally. Still, it was that or keep searching on his own, a pursuit that was feeling less and less productive – and that was taking more and more time away from what he actually wanted to be doing.

Deciding it didn't hurt to ask, he opened a DM to Trina. *Hey, back when you were applying to jobs, didn't you mention a consultant giving you some useful advice early on?* he typed. *Am I remembering that right?*

Within a few minutes, he saw the three dots at the bottom of the screen signaling that Trina was replying. She was quick. That was good. He wasn't sure how much longer his nerve would hold out.

Yes, she replied. *Out of Architecture. You should look them up!*

"Alright," Najee sighed. "Here we go."

#

A week later, Najee found himself on a call with Jake and Erin, rhapsodizing about his dreams of reforming architectural technology. Or maybe it was his vision of reimagining technological architecture. It had been a long time since someone was willing to hear him out – to listen to his dreams and plans and big ideas – and he found himself getting a little carried away.

"The thing is, it doesn't make any sense to me why architects aren't embracing the chance to explore more emerging technologies," he rambled. "I get that there's a lot of tools, but if you can make an impact on how a client perceives the design, then shouldn't it be worth investing in people who want to push the boundaries?"

"Sure," Jake replied.

"I mean – I was listening to a podcast the other day, and they were talking about how firms use VR and saying that it isn't a realistic addition to most projects. And I was like, okay, but so much of the heavy lifting is already done just by having the 3D model ready to go. Why wouldn't you take advantage of having someone on the team who can bring the Revit model into Unity or something similar?" He paused, realizing he'd gotten a bit off track. "You know?"

Within the first five minutes of the call, Najee knew he'd been wrong to dread this process. In fact, he was feeling more emboldened than ever. Erin and Jake had set up the first call, as they always did, just to get to know him. They asked him about his dreams for the future, about where he saw his career going, about all he wanted to accomplish. He'd never doubted his passion for technology – he truly believed it could save humans from their own hubris.

"So I guess the thing is," Najee continued, "I keep thinking maybe I should have gotten a degree in Computer Science, you know? Because some of my friends, they have a lot of the skills I have, but it just seems like – I don't know. Do I need to just suck it up and go back and get a master's?"

"We hear this a lot," Jake replied, "but let's slow down, because I don't know if we've really explored all of the options for you yet, especially since you've got tech internships under your belt, so you aren't starting totally from scratch. You've talked about a few different aspects of tech – you mentioned web design and maybe working on UX for mobile apps – what is it that makes you value projects like those?"

Najee paused. He'd never thought of it that way – that rather than thinking about how valuable he could be to a particular company, he might start by thinking about what types of companies *he* valued.

"I guess…" he trailed off. Then, after a pause, "I'm not sure."

"I think that could be something you think about, and maybe take some notes about between now and the next time we talk," Erin chimed in. "Another way of thinking about this could also be – how do you want to spend your day? What kinds of things do you want to be doing?"

That one was easier. Najee knew that the place he excelled above most of his architecture school cohort was in coding. "I'm passionate about web design," he answered confidently. "And I would really like to work more with coding."

"Okay, that's great!" Jake replied. "What language do you feel most comfortable with?"

"I used C# for my Grasshopper projects, but lately I've been teaching myself JavaScript for these websites," Najee answered quickly.

"Got it! Tell me more. Are you typically starting these projects from scratch or modifying an existing code base?"

He wasn't expecting this question. "Oh," he said. "I guess…Yeah, I would typically start with a GitHub repository, or I might find bits and pieces of what I need on Stack Overflow. But then I have done a lot of mods and customization for different projects in school."

"That's a great place to start," Erin interjected. "Have you studied any software best practices like DevOps or Agile?"

He hadn't.

"That's fine, though," Jake added. "But we do want to get a sense of what you know and don't know. When you work in JavaScript can you craft a basic FOR loop? Things like that?"

Najee's heart sank, and he could feel himself getting defensive. "I guess I do need to go back to school, maybe."

"Not necessarily," Erin said. "That's not at all what we're saying. The key is that you want to make sure you really have a sense of what you know before you start thinking about which jobs are a good fit."

"And listen – we don't know how to do most of that either," Jake chuckled. "We just know that those are the kinds of things that come up with hiring managers."

"Oh," Najee said. It was a lot to process, but he felt reassured by their confidence in him.

"Honestly, it's fine, though. One thing I would suggest would be to do a bootcamp."

"That's what I was thinking too," Erin added. "I would definitely do one of the less expensive ones, but one that will still test your skills. I think that would be a great way to move forward."

Najee paused. "I guess I always thought of those for beginner level, though. I think I've got the basics, so that's why I was thinking maybe a master's would be a better route."

This was a common response in Erin and Jake's experience, so they were prepared. "Look," Jake said. "Let's say you get there and you already know how to do everything. What have you lost? You've got a certification, a chance to practice things and maybe even hone some of those skills even more, and you'll have a better sense of where you fit in the scheme of aspiring coders. And if you get there and you *don't* know everything, then you'll have a chance to learn it."

Najee hadn't thought of it that way. He was a quick learner, and he was used to being able to fight his way through, picking up the skills he needed along the way. It was the concept of the "army of one" that was so prevalent among architecture students and practicing architects alike – the idea of bringing a variety of skills to the table, the most crucial being the ability to figure things out.

"I guess I just thought…" Najee started. "I mean, I can figure stuff out on the job. If I can get my foot in the door, I think I could go from there."

"I see what you're saying – 'fake it 'til you make it,' right?" Erin asked.

"Yes, exactly!"

"So, there is definitely a time and place for that. But it's not going to fly in the tech industry, you can only bullshit your way so far" Erin said. "It's crucial that you are honest about what you know. You don't want to wind up in a job where you don't know what you're doing. And there's a whole other language in the tech world – just like there is with architecture – so you want to make sure you can 'talk the talk.'"

Najee nodded. That made sense. He remembered feeling uncomfortable with some of the architecture language when he started in the program, so it made sense that he would have to develop insider terminology specific to the tech industry.

"You can do this," Jake added. "Look at it as a chance to try out what it's like to work in tech – just a little taste. We've done this with a lot of clients."

"You don't know what you don't know." Erin put a button on the conversation.

Najee had to admit that he was curious. He had shrugged off the idea of a bootcamp, he realized, in part because he didn't want to admit he needed one. And, honestly, he probably wouldn't have needed one if he'd chosen to stay in architecture. Now it became clear that this was a first step – something tangible that he could do – to move forward with the career he wanted.

That evening he signed up for a coding bootcamp. After hitting the submit button, he had a brief moment of doubt. The same feeling he had walking into studio for the first time thinking, *Do I really know what I'm doing here?*

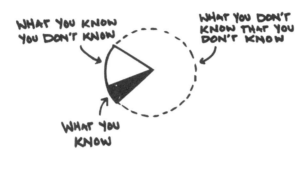

#

It would be difficult to overstate how much Najee loved bootcamp. Here was an opportunity to fully immerse himself into the work he loved most, and, while some of the other students in the bootcamp seemed a bit overwhelmed by the pace, his experience in architecture school meant that he was perfectly prepared for the volume and speed of the work expectations. He learned much more than he had anticipated and felt his confidence grow in a way he had never experienced before. He had been so certain of his design abilities that he hadn't even realized what it could feel like to gain a sense of confidence in the technical elements as well. He hadn't needed to ask Milo for help with anything for weeks, and he felt like he could even go toe-to-toe with his roommate – at least in some areas.

Before he'd even finished the program, he had reached out to Jake and Erin to let them know how much he loved it – and to schedule an appointment with them once he'd completed the bootcamp.

As they continued to explore options on the next call, Najee realized that there was a lot he didn't know about the tech industry. "Maybe I should go to industry bootcamp," he joked. But in reality, working with Erin and Jake had become a sort of industry bootcamp. He'd had no idea about the structure of the tech industry – even though he had quite a few friends who worked in tech – and he kicked himself for not realizing that he could search for entry-level positions rather than wading through thousands of job posts that he wouldn't be qualified for anyway.

"One thing that can help put things in perspective," Jake mentioned, "is that sometimes hiring managers are looking for something very particular from a new hire. I get that it's easy to get caught up in trying to figure out the reasons you didn't get this or that job, but the truth is that you're always going to be missing a lot of context. You don't know if they're replacing someone who had been there for thirty years and they just need that person to do the one thing you don't know how to do. So just keep that in mind for your own mental health."

"But that's the thing," Najee said. "I think I'm a person who can learn a new skill really quickly. So maybe I *am* the right person for that job."

Najee certainly wasn't wrong. Architects bring a lot to the table in any career, and the ability to self-teach can be a major selling point. And yet, as Jake continued, "it's not about faking it upfront. You need to be very honest and very explicit about your skills and your depth and your lack of certain things. And if you do that, regardless of whether or not you get hired, it will be the right decision."

"You don't want to find yourself in a job you can't do," Erin added.

Jake and Erin knew that this was good advice, but not easy to digest. The culture of architecture can encourage a sense that admitting weakness is career suicide. The idea that we need to "figure it out," is pervasive from the first year of architecture school throughout the stages of a career in the field. And this is an important and highly transferrable skill that architects bring with them when they leave the field.

But it often goes hand in hand with assumptions about the structure of industry that ignore the fact that teamwork is highly valued in non-architecture careers. You are not expected to know everything and, in fact, it is much more valuable to specialize in a particular area and then work with others to develop strong team-based projects.

Bootcamp had given Najee a taste of this. Over the next several months, Erin and Jake would connect him with key people in the industry – people who might serve as mentors for Najee, or who were looking to fill a position that would benefit from his experience in architecture school. Each time, Najee reminded himself to be humble, to practice being honest about what he knew and what he still needed to learn. He was a confident person by nature, maybe even cocky, but he knew he needed to express an openness not only to learning but to working with others who knew more than he did in particular areas.

"You don't know what you don't know," Erin had said, and that advice had stuck with him.

Once all was said and done, Najee had applied for quite a few jobs with a variety of tech companies. He'd chosen to stick with established companies, worrying that a start-up might not offer enough stability, and in the end, he finally got a call from a team leader at Microsoft.

Najee texted Milo right away, maybe a little out of competitiveness but mostly because he wanted to share the news with his friend. Milo had come home that afternoon with a six-pack of Najee's favorite craft beer, and they had toasted to the future.

"That's awesome, man," Milo had said.

"Yeah," Najee laughed, "I guess it was a good thing I deleted that interview email."

That decision, randomly made in a moment of procrastination, had set Najee careening down a path toward the place he was now – a place he couldn't have even imagined those months back when he first set out to apply for architecture jobs.

It was strange, but when he used to fantasize about revolutionizing architecture, it always felt like the biggest, boldest move anyone could make. Now, he thought, he was more invested in new projects – in bringing his architecture sensibilities to the tech industry. Somebody else could focus on bringing more tech to architecture.

You don't know what you don't know. And now he knew how much could be gained by being honest with yourself – what he'd learned from the whole experience was that humbling yourself, asking for help, and learning new things were truly valuable.

CHAPTER 12
THE FASHIONISTX

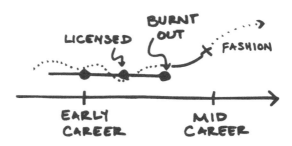

Sydney stared at the bedroom ceiling. The line where the wall paint met the ceiling paint made a slight dip just above the foot of the bed, and their eyes mindlessly traced the contorted border – just one more thing they couldn't control.

For six years, Sydney had told themself that everything would change once licensure was done. *Just hold on a little longer.* Then, *two more exams.* Then, *the hours are starting to add up. Just another month or two.* They had steadied themselves with an internal voice that vacillated between a lullaby and a battle cry. When Sydney believed they couldn't go on any further – a point of desperation that happened with relative frequency as the stress of working toward licensure increased alongside their growing responsibilities at the firm – that voice was always there, first cheering them on and later dragging them over the finish line.

It was a strange feeling to have reached the goal – to have seen that last item on the licensure dashboard screen flip to "complete," to have passed the last of the exams, logged the 3,080 hours – and to realize that maybe they had grown more invested in the challenge of the licensure process than they were in actually becoming an architect. The process itself had become their identity. Working toward licensure had been their reason for getting up every morning, and with that process behind them, life had started to feel alarmingly unstable.

DOI: 10.4324/9781003300922-16

They turned their head and reached for their phone. 3:39 am. Replacing the phone on the nightstand, face down to mask the taunting glare of the screen, they buried their face in the pillow. Sydney couldn't seem to stop their mind from ruminating, turning over and over the feelings of disappointment – sometimes, in their darkest moments, even feelings of betrayal – at the sense that all of this work had been for nothing. Maybe they'd had one shot at this creative dream life, but they had chosen incorrectly. Architecture wasn't what they thought it would be, and now they were trapped in it. The magical promise of being able to call yourself an architect, it turned out, meant very little when you were still stuck in an unfulfilling job with no escape hatch in sight.

Sydney rolled over and adjusted the comforter. They desperately needed sleep, but the world outside seemed far too quiet compared to the buzz of an endlessly scrolling brain. They clamped their eyes shut, feeling entirely hopeless. Sleep wasn't going to happen tonight – might as well make some coffee.

Sydney's long-haired calico, Ava, was curled up on the purple velvet armchair in the corner, apparently sleeping soundly. Their tossing and turning seemed not to have bothered her at all.

"Show off," Sydney whispered, scratching the cat behind her ears. "At least one of us gets to sleep, I guess."

Sydney stumbled through their morning routine, despite the abysmally early hour and their total lack of sleep. They figured they might as well head into the firm. They could get some work done before others started filtering in. There would be no catching up this week – Sydney was up against a huge project deadline with another waiting in the queue – but at least they could get a head start on the day.

Yawning, they pulled the apartment door shut behind them, spilling a few drips of coffee down the front of their blouse in the process. *Great.* Maybe that's the real reason architects always wear black, they thought. As usual, it was going to be a rough day.

Pushing through the front door of their building, Sydney was struck with a gust of wind, unseasonably chilly for a September morning, and the dark, expansive stillness of the early morning. They barely noticed, their mind already on the workday ahead. There were a few hours left on the renderings. Then they would need to shift focus to check over the intern's work, in case there were corrections needed. They knew they were missing something, but they couldn't quite put their finger on it.

The insistent buzz-buzz-buzzzz of Sydney's cell phone drew their attention, and they reached into their saddle bag to grab the phone. *Who could be calling at this ungodly hour?*

Sydney's heart skipped a beat. It was their sister. They fumbled to balance their coffee and bag while bringing the phone to their ear.

"Stella?" they said. "Everything okay?"

There was a wet sniffle on the other end of the line, and Sydney felt something like panic surge through their exhausted body.

"Stella?" they said, growing more insistent.

"No," came her sister's voice. "No, I mean, yes, it's me."

"What's going on?"

"I meant, no, everything isn't okay," her sister replied, the last word morphing into something like a wail. Stella had a propensity for drama, but Sydney could tell that something was very, very wrong.

"What's going on?" Sydney nearly screamed into the phone. Living nearly a thousand miles from their family and working the ridiculous hours of an early-career architect meant that Sydney wasn't always in the loop. Every time a family member called out of the blue, they had a little moment of panic. Usually everything was okay. This time, it wasn't.

"GeeGee," her sister sniffled, "had a stroke."

Sydney felt their fight-or-flight response kick into quick action. "Is she in the hospital? She's okay, right? I don't know if I can – no, never mind, I'll come as soon as I can." *Go inside. Pack some clothes. Book a flight. Call a Lyft. Shit, could they find somebody to feed Ava? They would have to leave a k –*

"Syd," their sister said, suddenly strangely quiet. "She died."

Sydney felt their legs go slack, and they slid down to crouch onto the filthy pavement. Suddenly, they couldn't catch their breath. GeeGee was gone. The woman who had raised Sydney and Stella from early childhood. Who had stepped in when their father left and their mother couldn't keep it together. Gone.

When had they spoken last? With that devastating thought, Sydney felt a wave of nausea flow through them. It escaped their mouth as a wet sob.

They turned and stumbled back up the stairs, flopped into bed, and wept until they passed out, the relief of sleep finally settling over them like a stormy fog.

#

Sydney gasped awake several hours later, thinking first of their work and only moments later about where they were and why. In a single, panicked movement, they grabbed their phone from the bedside table and dialed the firm's office number. When the receptionist tried to forward the call to their project manager, there was no answer. It was just as well, honestly. Sydney wasn't sure they could hold it together if they had to actually talk to the PM. When voicemail picked up, they left a message letting him know what had happened and that they needed to make arrangements to fly back to Wisconsin for the funeral.

A small, pitiful whimper escaped Sydney's lips. They had spoken to GeeGee for the last time. There would never again be an overly warm summer walk, GeeGee complaining constantly about the humidity but refusing to turn back early. No more snowball cookies – nobody else came close to GeeGee's recipe. She would never hear GeeGee's fingers glide gracefully over the antique piano. A tear welled in Sydney's eye and they wiped it away before it could fall. They could almost feel their grief mingling with their guilt and regret for putting their family on the back burner for so long. Too long.

It was all a poignant reminder of the sense of hopelessness that was keeping them up most nights in recent memory – the feeling of being totally isolated from family and friends. They were a cog in the wheel of a huge corporate firm. A firm that might miss them today, scrambling to meet deadlines as they were. But, Sydney wondered, if it had been them who'd died, how long would the firm wait to replace them? Would a single coworker mourn them? How long would it take before their absence registered with the lead architect they'd worked under for six years?

A few minutes later, the email app on their phone dinged, and Sydney swiped to reveal a reply from their PM. *Yeah,* the response read. *I guess it's fine. There's a lot to do here, but I guess we'll have to figure it out without you.* It would have been a shockingly dismissive email if it weren't so totally on brand for the firm in general and the PM in particular. *We'll need you all day tomorrow though, so please plan to be here all day. It's a grandparent, right? Not immediate family? I assume the funeral isn't for a few days,* the message concluded.

There is something about grief that seems to intensify all of your other emotions, somehow forcing them down into your gut like a heavy, fiery boulder. They resisted the urge to hurl the phone against the wall.

GeeGee was gone. And they had sacrificed their last possible years with her to live here. To work at this firm.

For what? GeeGee had told them to go to the big city and make a name for themself, not that GeeGee had any idea what New York was like – or what it might mean to "make a name for oneself" in architecture. But maybe Sydney didn't either. After all, what did they have to show for those years of sacrifice? They were nearing 30 and more miserable than ever. They hadn't had time to build relationships outside of work. They had dated a few people but never had the mental or emotional energy to spare on any kind of relationship. They basically worked and slept, with the odd meal squeezed in here and there. Was this the dream they'd had for their life? Was this what GeeGee had imagined they were doing?

Why had they fought their way through architecture school, and why hadn't anyone told them that the creative work they loved there would be miles away from the practical work they did at their actual job? They had always felt like an outcast back in school, but that only motivated them more. Then they'd thought that first real job might be the turning point. But while there was less overt animosity, the firm was still a space where they – and everybody they knew – felt overworked and undervalued.

They had certainly "paid their dues." They had rushed around to finish a set of renderings that would never see the light of day – the project architect had decided the project wasn't yet ready to show before totally forgetting about the renderings they'd completed. They had reworked most of a nearly finished model when the project architect decided at the last minute to go in a different direction. They had listened as the lead architect excoriated the team for a project on which they were not "feeling the love" – he argued that the team, who had worked themselves to the bone on the project – should have stayed later, come in earlier, worked harder.

Sydney had given so much to the job over the years, a job that seemed determined to keep taking until there was nothing left. Licensure, they had once believed, would be the last line in the sand; the last sign that they had fought through the bullshit of overwork and undervalue and emerged an architect on the other side. This achievement was supposed to mark the moment when they could finally embody what they had imagined in architecture school and in their early career. Only now, they couldn't even remember what that image had looked like. Why had they ever wanted this life in the first place?

Ava hopped up on the bed next to Sydney, as if to remind them of one positive aspect of their life. "Come here, sweetie," they said, stroking the cat's head. The small act of comfort inexplicably brought Sydney to tears. They had been miserable for so long, surviving only by tamping down the feelings of desperation, isolation, fatigue, and hopelessness. A couple of years into architecture school, they had started to take anti-depressants. The next year, they added anxiety medication. They'd now started on B-12 and vitamin D supplements for mood. Nothing seemed to stave off the depression anymore.

Sydney felt a familiar fire growing in their gut. The injustice of needing psychotropic medication just to survive a day at work – every day at work – crashed over them. What other profession would rationally ask this of employees? Where else would professionals with Ivy League degrees be repeatedly told they weren't good enough? They should have loved their job, given their passion for craft and design. So why was it feeling more and more like a prison sentence?

Sydney put their hand to their face, closed their eyes, and took a deep breath. They felt a whimper climbing up their throat, and they suppressed it by reaching for their phone. Mindless scrolling – it was the mental health care you got if you had terrible insurance and no time for therapy appointments. But the scrolling only set their mind spinning into the familiar spiral of hate. Beautiful images passed in front of their eyes, but they barely even saw them. The woman who had loved them most in this world was gone, and what did their project manager have to say about it? Only that they would have to come in tomorrow. No sense of concern. Not even shock. Just a blasé reiteration that the firm believed it was more important than Sydney's family.

This was not how they were raised. They opened their travel app and booked a ticket on the late-night flight home the next evening – it was the earliest flight they could afford – then placed the phone on their nightstand. The sun had only just begun its descent, but Sydney's head was throbbing, and they were so, so tired. They climbed into bed and tossed back a few ibuprofen. For the second time that day, they cried themself to sleep.

#

The next few days were a blur of grief and defiance. Something had snapped in Sydney, and there was simply no going back to how things had been. The loss of a caregiver can do that to a person. The loss of a caregiver with a generous helping of employer indifference is even more effective.

The morning after GeeGee passed, Sydney had gasped awake before their alarm, forgetting for a moment the events of the previous day. They sat bolt upright, frantically cursing themself for forgetting to turn on their alarm. Then it all came flooding back to them. Fixing their lips into a tight grimace, they laid back down, propped their head on some pillows, and reached for their phone.

First, they emailed the firm. They were taking the entire day off. They knew their project manager wouldn't like it – perhaps they would get reprimanded, maybe even fired – but they weren't feeling particularly concerned about that at the moment.

Then, they began to search. The plethora of blogs and articles about people's dissatisfaction with architecture was both shocking and deeply saddening. There was a lot of advice, much of it conflicting. Eventually, a series of posts and links and referrals brought them to Out of Architecture. They immediately booked an introductory call, and Jake and Erin were able to squeeze in an initial appointment early the next week. Sydney would take the call from Wisconsin. They needed some time home, and their neighbor had agreed to feed Ava. It wasn't like Sydney to behave rashly, but the more they thought about it, the more it seemed right.

#

At that first phone meeting, Sydney had poured out the sense of dissatisfaction and hurt that had led them to this point of career crisis. It had been a comforting place to start, and within a few days they officially took a short leave of absence with a promise to return to the firm as a part-time employee. Erin and Jake suggested – and Sydney agreed – that the first priority was to quell the burnout. They could see no way of doing that while maintaining their current schedule and managing a trip home.

Now Jake and Erin's faces popped up on a follow-up Zoom call, and Sydney felt hope for the first time in years.

"I love your top," Erin commented, indicating Sydney's military green origami-inspired jacket.

"I was noticing that, too," Jake added. "Very architectural."

"Oh," Sydney replied, caught off guard. "Thank you. Their hand went to one brass button, "it's actually a jacket. I found this fabric on sale – "

"Did you design that?" Erin asked enthusiastically, accidentally cutting them off.

"I did! I wanted something casual that still spoke to my aesthetic. And I can never find jackets that fit right off the rack. My torso is too long," they shrugged. They typically had to excuse their clothing with other architects. Sometimes they gave in and wore the expected all-black ensemble – architects' clothing was never supposed to overshadow the work – but this period of defiance had reminded them that clothing had been the one way they could express themselves, even under what felt increasingly like the tyranny of the firm's work expectations.

"So," Jake started. "We'd planned to talk about other career routes you might take today. And we didn't plan this necessarily, but I'm curious if you ever thought of fashion as a career path."

"I mean," Erin said, "it looks like you're a talented apparel designer!"

Sydney raised their eyebrows, considering this. They had always used fashion as a creative outlet, often designing their own clothes – not only out of the necessity of getting a good fit, but because one couldn't find clothing that fit Sydney's style at Target or Old Navy. If they wanted to look sharp – and they definitely did – they had to figure out how to make the clothes themselves. With GeeGee's vintage sewing machine and the occasional tutoring session, Sydney had taught themself to sew as a teenager. While Sydney saw it as a natural extension of their design sensibility, all of these years later, they took their skills for granted.

Now, they realized, it was actually a natural extension of their *architectural* design sensibility.

"But," Sydney continued with trepidation, "I'm not a fashion designer."

"It seems like you are," Jake said.

A flood of anxiety and curiosity washed over Sydney. They had worked for almost a third of their life to be able to call themself an architect. Years of school, followed by years of intern and junior-level work, years of preparing for the exams, and another year of actually completing them. Not to mention the financial investment.

How did someone walk away from all that?

"I guess I'm just not sure how to be anything other than an architect," Sydney said, a hot well of tears growing at the corners of their eyes. "Who am I if I'm not an architect?"

"You're much more than that one thing, Sydney," Erin said. "Honestly you might be surprised to know that we see this a lot. But we always push back against it. There is much more to your identity than just 'architect.' You're not just one noun."

This was a topic Jake and Erin had spoken about a lot recently – the idea of finding your noun. It was easy to pack your self-worth into the defining terminology of your career. This was particularly poignant in architecture, a field that required college-educated graduates to continue to jump through years of hurdles before one could claim a professional title.

So much time, energy, emotion, and money got packed into that one little noun – architect – it was often difficult for their clients to imagine themselves beyond the term.

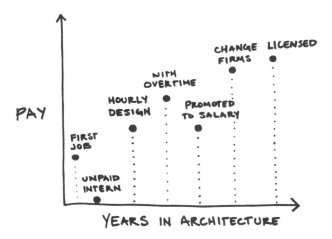

The rest of their conversation that day centered on the imperative of shifting Sydney's mental framework – of thinking about how they might reconcile their desire to build a fulfilling career outside of architecture with their emotional investment in the architect title. This transition looked different for everyone. Sometimes, people left architecture and never looked back. Other times, people diversified their interests, going part-time in architecture while exploring other opportunities. Some people wanted licensure above all else, while others were happy to dismiss what they saw as an antiquated procedure.

The thing that was true for nearly everyone, though, was that leaving a profession required a mental and emotional shift. It meant that Out of Architecture was always a space where people explored their identities as much as their career options. But once they were able to reimagine themselves in other roles, the move out of the field was much easier. It allowed them to understand their noun – their career-assigned identity – as only a part of who they are. And it allowed them to realize that they could always imagine another noun for themselves, despite what those in the field might indicate.

Sydney left that call with a renewed sense of dedication to figuring out who they were. Or, perhaps more accurately, who they wanted to be. They had truly never imagined that their interest in fashion could extend beyond the necessity of dressing themself stylishly and affordably. What might it mean to work in fashion, then? Who could they be in that industry? And how did you redefine yourself after years of dedication to one particular field?

When Sydney finally got back to their apartment, they were greeted by a stack of boxes and a pile of junk mail.

"I just left it all there on the table for you," their neighbor said. "And Ava was a peach."

Sydney smiled. "I really appreciate you so much," they said. "Thank you."

As they sorted through the miscellaneous packages and envelopes, one small, square package caught their eye. Once opened, that package would all but wipe away Sydney's resolve to build a new noun for themself. Inside the box was the cylinder they had spent the last decade working towards. A self-inking stamp bearing their name. And the word, "architect."

Something like mourning settled in their heart. This process of redefinition wasn't going to be easy.

#

"You may not know how to do this yet, but you can do it," Sydney repeated to themself. Simple words from their last meeting with Out of Architecture, but comforting nonetheless as they sipped their coffee and anticipated another contact meeting. Erin and Jake had reassured Sydney that getting to know a few people working in the apparel industry would help them to see how their future might unfold in this new world.

It was an intimidating prospect for an introvert, but there was something calming about being given instructions in the middle of a crisis. The element of the unknown was, in many ways, the worst part. Jake and Erin had explained the whole process, pointing out the parts that might be more difficult or stressful, but assuring Sydney that everything would be fine. The company had coached many people through the process before, so even though Sydney felt utterly panicked about embarking on such a major life change, they had to trust that Jake and Erin knew how to do this.

A couple of weeks following their last appointment, Jake had sent a few emails, introducing Sydney to a few contacts in fashion and apparel-based careers. Sydney still wasn't completely convinced that they could work effectively in fashion, but Erin had made a compelling case that apparel and architecture had more in common than not. In apparel, she had pointed out, you created patterns. These weren't so different from building plans – both flat representations of what would become three-dimensional objects. What was a pattern but an assembly drawing? An exploded axon, except for a garment rather than a building. Apparel design, Jake added, was about pulling apart the pieces, imagining what the final product would look like, and then deconstructing it to build it up again. That was precisely the same process architects used.

Sydney kicked themself for not realizing this before.

Now, as they headed into their third meeting, many of the nerves had gone – at least they were no longer afraid of being laughed out of the coffee shop – but doubt still lingered about the ability to transition into apparel in a way that would be creatively fulfilling. At least it couldn't be less fulfilling than architecture, they thought to themselves, taking a sip of their latte.

"Are you Sydney?"

They looked up from their coffee to see a smiling blonde woman approaching them. The woman was dressed in a bold floral-print velvet jacket and dark skinny jeans. "Yes! Hi!" Sydney said, compulsively adding, "That jacket is fantastic."

"Thank you," the woman replied graciously. "It's a sample. Perks of the job."

The woman was a contact of Jake's, and Sydney was particularly eager to meet her. She hadn't worked in architecture as long as Sydney – it had only taken her a year to realize the profession wasn't for her – but she had experience in the field. Sydney thought this could go one of two ways. On one hand, Sydney knew if they were really going to take the leap into garment design, they would need a model for how to effectively make the move.

On the other, Sydney worried that their old familiar noun would come back to haunt them. Would the woman expect them to talk about the business of architecture? And if so, how could they possibly have that conversation without coming across as a horrible, miserable person? Would this woman think Sydney was creatively bankrupt? That they couldn't hack it in this field? That they were just another entitled millennial who didn't have the fortitude to pay their dues? And if they couldn't make it as an architect, how could they possibly convince this person – who they now saw was stylish, impeccably pulled together, and the picture of a fashion professional – that they would be an asset to her network?

"It's so nice to meet a fellow defector!" the woman said with a delicate laugh, and Sydney felt their shoulders relax just a little.

They grinned. Sydney had a tendency to be a little awkward at small talk, but Erin and Jake had coached them. You don't need to try to impress her, the two had said. You're just there to learn about her experiences and make a connection. "It's great to meet you, too," they said sincerely.

Over the next hour, the two hit it off. This woman seemed to have an answer for every fear Sydney had. Maybe even more than that, it was just nice to feel validated.

Finally, the woman retrieved her bag, signaling the end of the meeting. "It was so great to talk with you," she said. "I've gotta run – I have another meeting at three, but I wanted to say – " Here, the woman seemed to deliberately look Sydney in the eye. "You can do this. I know it's really scary. I went through that, too. But I am so glad I took the leap."

When Sydney wrote to thank the woman, it was perhaps the most sincere email they had ever sent. They had been plagued with self-doubt, and they knew that some of that would linger – trauma like they had experienced in their early career didn't simply vanish overnight. But meeting this woman truly gave them hope. It was incredibly destabilizing to change one's noun – so much of their identity had been poured into the prospect of officially becoming an architect – but Sydney felt reassured that doing so just took some hard work and perseverance. And they had that in spades.

Jake and Erin had been clear that the change wouldn't happen overnight. That a realistic timeline for a job transition was typically two months or so. But within a few weeks, Sydney had received a follow-up email from one of their new contacts. The woman had come across an opening at a major retailer and wondered whether Sydney would be interested in a referral.

Suddenly, it became clear: when it came to changing your noun, there was no way out but through. You simply had to take a leap of faith. Sydney wrote back to the woman, graciously accepting the offer for a referral, and immediately sent a second email to Erin and Jake. If they were going to get this job, they needed some coaching.

Then they picked up the rubber stamp from their coffee table where it had rested, still in its box, since the day Sydney returned to New York. They tossed the box into the recycling bin, then placed the stamp purposefully on the bookcase, a reminder that they had fought their way to a title once before. They were ready to do it again.

CHAPTER 13
THE QUESTIONER

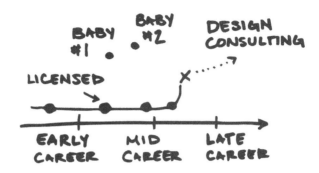

Tia took a deep breath in and slowly blew it out, focusing on the way the breath caught in her throat as she exhaled. Her chest felt uncomfortably tight. *Keep breathing.* Her fingers loosened slightly on the steering wheel. She was going faster than she intended, the car racing at the same pace as her mind.

"Deep breath. One more," she said aloud. She'd carried this ritual through architecture school, through her early years on the job, through the rough spots when she was holding together her marriage, through the stress of caring for two babies while balancing demanding expectations at work. Her mother had taught her this: *Take a deep breath in, then blow it out slowly. Center yourself.*

What would her mother think of her now, she wondered. Late for another Little League practice, and for what? For a bullshit meeting about a bullshit project that she couldn't even believe the firm was entertaining. Just thinking about it made her heart rate climb again. The firm was a company. Of course she knew that. Their entire goal was to make money. That had become increasingly clear over the past several years, as the firm had taken on skyscraper after skyscraper, glitzy high-rises and luxury condos and whatever other structure some disgustingly rich person could dream up.

And now, in all likelihood, they would be designing a prison. It would certainly be a departure from the extravagance of some of the firm's recent projects. This

DOI: 10.4324/9781003300922-17

one wasn't designed to feel rich. It was designed to make the client rich. *Imprisoning people to make a buck.* The idea turned Tia's stomach. "Don't say it like that," her colleague had said. "It's not like the company actually puts people in prison. Just think of it as any other building. They're just housing people, if you really think about it." Tia didn't find this argument convincing. In fact, she found it offensive. And the meeting with the client hadn't helped at all, with the constant talk of efficiency and the consultant's frequent use of the phrase "bottom line."

Tia pulled into the school parking lot. She'd missed most of Jayden's practices, and she had resolved to be present – physically and mentally – at this one. The sun beat down on her as she hurried toward the diamond. It was on the warm side, but it felt good after being cooped up at the office all day. She could never understand why a company so focused on profits was so aggressive with their air conditioning.

Tia climbed the bleachers, scanning for the sight of a familiar face. She thought she recognized a couple of parents. Vaguely. But everyone else seemed to know each other, and she couldn't even match these parents with their kids – Jayden's friends and teammates. Tia knew she didn't spend enough time at these types of events, and she felt guilty for it every single day. Nothing to be done about it, she thought. At least she was here now. Barely.

As she claimed a seat, a smattering of applause rose from the stands along with one lone, "Thatta way!" Tia searched the diamond for Jayden and found him in the dugout, chatting with a much shorter child whose cap seemed comically oversized. She waved, but the two were obviously in the middle of an intense first-grade conversation – about what, she couldn't even imagine.

Just then, Tia's phone dinged. Instinctively, she pulled it from her purse and swiped right to open the message from the partner.

Tia, it read, *I just wanted to thank you for sharing your thoughts on this new project. The firm really needs this contract, so we went ahead and signed on. I know you had some reservations. Wanted to reassure you that you have nothing to worry about. We know you are a person who can step outside her comfort zone and be a leader here.*

So much for the deep breathing exercises. The tension had instantly flooded back into her shoulders, her jaw, her entire body. She tapped the arrow to reply. *We need to talk more,* she wrote, than deleted the words. *Can we please – .* Deleted again. She dropped the phone to her lap, staring at the message. Was it condescending, or was she just reading into it because she was upset about the decision? *Whatever.* She couldn't deal with it now. She'd sped out to the diamond for J's game, and she wasn't about to let this distract her. She closed the email, then refreshed her inbox. Mostly junk. A confirmation email reminding her she'd agreed to guest lecture at her alma mater tomorrow. *I'll be there!* she wrote back quickly. Unable to resist the urge to hate-read, she opened the partner's message again. *You have nothing to worry about*, she read again, seething. That guy is a piece of work, she thought, dropping her phone into her purse.

She looked up to see Jayden standing on first base and grinning ear to ear. How had she missed it? She'd looked down for no more than 15 seconds. Maybe 20. It was like someone had punched her in the stomach. Jayden had been begging her to come to practice for weeks. Here she was, and she couldn't even put work aside for long enough to watch him get his hit. From the field, Jayden looked right at her, his grin radiant. Tia forced herself to smile, fighting back pangs of guilt and anger. She raised her hand and waved at her son, and he waved back before rotating his hand into a high-five with his coach.

Tia rubbed her eyes and tried to calm the shakiness of her breath. Sometimes it seemed like her entire life was just a constant, never-ending roller coaster of stress and breathing exercises. The life in her work-life balance revolved around trying to calm herself down from work, only to head back in the next day and start the cycle of stress all over again.

No, she thought, that was too far. Sure, her job was stressful – weren't all careers? But mostly she liked her work. She had pushed through the grind of her early career and, just as she'd been promised, she had finally reached a point where she could do the things she loved. And how could she complain about designing high-budget project after high-budget project? For the most part, Tia felt fortunate to have finally made it this far.

And, she reminded herself, there was certainly a time when leaving at five to attend J's practice would have been out of the question. Of course, she had asked to leave at 4:30, but the young, aspiring architects she would speak with in tomorrow's class would have to wait at least a decade for that type of privilege.

"Mom!" Jayden shouted, bringing her back to the stands. He was leaning against the chain-link fence, his fingers laced through the diamonds and his face pressed against the metal links. "Did you see me?"

She swallowed hard, then grinned. This time it wasn't forced at all. As much as her parental guilt had chosen this moment to refresh itself, the sight of her kid – beaming with pride from behind the fence – was enough to bring her back to a much more joyful place.

"You know it!" she exclaimed. "You were great!" Sometimes a little white lie was worth it.

#

Tia considered it her responsibility to be completely honest and up front with aspiring architects. The job was hard enough as it was – especially in those first several years after school – and she was grateful that her mentors had been honest with her about things. Her willingness to level with students was, she imagined, one of the reasons she was asked back to the Professional Practice class year after year.

The next morning as she prepared for the lecture, she scrawled in her notebook, *Never forget the financial aspect of architecture.* It was a poignant reminder of the firm's recent client decisions and the third bullet point she'd listed after, *Be flexible about your work assignments* and *Licensure is expensive.* It had always nagged at her the way people talked about architecture as though it was somehow separate from the economy, as though the forces of supply and demand didn't apply to this business. She'd certainly gotten a lesson in that, lately, as the firm turned its focus more and more toward high-ticket clients and major competitions. The higher the budget, the more room to push design boundaries, her colleagues frequently reminded her. And it was true that she had loved the last high-rise she worked on. It had given her many of the opportunities to innovate that she had dreamt of as a student.

What she hadn't dreamt of – certainly not as a student, and even less so now that she had officially paid her dues – was the idea that this profession would lead her to a project that was so completely out of sync with her ethics. Tia had followed the growing conversation about US incarceration rates. She didn't consider herself a political person, but she was troubled by some of the statistics she'd seen circulating around social media. It was only recently that she had learned about private prisons – up until then, she had assumed prison was a government-run operation, unfortunate but necessary to maintain public safety. Now she was being asked to design one of these for-profit structures. No – not being asked. Being told. She had objected in the meeting yesterday, but her concerns had obviously been interpreted as expressions of insecurity rather than the ethical challenges she had intended them to be. She had always believed that this profession could truly change the world. But she hadn't imagined it would do so in this way.

Behind her, Tia heard a series of sleepy footfalls. She turned from her perch at the kitchen island to see her littlest stumbling in. Joy wandered down the hall with one fist rubbing at her eyes, the other lazily at her side. All she was missing was a floppy teddy bear.

Tia stretched out her arms, and Joy climbed onto her lap.

"Good morning, sunshine," she said, giving the preschooler a peck on the cheek. Joy's hand immediately wiped at the spot, and Tia responded by showering her with more kisses.

The little girl giggled. "Knock it off, Mommy," she said, a phrase older than her years that she had probably picked up from some cartoon.

"I can't help it! You're just so cute!" Tia said, nuzzling the girl's neck. Even as she said it, Joy was already struggling to get down. She had always been a busy kid, usually quiet but never still. She reminded Tia of herself in that way – always more to do than could be done in a day. "Why don't you go get your brother up?"

"Okay," Joy said, although she was already halfway through the living room when she replied.

The house was stirring, Tia realized. Plan time was over. She jotted a few more ideas into her notebook, then tucked it away in her purse and tossed back the last sip of her tepid coffee.

"Morning," Tia's husband said making a beeline for the coffee maker.

"Good morning," she replied, pushing her mug across the island. "Just a tiny bit," she requested, "I've gotta run here in a second."

"Are you good to pick J up from school this afternoon?" he asked, tipping the carafe.

"That's plenty," she said. Then his question hit her. "Oh my God," she said. "I can't believe I forgot to tell you. I have to do that class tonight, so I was just gonna stay at the office until then. But I can – "

"No, no, don't stress yourself out. I can get him. Or I'll have my mom pick him up. We've got you covered, Professor Jeffries."

Tia grinned and rolled her eyes at him. "I'm visiting a class," she said. "Don't get carried away."

#

The day had passed much as Tia thought it would. She had tried – mostly successfully – to push the notorious prison project out of her mind, focusing instead on the project that needed to be completed first. There was no point in protesting this new contract, anyway. The firm was moving forward, and her personal ethics would never be enough to derail a big-ticket project this like one.

But as she glanced around the classroom later that evening, she felt her own dissonance surfacing like bile. She'd gone through her list of advice – Tia's Tips, she'd called it, then laughed at herself. Raising a six-year-old and a four-year-old certainly hadn't made her any *less* dorky. The list, she noticed as she talked through her points, was solely focused on money. It wasn't that she had planned it that way. In fact, a lot of her points were meant to encourage students to try new things and to bring a good attitude to the work. But when she explained her points, she noticed that all of her reasoning came back to the financial viability of the firm.

She hadn't always seen things this way, had she?

"Thanks for all of that helpful advice, Tia," the professor said. Then, expectantly, "We have a good amount of time for questions, if anybody has them?"

The question-and-answer session was nothing out of the ordinary. Questions about the types of projects she worked on, tips for finding a job that was a good fit, advice for women in architecture. She'd given these answers many times before. Typically she loved chatting with students – bright-eyed and hopeful behind the glaze of fatigue. But her heart wasn't in it today. She kept thinking about herself all those years ago, when she had sat in a class like this. Had she imagined herself thinking of money above all else? She knew she hadn't. Tia had been as hopeful and optimistic as these students. She had truly believed that architecture could change the world for the better, that design could improve people's lives.

At the end of the class session, one student approached her, a contagious smile filling his face.

"Hi, Miss Jeffries," he said.

"Oh, call me Tia," she interrupted him, accepting his proffered handshake.

"Tia," he corrected. "Sorry."

She smiled as reassuringly as she could, shaking her head.

"I don't know if you remember my dad," the student continued. "Troy Halliwell?"

"Oh, of course!" Tia exclaimed. She and Troy had worked together at her first job, over a decade ago at this point. "How's he doing?" Then, gasping at the realization, "Are you Jonah? You were just a kid the last time I saw you!" She suddenly felt unbelievably old. College students could do that to you.

"Yeah," he continued. "He's doing good. Still at the same firm." A few seconds of silence followed.

"So, what are *your* plans?" Tia asked, hoping this would be a more fruitful route of conversation.

"Well, I haven't really told many people," he said conspiratorially, "but I'm actually thinking of trying to move away from architecture a bit."

This was a new one for Tia. She'd talked with many architecture students over the years, and they always had the same future plans – big name firm, licensure, aspirations of making partner. She found herself at a loss for words.

It turned out that was fine with Jonah, who rambled on. "We had a guest company come talk a couple of months back, and they help people find work outside of architecture, so I called them, and it's really good. I'm excited about it!"

"Oh, yeah?" Tia said, her curiosity piqued.

"Yeah! The company is called 'Out of Architecture,'" Jonah replied to her unasked question.

"That's really interesting. What did your dad say when you told him?"

"Well, he didn't know how to react at first," Jonah's voice trailed off, and Tia found herself with more questions than responses. She was enthralled with this new idea. An entire company that existed for the purpose of helping architects leave architecture. She would never have guessed that so many architects were leaving the field. Did that mean that there were others, like her, who were questioning the profession? Maybe even someone she knew? Architecture was notorious for burning people out. But could it be true that an entire coaching industry's worth of early career practitioners were defecting? The idea was fascinating, but she needed to do a bit more research before she was willing to make her interest public.

"That's so great, Jonah," she said, slinging her bag over her shoulder. She wouldn't make it home in time for the kids' bedtime, but she was eager to get home nonetheless. "Please tell your dad I said, 'hello.' And it was so nice to see you again!"

They parted ways, and Tia chatted briefly with the professor, but even as she made her way home, she couldn't shake this idea. Out of Architecture. Something about it was intriguing. She wrote an email to herself just as she was starting the ignition, "Out of Architecture?"

#

Two weeks later, Tia was face-to-face – or the Zoom equivalent – with Jake and Erin. The idea, it turned out, was too compelling to put aside, and she had contacted them soon after her conversation with Jonah. She began by telling them about her discomfort with the prison project, her sense that the job had already veered away from her ethics, her disappointment with work-life balance. Tia didn't like to complain, so she typically didn't, but it felt good to let herself feel all of this, to let her guard down from being the projection of strength she had built up as a defense against the male-dominated world of architecture.

"The thing is," Tia said hesitantly, "I really feel almost guilty complaining. I have a good job. I really do feel valued by my firm, usually." *Prison project aside*, she thought. "But I keep wondering if it's time for a change."

"That's really nothing to feel guilty about," Erin said. "You are entitled to explore your options. But I wanted to go back to the word you used – and I'm glad you used it – of saying you feel valued. We talk a lot about value, and one thing to keep in mind is that there are a lot of things to value about your job. A lot of times people want to feel more valued by their firm. It's great that you don't feel undervalued. But there are other things that are perfectly fine to want. So, I guess what I'm asking is – putting your firm aside – what do *you* value?"

This was an interesting proposition. What *did* she value? So much of Tia's early career had been focused on paying bills, on getting enough stability to start their family. Then, once Jayden was born, and Joy two years later, it had really become about making it through the day-to-day.

"Another way of looking at this," Jake interjected, "is to think about what your ideal week might look like."

"Oh, I have some ideas on that front," Tia laughed.

"That's good!" Erin said. "So I would say, why don't you write out an ideal week? Open your calendar up to a week a couple years from now and fill it in with what you would want your week to look like. Then, we can meet again and look things over."

Tia loved the idea, and they had ended the call so she would have some time to work on her ideal calendar while her husband made dinner. She closed her laptop, grabbed her notebook, and headed into the kitchen where Joy was coloring and Jayden was filling out a spelling worksheet.

"How'd it go?" Tia's husband asked.

"It was really great," she replied. Jayden looked up from his worksheet, as Tia slid onto the stool next to him. "I have some homework, though."

"In your office?" Joy asked.

"You know what?" Tia replied. "I don't think so. I think I'm gonna work on it right here." She opened her notebook and drew out a week, just as she typically would. But this time, it wasn't packed with meetings that had been arranged weeks in advance. This time the entire page was a blank slate.

"What's the homework?" her husband asked.

"I've gotta make a calendar with all the things I like to do on it." Her answer had been as much for the kids as for him, and they took note.

"Are you gonna put my practices on it?" Jayden asked expectantly.

"And the park," Joy added.

Tia smiled and wrapped an arm around Jayden. "You know what? I think I will."

Tia had been excited about this homework assignment since Erin mentioned it, and it did not disappoint. She loved her work, so of course, she listed plenty of time for design projects. She was nothing if not an overachiever, and she wanted to be as specific as possible, detailing out the types of tasks she enjoyed – as Jake and Erin had encouraged her to do – as well as the types of projects she would want to work on. This was all an exercise in fantasy, after all, so she figured she might as well dream big.

Thinking about the work she really enjoyed was honestly somewhat surprising to Tia. She hadn't *hated* working on the firm's high-budget projects, but something about her visit to the class had gotten her thinking about the projects she'd been drawn to in school. She had dreamed of working for non-profit clients – schools, libraries, domestic violence shelters. She loved the idea that beautiful design could be more than eye candy – it could actually help people.

HIDDEN JOB MARKET

Although she had dutifully done her homework – mapping out an entire week of her dream job and home life – she kicked off her next Out of Architecture meeting with this notion of more charitable work. "But," she said, finishing her spiel, "I really can't afford to take a big pay cut."

"You're thinking about this idea that nonprofits don't pay much, right?" Jake asked.

Tia nodded.

"That's actually a myth," Erin chimed in. "Some nonprofits don't pay well," then under her breath, "some for-profits don't pay well either." She smiled at that. "You just have to find the right company."

"It's all about what you value, like we were talking about last time," Jake said. "You might not be able to get everything you want, but looking at what you sent over, I really think you can find something that would be a good fit."

This was blowing Tia's mind. She had always assumed that, once you were established in your company, you were kind of stuck there. That changing careers would be basically impossible unless you were willing to start over with an entry-level job.

"I looked at a couple of places – I know a couple of people who went to IDEO, so I looked there. I didn't see much there."

"One thing to keep in mind," Jake said, "is that

something like 80 percent of jobs are never listed – we call it 'the hidden job market.'

You'd only get those jobs through referrals. So if you know some people, that's great."

"Have you talked to your contacts there?" Erin asked.

"Well," Tia started, tentatively, "I maybe am pushing it to call them 'contacts.' I haven't talked with them in a while. Should I just, what? Call them out of the blue? And won't they wonder why I'm trying to leave my current job?"

Erin and Jake had worked with a lot of clients who felt hesitant about using their networks. But very often, this was the challenge that hid the greatest reward. If they could just get past the discomfort of asking for help, they could often find a much better job than if they stuck with scanning the job websites.

"We can help you figure out how to reach out," Erin said. "Maybe even put together a template you can use to email if you'd be more comfortable that way."

Jake nodded, "But the thing is, you don't know what your contacts might be sitting on. They might have just gotten a big email blast from recruiting saying that they're looking for a position. They might be hiring for a role. They might be leaving their job and want you to fill it. And I think everyone likes to support other people. I think the personal relationships are stronger than the bond that people have with their company."

Tia could definitely see that perspective now that she thought about it.

"No one is gonna be upset with you about leaving your company," Jake continued. "They're gonna say, 'oh wow, I'm excited that you're interested in what I do, and here's my best stab at helping you.'"

"You really think so?" Tia asked hopefully.

"Absolutely," Jake said.

From there, the three of them worked together to build a plan. It was an approach that spoke to Tia's Type-A personality, with the excitement of new possibilities drowning out her fears about a career change – well, almost.

By the end of the week, Tia had gulped down her anxiety and composed an email to her contact at IDEO. She took a deep breath in, and let it slowly out, then pressed "send" before she could change her mind. He replied almost immediately and, thanks to Jake and Erin's coaching, Tia was open and honest about her interest in working for the company. Just as the two had assured her, her old friend seemed genuinely pleased that she had reached out to him. And as uncomfortable as she had felt initially – this idea of being totally transparent about your motives for reconnecting with someone was totally foreign to her – Tia pushed forward and found herself growing more and more confident about the possibilities for leaving her current role and finding something that would serve her and her family even better.

It took a few weeks, but soon her contact at IDEO had contacted her with a position posting that looked great. Tia quickly put together her application, checking in with Jake and Erin along the way. Only a couple of short months earlier, she had been laboring away at her job, pushing aside the thought that things could be better. Now, she found herself eager and hopeful in a way she hadn't been since she finished school. There were big things on the horizon. She could feel it.

#

Around the end of the month, Tia hopped back on a follow-up call with Erin and Jake. "I didn't get the job," she said, holding her face steady.

"That's really okay," Jake started, "sometimes it takes a while – "

"But I got offered a different one!"

"Oh, wow! That's awesome," Erin said.

Jake grinned, shaking his head at her prank. "Congratulations. Well-deserved," he said.

Throughout the process, Jake and Erin were her close confidants, so when the good news struck a couple of months after that initial meeting, she immediately scheduled a call with them. She hadn't gotten the job she had initially applied for, but, right in line with this new-to-her idea of the hidden job market, she'd soon gotten a call asking her to apply for a different position. The company was building a new team – Tia had applied to be part of it. In the end, though, the new team had drafted a designer from an existing team, which left a position open in a different area of the company. The hiring manager knew right away that Tia would be a great fit.

"The salary is about the same as I'm making now," she told Erin and Jake, "but talking with people over there, this team is really big on keeping workers to a 40-hour week. And they're open to flex time, too, so I can move things around when I need to. And the projects there…"

Tia trailed off, dreamily.

"No private prisons, I guess?" Erin said dryly.

Tia nodded, almost in disbelief of this new direction in her career, and in her life. After all, as excited as she was about these new projects, she was absolutely over the moon at the prospect of never missing another Little League practice.

"I just can't thank you enough," she said, a huge grin spreading across her face. "I mean, I used to know this guy at IDEO, but I really thought that connection had fizzled out. I never would have been so explicit with him on my own. And you were totally right! He was really happy to help."

"That's just working your network," Jake said. "We're glad to help."

Tia had learned a lot about herself over the past few months. She had liked working in corporate architecture, but it was time for a change. And it turned out, she was up for the challenge.

She had a few weeks before she started at her new company and enough savings to take a week off between ending her time at her former firm and starting at the new job. That week, she wouldn't put any work on her schedule – that week would be all Little League and trips to the park. Jayden and Joy's dream calendar. *Her* dream calendar. She took a deep breath and let it out, settling into a new and unexpected sense of peace and calm. Tia was really looking forward to taking this new step into a career. She thought – and believed – that this might be the thing that finally let her breathe a little easier.

CHAPTER 14

THE ASSOCIATE PRINCIPAL

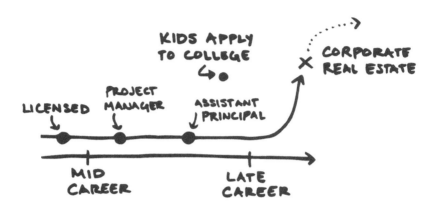

Thomas looked up at the sky and blinked at the cloud-covered sunlight. The forecast this morning had been clear, but he thought it looked like rain. There was a tinge of dark grey in the clouds to the east, and he'd noticed the wind picking up. He checked his watch – 1:53. They had better get started soon, or this whole thing would be rained out.

The thought sent a jolt racing across his skin. He'd tried to shrug off the event – just another ribbon-cutting ceremony – but in reality, this building was his baby. It was his chance to prove his architectural prowess, to really test his chops, something he was truly proud of. The structure sprawled out on every side, an ambitious blend of library space, government offices, childcare facilities, and classrooms. It was a place that could truly bring together the small suburban community in a way that the former library building hadn't. This wasn't just a space to house books – it was a true gathering place.

And now, people were starting to congregate for its official opening. He wasn't the type to get excited, but he was looking forward to the indirect praise he would receive from the "oohs" and "ahhs" of the building's new visitors.

DOI: 10.4324/9781003300922-18

Thomas walked a few feet toward the building's west entryway to calm the butterflies in his stomach. His wife had suggested that Thomas might be asked to join the firm's principal on the ceremony stage. "I'm sure Jim can handle it," he'd said, certain his boss wouldn't want to share the limelight with a lowly project manager like himself. He shook his head in a vain attempt to shed his feelings of inadequacy. Or maybe disrespect. It was difficult to articulate the way Jim made him feel, a problem further complicated by his typical refusal to think about it at all. Thomas believed that Jim's heart was in the right place, but something about the man made him feel incredibly small.

"I'm not late, am I?"

Thomas turned to see his wife making her way toward him. She was dressed in an outfit typically reserved for church, with high-heeled shoes that seemed ill-advised for wading across the center's lawn.

"I didn't miss it, did I?" she continued, checking the time on her phone and glancing at him expectantly. "I thought they would at least be up there on the platform. Did they push the time back?"

Thomas shook his head. "You know the government," he half-joked, squinting up at the make-shift stage. When he looked back at his wife, her eyes were buried in her phone. Just as well, he thought, jamming his hands into the pockets of his slacks.

At two o'clock on the dot, a middle-aged woman in a blue skirt suit ascended the platform. There were several moments of audio awkwardness, as she struggled to make sense of the microphone set-up, before the woman introduced herself as a city council representative for the small suburb that the community center would serve. Reading a statement from a notecard, she welcomed the small, but respectable, crowd to the event. Then she brought the others onto the stage, introducing each of them as they stepped up wobbly stairs onto the platform.

There was a second city council representative, the director and associate director of the new center, and, of course, Jim.

The next name made Thomas feel as though his lunch might make a repeat appearance: Hudson Cresswell, Jim's brother-in-law. He was in his early thirties, Thomas guessed, the husband of Jim's wife's sister, and had joined the firm a few years earlier as a Project Architect – a role typically reserved for people much older and with much more experience. People like Thomas.

Thomas felt his ears ringing, as the world seemed to collapse around him. He felt rage growing in the pit of his stomach.

It must have shown on his face, because he felt his wife wrap her hand around his elbow and give his arm a firm squeeze. He couldn't move. He could only stand, slack-jawed, and stare.

Truthfully, he had hated Hudson the minute he laid eyes on him. He could tell right away that the kid was slick. He dressed like a high-end real estate agent with a haircut that looked like it cost as much as Thomas's mortgage payment.

Jim was speaking now, but Thomas couldn't make out the words.

"It's your building," his wife whispered, positioning her head just behind his shoulder. "You did well."

It *was* his building. And he had done well. That was part of the problem. He had given 22 years to this firm – the best years of his life. He had seen others in his school cohort – even others in the years behind him – step into partner and principal roles at the firms. He should have *at least* been up on that stage.

He thought he felt a raindrop. "Maybe we should head out. Try and beat the rain."

His wife gave him a pitying look. "Come on," she said. "Don't let this ruin the day. Stick around and talk to Jim. I'm sure he'll have some nice words to say. And don't you want to see how people react to the building? I'm sure everyone will love it."

Jim was still on stage, wrapping up his statement: "thank the members of my firm...invaluable support..." Thomas's stomach flipped. He answered his wife by remaining planted in place. Around him, there was a smattering of applause. Thomas pulled out his phone and tapped the screen. No messages. He refreshed the feed just in case. Praying for a distraction.

"Thomas!" Jim's voice rang out moments later, not from the microphone, but from a few yards in front of him. His boss approached him with an outstretched hand. Thomas took Jim's hand out of habit, silently cursing himself for being such a pushover.

"Jim," he said, extending a hand firmly and forcing a smile.

"Hey, congratulations," Jim cooed. "This center is a major accomplishment. We couldn't have done it without you."

Before Thomas could gather his thoughts, the sheen of Hudson's well-coiffed hair appeared behind their boss. Thomas self-consciously smoothed his tie.

"Thomas," Hudson said, extending his hand – Thomas shook it with an unprecedented level of self-revulsion – "glad you could make it."

"I – " Thomas started. *Glad you could make it? It was* his *damn project.*

His wife raised a hand to waist level and looked up at the sky. "Oop," she said, "I think I felt a drop." Then, nervously, "Did you feel that?"

In the next few seconds, they all did. The sky opened up, and the group offered hasty good-byes as they made their way through the now damp lawn to the fresh concrete of the parking lot. Thomas's wife wrapped herself around his arm – she was definitely wearing the wrong shoes for the occasion – "I'm very proud of you," she said.

Somehow it only made him feel worse.

#

Thomas had always been a realist. He was stoic and quiet, trying never to make a fuss. But this moment had stung in a way he hadn't been prepared for. He tried not to think about it, but he couldn't seem to move without renewing the irritation.

As he sat at his desk looking over the parameters for the firm's newest project – a project *he* had brought in through a referral – he found that he couldn't concentrate. All he could think of was Hudson's smug face. *Glad you could make it,* he'd said. Thomas had thought he might be recognized at the ceremony. Now he just felt foolish. Humiliated. His wife had even come to the site – to the opening of *his* project – and now he just felt embarrassed.

And jealous. Hudson had slithered into the role that had been earmarked for Thomas for years. Jim wouldn't retire for at least another decade, but until now, Thomas had felt sure that Jim was looking at him as his replacement. He had thought that he might be promoted to principal, then take over the company once Jim stepped down. He had imagined the moment so clearly in his mind – and he had worked hard to usher in that reality, only to see it slowly slipping away.

He opened Outlook and clicked "new message." If he was going to assert his right as Jim's predecessor, he couldn't wait any longer. The least his boss could do was meet with him and hear him out.

Jim, he typed. *Wondering if we could set up a meeting in the next couple of days. Want to talk about my role –* He stopped and deleted that last sentence. He hadn't negotiated anything, aside from client contracts, in quite a number of years. But he thought he'd heard that you should leave things open. Don't give the other side time to prepare. The element of surprise and all that.

At the same time, he didn't want to upset Jim. Realistically, this was a job. It was a good job with longevity, and Thomas's oldest son was looking at colleges at the moment, the reality of tuition bills looming on the horizon.

He decided he would leave the topic of the meeting open. That way, he could feel out Jim's mood, and sidestep if things started to go south.

Thanks, he wrote, then typed his name and clicked "send."

Okay, he said with a sigh. Thomas closed the Outlook window and tried again to focus on the document in front of him, moving the cursor over the text absent-mindedly.

Not five minutes later, he looked up to see Jim leaning into the door of his office.

"Good morning," Jim said cheerfully.

"Good morning," Thomas returned, his heart suddenly racing.

"I've got a few minutes, so I thought we could just talk now?"

"Sure," Thomas said. *Why hadn't he accounted for this possibility?* He'd assumed he would have some time to prepare – to at least figure out what he was asking for – but this would have to do. To put off the meeting now would seem overly fussy. "Come in."

Jim plopped down in the chair Thomas reserved for clients and leaned back, casually flopping his right ankle over his left knee. Jim was a tall man, but even so, the amount of space he was taking up was impressive…and a little intimidating. "How's everything going?" he asked.

"Good, good," Thomas said automatically.

Jim nodded. "Hey, I wanted to say – great work bringing in the Milligan project." The Milligan project was for a new office park in midtown, a type of client that the firm didn't often land. Thomas had brought it in by referral. It was a high-traffic area, and it had the potential to bring the firm a lot of visibility. "I think we're all pretty excited to work on that building."

Thomas felt his confidence swell. He'd been so focused on the community center that he'd forgotten that he could highlight his recent success with new clients as well. "Sure, yes," he replied. "I've gotten really – " he started to say lucky, but quickly caught himself. " – well, I've been trying to be more strategic about the types of clients I bring in. Just thinking about the firm moving forward."

"It's been noticed," Jim said with a warm smile. "Hudson and I were just talking about this approach to expand our reach. Residential projects have been our bread and butter, but with the new developments in midtown, there's a lot of opportunity in that area." Jim shifted in his chair slightly and extended his arm to reveal his watch, furrowing his brow slightly at the time.

Your Career Is a Design Problem

"I wanted to follow up on that, actually," Thomas said, seeing an opening, "that idea of the firm's future. I wanted to talk about having more of a stake in the company. Of *me* having more of a stake in the company, I mean. Leveling up."

"Ah," Jim said, nodding.

Thomas plowed ahead. He needed to get this out.

"I'm glad we have so much work lately. And, speaking of, Jason is headed to college next year, and with tuition – I guess what I'm saying is, I wanted to see what you thought about me maybe taking more ownership in the firm, just, I mean, not necessarily now, but in the future."

Jim was grimacing in a way that made Thomas feel incredibly uncomfortable, his lips drawn into a tight line. He took an audible breath, then exhaled. "Thomas, I don't want you to take the wrong thing away from this – this firm wouldn't be what it is without you. I'm just not sure how things are looking, budget-wise."

Thomas nodded. "Sure, right."

"Tell you what: let's be sure to make time at the end of the year to talk this over. We'll have a better sense of things then."

"That makes sense," Thomas said, begrudgingly. This was always Jim's move. He was constantly kicking the can down the road, putting off any real discussion of change in the organization. Except, of course, when it came to Hudson.

"I'm really sorry I can't do more. But I do want to just say again – you're doing a great job. I really appreciate you."

Jim leaned forward to stand, and Thomas followed his lead, extending a handshake to his boss. Jim grasped his hand, then headed back toward the door.

"Thanks for taking the time," Thomas offered into the ether, but Jim was gone before he could get the words out, replaced in the doorway with the intern.

"I brought your mail," he said, handing Thomas a stack of papers. Thomas thanked him and collapsed back into his chair.

Piece by piece, he went through the mail, tossing most of the items into the bin for recycling. But the glossy cover of his college alumni magazine caught his eye. He flipped through the pages distractedly, scanning for familiar names. A woman in the cohort above him had just scored a major competition. A professor of his was retiring. An acquaintance of his had passed away.

Then his eyes stopped on a paragraph noting two architecture alumni, Erin Pellegrino and Jake Rudin, who had given a talk recently on the possibilities for architects to work in careers outside of the traditional field. The title of the talk was interesting – "Out of Architecture" – also the name of their company, he read.

"Huh," he said aloud, mulling the idea over in his head. Typically he tossed the magazine straight into the recycling bin. Today, he grabbed a sticky note from his desk and marked the paragraph. Maybe he was feeling just frustrated enough to see what they had to offer.

#

Less than a week later, Thomas found himself in his home office, struggling to believe what he was about to do. He'd been an architect for almost half of his life. His firm had been his home through Jason's birth, and later, Casey's. He'd known his boss nearly as long as he'd known his own wife. He had always imagined himself as Jim's protege – the employee who was "like a son" – poised to take over the business he had invested 50 to 60 hours in every week for the past two decades. When he started at the firm, Bill Clinton had been president. Randy Travis had played on every country station. He'd been 20 pounds lighter with much more hair, he liked to joke.

But when it came down to it, Thomas knew that this was just a job. Sure, he had invested in the company, and he liked Jim well enough. But jobs were jobs, and if this Out of Architecture company could help him find a better one, then so be it. It wasn't personal, after all. It was just business.

He searched back through his email to retrieve the Zoom link, and clicked to open the application.

"Hello," Jake said, his image filling the screen first followed shortly by Erin's. "Thomas – it's nice to meet you!"

"Yes, hello," he replied. "You too."

"It's nice to meet you," Erin said. "Glad we could find a time."

"You too," Thomas said again, this time to Erin. "I appreciate it." The three waded through some quick pleasantries, but Thomas was ready to dive in. "Can you tell me what you guys do?" he asked. "Are you guys headhunters, I guess?"

Thomas wasn't the first to ask this, and Jake had a quick answer. "We aren't headhunters," he replied, "although we do have a lot of industry connections that we can use to help clients network and find open positions. But it's much more organic than that. We make sure that you have everything you need to succeed in your career search. We work for our clients."

"We're more like career consultants," Erin added.

"I see," Thomas said, checking his notes. It felt strange to need a career coach at this stage in his life, and, although he hadn't planned to share it on the call, he said so.

"I can see that it would be uncomfortable," Erin said. "A lot of our clients feel that way, though. Even clients who are still in school or recently graduated can feel strange considering a new path."

Thomas thought of his own son. Jason wasn't planning to pursue architecture – in that way, he'd followed more in his mother's footsteps and planned to major in psychology. Yet, he imagined how his son would feel if, on finishing his degree, Jason realized he'd chosen the wrong major. He felt a pang of empathy. "Do you have a lot of clients who are still in school?" he asked.

"Quite a few," Jake responded. "We give talks to student groups sometimes, and we always get a lot of interest from students who aren't interested in the kinds of limitations they see in the traditional field."

"Huh," Thomas responded. The idea was incredibly relatable to him, as someone who had worked for 22 years at the same firm and couldn't even negotiate for a basic promotion and the raise his family needed.

"Can we ask what kinds of things you're looking for?" Erin interjected. "It might help to know what brought you to reach out."

Thomas was upfront with them. He wasn't one to mince words, and really what he wanted was simple. He wanted autonomy – a company that could trust him in a leadership position – and he wanted more money.

"For someone with your level of experience," Jake responded, "I think we could come up with quite a few options. Consulting comes to mind. We could look at corporate real estate. Or a major retail brand, something like that."

"You know, I actually had a friend who went into consulting," Thomas said. He could feel himself growing more and more invested in this idea of leaving the firm. Of leaving the profession. It was like he had only needed a little push – just a blurb in the alumni magazine – and he was ready to make a leap. Or, more accurately, to start looking for some new places to land.

It was refreshing, honestly. He had been nervous about the idea of moving out of his comfort zone – that was why they called it a "comfort zone" after all – but the more he thought about this idea of moving out of architecture, the more interested he became. After his meeting with Jim – a meeting that had resulted in being put off yet again – he felt a strange sense of excitement about the prospect of being able to leverage his experience at a new company in a different field.

The three talked for another 30 minutes or so, Erin and Jake focusing on the opportunities that exist for people like Thomas. Opportunities he had never dreamt of. As the conversation drew to a natural conclusion, Jake asked whether Thomas had any other questions.

"No, I don't think so. Not at this point," Thomas replied. "Why don't you put together a proposal, and that will give us something to talk about."

Jake and Erin agreed and the three set up a meeting for the next week. As Thomas closed the Zoom window, he sat back in his chair and grinned. His head was swimming with possibilities.

He rose from his office chair and made his way into the dining room.

"How was your meeting?" his wife asked.

"Really great, actually," Thomas said, picking up a folded piece of paper from the table. "What's this?"

His wife beamed. "Look at it yourself."

He scanned the letter, addressed to his son. *We are pleased to inform you…largest scholarship we offer…welcome you to campus.*

"Jason got a scholarship!" she exclaimed.

"I thought he already had his mind set on Dartmouth," Thomas said, surprised at the community college letterhead.

"This is a good thing," his wife scolded him. "He's worried about student debt. This way he can go for nearly free without having to take out loans. It even has a book stipend."

Thomas felt his heart sink. All he had wanted from life was a secure financial future. The ability to send his kids to good colleges. To retire comfortably.

"Is this where he wants to go, though?" Thomas asked.

His wife approached him and wrapped her arms around his neck. "He's happy," she said. "There are a lot of options to consider, and this is just one more possibility."

There *were* a lot of possibilities for a kid like Jason. The stream of mail that had piled up on the dining room table over the past few months proved that well enough. Just a week ago, Thomas would have said that he was too far along in his career to make a change, but maybe he should be more like his son. More like his wife. Maybe he should consider all of his options. Maybe this was finally the chance he needed to make sure Jason – and later Casey – had all the options they needed, too.

#

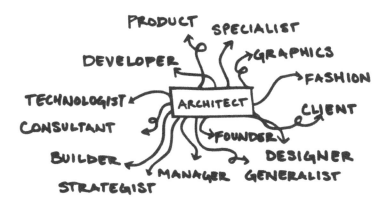

The next couple of months were a flurry of activity. The enthusiasm Thomas had felt working on the community center project paled in comparison to his zeal for rebuilding his career.

> *Jake and Erin had told him to think of his career as a design problem, and that had proven to be some of the most useful advice he'd ever received.*

It allowed him to think about his limitations – things like relocation or entry-level positions were off the table. And it also helped him to think about the value he could bring to a variety of companies. He had always known he was valuable to Jim, but thinking about the things he could bring to a job beyond architecture made him feel like an asset in a way he hadn't before.

Erin and Jake hadn't only equipped him with good advice. They had sent along a package of career tracks. All of the options Jake had listed on the first call were there, along with a couple of other ideas. The document included all of the relevant information about the type of career, the target salary ranges for specific roles within that field, exemplary job postings, and outlines of companies within 20 miles of his home that fit the bill.

He had been so intrigued by the beautifully designed document that he dove right in, applying to a number of roles, always with support from Out of Architecture. They acted as an accelerant to a process that otherwise would have likely dragged on for more time than he cared to admit. You *could* teach an old dog new tricks, it turned out, and he found his energy renewed at this opportunity to explore career options.

Now, five months from that first call, he had requested a new appointment with Erin and Jake. He found himself in the best type of predicament, having received two competing offers – one from a small consulting firm and the other in corporate real estate.

"That's excellent news. Congratulations," Erin started.

"Great work," Jake added. "Do you have a sense of which you might lean toward?"

"Whichever pays more," Thomas said, half joking. "Seriously, though. One offer was a little higher, and the other has more team management aspects. I think I'd lean toward the better compensation package."

"Makes sense," Jake replied. "Then I think the thing we want to talk about is the offers themselves. Tell us more about what was included."

It felt surreal to describe these compensation packages, both in the range of $150,000, and to ask whether they were actually strong offers, but that's exactly what Thomas did. This was his one shot, he figured, and he wanted to make it count.

Erin and Jake had the same goal, teasing out the finer details of the offers and coaching Thomas to look beyond the salary to consider things like 401K, health benefits, a starting bonus, and a relocation package.

At the last point, Thomas stopped them. "I'm not relocating, though."

Jake nodded. "But if the money is set aside, there's no reason you couldn't ask for that to be included in a different form."

"Ah," Thomas said, "of course! That's great!"

He was amazed at how this process had brought out a new side of him. He had felt so run-down, so tired, for so long. And now, with the prospect of a big life change, he didn't feel nervous – not much, at least. He felt genuinely excited.

Armed with his newfound negotiation strategies, Thomas felt much more confident than he had the day Jim visited his office. So when he picked up the phone that afternoon to call the hiring manager, he approached it like the professional he knew he was.

When he emerged from his home office, grinning like a man with a secret, his wife nervously demanded details.

"Well, let me ask you this," he said. "What's Jason's top choice? Not the one he thinks we can afford – the one he really wants to go to."

His wife raised her eyebrows. "You know he's wanted to go to Dartmouth since he was a kid," she said. "And he really liked their psych program." She paused, sensing a set-up. "Why...?"

"Let's go tell him that he can pick wherever he wants," he said.

"You got it?" his wife exclaimed. He nodded, and she threw her arms around him. "You got the job!"

Within a few minutes, the family was all gathered in the living room as Thomas told his kids about his new job. He couldn't remember the last time they had looked so proud of him, and it made his heart swell.

Thomas had believed, erroneously, that once you were in a career, you stayed in that career. In truth, he had learned, people often changed not only their jobs, but their entire career trajectories. Making a better life for yourself wasn't only for young people with their whole lives ahead of them like Jason – it was just as important for someone like him: someone with a relatively stable job, a happy life, an established family, but who needed a change. He hadn't thought he could do it, but it turned out that Out of Architecture was right – his career was *still* a design problem. Just as it had been two decades earlier. The parameters were different, but the problem deserved just as much attention.

#

The next day, Thomas told Jake and Erin all about his new job on an impromptu call.

"Fantastic," Jake said.

"Congratulations," Erin followed up. "What are you most excited about?"

"The starting bonus," Thomas exclaimed, realizing that he was actually just as enthusiastic about the new position – a new corporate culture, a new work atmosphere, new colleagues, a new boss – as he was about the financial compensation. "I talked them up to a $21,000 starting bonus. That kind of money..." he paused. It hadn't really hit him yet how much his life was about to change. "I just can't thank you enough."

"We're glad it worked out," Jake said.

"It definitely did. And you know what?" Thomas asked expectantly. He waited for both of them to offer the requisite, "what?" before he continued. "Sitting down at the table and being able to tell my kids that they could have the education they've always wanted – on that first call, when you asked me about my goals? Well, that's what I should've said."

CONCLUSION

One of the fundamental facts of the architectural profession is that it can only operate as an extension of somebody else's initiative. There is no architecture without clients; therefore this strange profession cannot take initiatives or decide what its own agenda should be. So it will always establish its agenda indirectly, through a particular interpretation of demands.

– Rem Koolhaas[1]

In the quotation above, Koolhaas points to an excuse that is frequently offered when architecture is faced with an opportunity to grow and change. It functions as a justification for refusing to become more equitable and humane – and, as a result, more conducive to strong, innovative design. Koolhaas's excuse, put more simply, is the market – a force that is not unique to architecture.

What is unique to our field is a particular refusal to change, even after years of public conversation about the professional hazards – from general malaise to total burnout – that consistently plague emerging and established architects. To believe Koolhaas's analysis is to believe that architecture as a profession can never adapt because clients are somehow invested in the business of our practice. Therefore, the business of our practice must remain hopelessly rooted in the past in order to satisfy our clients.

Nonsense.

We see Koolhaas's statement as the worst type of tautology, an impractical and self-defeating ouroboros that bases all future professional prospects on a faulty premise. Koolhaas believes that it is clients who are holding architecture back from growth, despite the fact that a recent *Architect's Journal* study found that over 90 percent of the general public did not realize the extent of architects' professional tasks.[2]

Clients do not hold the profession back. Only the profession holds the profession back.

Throughout this book, we have demonstrated the tendency for architecture to eat its own. Too often, the profession utterly ignores and disregards market demands. Certainly those demands include, as Koolhaas states, keeping traditional architecture clients happy. But market demands also include the need for workers to make a living wage, for firms to maintain financial sustainability, and for the profession as a whole to meet a changing world with changing models. The architect's perceived role in society has not adapted to the changing demands of our profession – in response, we must re-present ourselves in order to show people what we do and to demonstrate the value we provide.

In the future, the need for architects' ideas and ways of thinking will be as important as our traditional roles. Perhaps even more so. Therefore, we offer a minor adjustment to Koolhaas's assertion:

One of the fundamental facts of architectural *design* is that it can only operate as an extension of somebody else's initiative. There is no *design* without clients; therefore, this strange *design process* cannot take initiatives or decide what its own agenda should be. So, it will always establish its agenda indirectly, through a particular interpretation of demands.[3]

Our point here is not to split hairs between "profession" and "design" as terms. Instead, our point is to reframe the focus of architecture away from the inhospitable world of the "profession" – with all of its religious and cult-like symbolism – and shift it back to the heart of architecture, to the passion that brought us to the art form in the first place.

Good design should never be self-referential in the way Koolhaas describes – it should always be relational, operating as an extension of other initiatives, whether on behalf of a particular client or an identified need in industry.

But that doesn't mean that the practice of design must always follow tradition.

This is why our approach to **Out of Architecture** *has centered both the process of leaving the profession – of moving out of architecture – and the acknowledgement that architectural training is a deeply valuable resource for individuals, industries, and society in general.*

Much of that value is best realized when the "strange process of design" is relocated, moved out of the traditional architectural profession and into areas that better nurture the passion, creativity, innovative thinking, and determination that architects can bring to the world's problems.

In other words, while *Out of Architecture* is a book about careers, it is not a book about business. It's a book about value.

#

Throughout the previous chapters, we have worked to highlight the competing conceptions of value at play when talented designers apply their skills in contexts that take them out of architecture. Working from our own narratives to a causal analysis and finally into a series of case studies, we have highlighted the consistent experiences of disillusionment and trauma that characterize professional architecture. Yet, we and our clients remain deeply passionate about the architectural art form, and we continue to extract value from our design training as we move through our endeavors both within the traditional field and out of architecture. This is the heart of our message: you are valuable, you deserve to be valued, and you deserve a career that respects and aligns with your personal values. This idea should be so obvious it does not need to be said.

But, clearly, it does.

Clients often struggle to embrace the value-based approach – as architects, we are not often given permission to think of ourselves or our goals in this way. Reframing the way we understand architects' career options thus begins by identifying the origins of toxic ways of thinking about value. We contend that many of these harmful approaches originate in the traditions of the studio education model which, perhaps unintentionally, can cement damaging myths in students' ways of understanding architecture. However, when we focus on solutions – particularly in reframing our approach to value so that the skills and priorities of individual workers are placed at the forefront of the conversation – we can carry the principles and aesthetics of architectural design into spaces of personal transformation.

#

We began *Out of Architecture* with a focus on love. Most architecture students begin their studies with a deep passion for the architectural art form – we were no exception. We fondly recall the feeling of being deliciously overwhelmed, the sense of having our minds pried open, and of suddenly seeing the world as something beautifully new, different, and unfamiliar. As students immersed in the early years of school, the feelings of being immersed in a love affair with your art – of having your mind blown in lecture after lecture, exercise after exercise – feel almost like a high. Our nostalgia for those years lives uncomfortably with our awareness of the potential for that passion to be exploited by a profession that consistently fails to pay its practitioners a fair wage. Even when salary isn't the primary issue – as in cases like Brian's job search – the sense of passion, love, and opportunity often vanish in the face of a profession severely misaligned with traditional architecture training. In other cases, like those of Najee and Sydney, a love affair with architecture emerges as a love affair with particular aspects of architecture – many of which are more highly valued outside of the traditional profession.

As crucial as that sense of passion is, the skills it leads to are even more important. Architecture students quickly learn that a love for the art form is a prerequisite – it can help students to persevere through the brutal expectations of architecture school, but it does not replace the hard work of skill development: the meticulous patience of learning to draw, the unprecedented stress of preparing for review, the uncertainty of patching together history, theory, and application. These require more than passion and love. They require a willingness to learn – and to learn how to learn. This was Najee's experience, as he waded through the somewhat unfamiliar territory of coding, and it was Thomas's experience as he navigated the challenging task of negotiation. Architects are well-trained in self-education – we are skilled at identifying a problem and coming up with the solution. This is no doubt part of what makes us insecure overachievers. We are naturally curious and inherently ambitious. We often struggle to ask for help from others, even when we need it.

And many of us desperately need help as we transition from school into our early careers. We find ourselves in a chasm of disconnect between the art form we loved and a profession that can be confusing, frustrating, and isolating. It is often at this point that we realize the harm of architecture's lack of focus on healthy team building – as we make our way into our first job and realize that there will be no formal assignment of roles. We are on our own, lost and flailing, and unsure of how to right the ship. For architects like Sydney, the solution seems to be licensure – if we can only hold on long enough to get that beautiful self-inking stamp with our name on it, maybe we'll finally be able to carve out some stability. But too often, as Sydney learned, very little changes after licensure. Dismissive principals are still dismissive principals. Mind-numbing projects are still mind-numbing projects. A feeling of being disconnected – from a job that should have been your dream job – remains, just as devastating as ever.

Too often, this is the point when the dream becomes a nightmare. It becomes clear that the underlying structures of architecture are unyielding, that even when partners and principals have the best of intentions, often the persistent undervaluing of the field's practitioners undercuts any potential avenues for more equitable change. Sometimes this issue comes in the form of a clearly inequitable approach – such as the idea of the "gentleman's profession" that has undergirded architecture from its founding – and in other cases, it is an apparently more benevolent framework – as when firms want to understand themselves as "families." In either case, as Tia and Thomas discovered, most architects never escape the structures that can turn this dream job into a seemingly inescapable career trap. Despite all the talk of "paying your dues," most architects never make it to the top echelon of the field. Within the traditional practice of architecture, most of us will experience the fallout of being persistently undervalued. As one recent client told us, even a reasonable salary means little when it is undermined by "terrible health insurance and constant verbal abuse."

#

We want to be perfectly clear that, while we have been critical of the more inhumane aspects of architectural training, our point isn't to rail against the studio method or architecture education in general. We are much more interested in how particular expectations and thought patterns that are ingrained in school eventually become mental blocks for architecture professionals. The imperative to throw your entire self into a project, for example, can be deeply satisfying. However, that sense of intellectual, emotional, and creative fulfillment can also foster an impulse to chase the elation of success – even when that sense comes at an unreasonable financial or psychological cost. Likewise, the stress of assembling the many moving parts that go into preparing for review – and the feeling of defeat when that review doesn't go the way you'd hoped – is what makes architects great. Being pushed to the very brink of your limits is the only way to emerge a truly excellent designer. But the toxic cycle of striving for perfectionism can also instill a sense of insecurity and an unconscious need to overachieve – to please that imaginary reviewer in your head. This can be a foundation on which exploitation is built.

Still, we acknowledge that issues like these – an intense passion for your craft and a drive toward perfectionism – are only problems when they are situated in an exploitative environment.

In a healthy, supportive context, these are the areas in which architects and architecture students thrive. And, for many talented designers, that context only exists outside of architecture.

As we draw this book to a close, we urge you to

take action in your own career.

This action may take a variety of forms, depending on the particular values you hold in your life and the specific skills and perspectives you can offer to the industries whose work aligns with those values. There is no one-size-fits-all approach to career counseling.

Still, as we have highlighted in the previous pages, there are some commonalities that emerge as we reflect on our clients', our friends', and our own transitions out of architecture.

First, we urge you to consider your experiences in architecture school, in the early years of your career, and, for more advanced readers, the ways you may have seen your own experiences reflected in a younger generation of students. As we highlighted in Part Two, the particular strains of thinking within architecture are widespread, not out of chance, but because they are baked into the profession. In order to truly change your career – and change your life – it is crucial that you reflect on the ways of thinking that are contributing to career toxicity, as well as the ways that your training in architecture may be leading you to self-sabotage. Many of these mental frameworks can be shifted to reflect a healthier – even beneficial – approach to work. But this requires the difficult work of self-reflection. We hope this book has offered you the tools to interrogate the trauma you may have experienced in school and on the job, and to rethink the way these experiences have oriented you toward a particular career vision.

Second, and relatedly, we encourage you to reflect on the things you loved about architecture in the first place. What was it that brought you to this strange, somewhat insular world? How did you hold on through years of challenging work schedules, through critiques that sometimes felt overly harsh and even devastating, through projects that seemed never-ending? If you were like us, you held on because you loved the craft. We hope *Out of Architecture* provided you with a space to reflect on these experiences, and we invite you to use the book as a tool for reflection, to think about the things you value about architecture. Particularly for our clients who are well advanced in careers they find unsatisfying, that love and passion for the craft can feel like a distant memory. We hope that you will use the stories collected in this book as a way to reconnect with your love of architecture and stoke your passion for design.

Finally, we hope that the case studies we included in Part Three of this book have provided you with some inspiration for practical ways of assessing your own career needs. Whether you are a recent graduate seeking entry into an emerging industry or a seasoned architect looking for a healthier work-life balance, the exercises we have offered our clients may be useful for you. We hope you will use these tools – things like mapping out your ideal week or conducting a quick job search and seeing what kinds of ads spark your interest – to consider how you might approach your own career as a design problem. And, if you should find yourself in need of more personalized career consulting, we hope you will reach out to our company – Out of Architecture – for assistance.

#

In fall 2019, Erin and an architecture student were chatting casually with a guest speaker in the Professional Practice class, a fellow MBA whose work focused on marketing and public relations. As the conversation progressed, with Erin and the student telling increasingly unsettling horror stories about their training, the guest speaker's eyes grew wider.

Finally, he interjected, "I don't get it. Why do you look back on these things fondly?"

Erin could only grin as he continued in utter disbelief.

"You drilled a hole in your finger. And you nearly cut off your thumb. It all sounds horrifying."

She replied with a question:

"Why does a soldier look back on bootcamp with nostalgia? Why cherish memories of waking up at five o'clock in the morning or of being screamed at by a drill sergeant? Because you saw yourself go through something that was really difficult. You saw yourself learn and grow and overcome impossible odds. The same is true for surviving architecture school."

We're not sure that guest speaker ever really understood. And maybe he couldn't. Maybe you have to suffer through the gauntlet of architecture training to truly understand how something so challenging can become something you love so deeply. When we look back at the challenges of our education and careers, we would do it all again. What we took away from the experience has made us better designers, more innovative thinkers, and stronger people.

Leaving the profession of architecture did not diminish those aspects at all. These are the prizes we gain through our training as architects, and they are much more broadly applicable than traditional practice would have us believe.

They are the things that make us who we are. And they can all be carried with us out of architecture.

NOTES

1   Rem Koolhaas and Bregtje van der Haak, *A Discussion on Koolhaas's Research with the Harvard Project on the City on Lagos, Nigeria*, July 5, 2002.
2   Max Thompson, "It's True: People Don't Know What Architects Do," *Architects' Journal*, July 19, 2012. Retrieved from www.architectsjournal.co.uk/archive/its-true-people-dont-know-what-architects-do.
3   Credit for the idea of revising Koolhaas's statement goes to Paul Nakazawa, who first revised this quotation by replacing the term "profession" with the term "business," a minor adjustment that we found to be incredibly profound, and that helped to inspire the way we think about architecture today.

INDEX

value 4–5, 104–105, 121, 179, 199; time 126

well-connected families 87–89; *see also* gentlemen's profession
Woods, Mary N. 84, 85

work cultures 64
work life balance 58–60; Tia, the questioner case study 172–183
Wright, Frank Lloyd 32

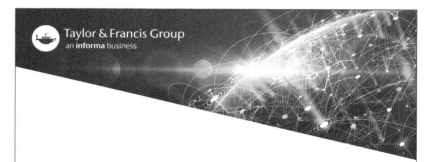